Do-All Computing in Distributed Systems

Cooperation in the Presence of Adversity

T0137768

Do-All Computing in Distributed Systems

Cooperation in the Presence of Adversity

by

Chryssis Georgiou
University of Cyprus
Cyprus

and

Alexander A. Shvartsman
Massachusetts Institute of Technology (MIT)
USA

 Springer

Chryssis Georgiou
University of Cyprus
Dept. Computer Science
P.O.Box 20537
1678 Nicosia, CYPRUS
chryssis@ucy.ac.cy

Alexander A. Shvartsman
University of Connecticut
Computer Science and Engineering
371 Fairfield Way
Storrs, CT 06268, USA
aas@cse.uconn.edu

Do-All Computing in Distributed Systems: Cooperation in the Presence of Adversity
by Chryssis Georgiou and Alexander A. Shvartsman

ISBN-13: 978-1-4419-4043-8   e-ISBN-13: 978-0-387-69045-2

Printed on acid-free paper.

9 8 7 6 5 4 3 2 1

springer.com

To my wife Agni, and son Yiorgo
CG

To Sana, my wife and best friend
AAS

Contents

List of Figures

List of Symbols

Foreword

Distributed computing was born in the late 1970s when researchers and practitioners started taking into account the intrinsic characteristics of physically distributed systems. The field then emerged as a specialized research area distinct from networking, operating systems, and parallel computing. *Distributed computing* arises when one has to solve a problem in terms of distributed entities, usually called processors, nodes, agents, sensors, peers, actors, processes, etc., such that each entity has only a partial knowledge of the many parameters involved in the problem that has to be solved. While parallel computing and real-time computing can be characterized respectively by the terms *efficiency* and *on time computing*, distributed computing can be characterized by the term *uncertainty*. This uncertainty is created by asynchrony, failures, unstable behaviors, non-monotonicity, system dynamism, mobility, connectivity instability, etc. Mastering one form or another of uncertainty is pervasive in all distributed computing problems.

The unprecedented growth of the Internet as a massive distributed network in the last decade created a platform for new distributed applications that in turn poses new challenges for distributed computing research. One such class of distributed applications is comprised of computing-intensive problems that in the past were relegated to the realm of massively parallel systems. The Internet, with its millions of interconnected computers, presents itself as a natural platform where the availability of massive distributed computing resources is seen as a compelling alternative to expensive specialized parallel supercomputers. Large networks, used as distributed supercomputers, scale much better than tightly-coupled parallel machines while providing much higher potential for parallel processing. However, harnessing the computing power contained within large networks is challenging because, unlike the applications developed for the controlled computing environments of purposefully-designed parallel systems, applications destined for distributed systems must exist in the environment fraught with uncertainty and adversity.

The field of distributed computing research, as many other areas of informatics, has traditionally encompassed both *science* and *engineering* dimensions. Roughly speaking, these can be seen as complementary facets: science is to understand and engineering is to build. With respect to distributed computing, we are often concerned with a *science of abstraction*, namely, creating the right model for a problem and devising the appropriate mechanizable techniques to solve it. This is particularly true in fault-tolerant, dynamic, large-scale distributed computing where finding models that are realistic while remaining abstract enough to be tractable, was, is, and still remains a real challenge.

The monograph by Chryssis Georgiou and Alex Shvartsman presents a very comprehensive study of massive cooperative computing in distributed settings in the presence of adversity. They focus on a problem that meaningfully abstracts a network supercomputing paradigm, specifically where distributed computing agents cooperate on performing a large number of independent tasks. Such a computation paradigm forms a cornerstone for solutions to several computation-intensive problems ranging from distributed search to distributed simulation and multi-agent collaboration. For the purposes of this study, the authors define *Do-All* as the problem of multiple processors in a network cooperatively performing a collection of independent tasks in the presence of adversity, such as processor failures, asynchrony, and breakdowns in communication. Achieving efficiency in such cooperation is difficult due to the dynamic characteristics of the distributed environments in which computing agents operate, including network failures, and processor failures that can range from the benign crash failures to the failures where faulty components may behave arbitrarily and even maliciously. The *Do-All* problem and its iterative version is used to identify the trade-offs between efficiency and fault-tolerance in distributed cooperative computing, and as a target for algorithm development. The ultimate goal is to develop algorithms that combine efficiency with fault-tolerance to the maximum extent possible, and that can serve as building blocks for network supercomputing applications and, more generally, for applications requiring distributed cooperation in the face of adversity.

During the last two decades, significant research was dedicated to studying the *Do-All* problem in various models of computation, including message-passing, partitionable networks, and shared-memory models under specific assumptions about synchrony/asynchrony and failures. This monograph presents in a coherent and rigorous manner the lower bound results and the most significant algorithmic solutions developed for *Do-All* in the message-passing model, including partitionable networks. The topics chosen for presentation include several relevant models of adversity commonly encountered in distributed computing and a variety of algorithmics illustrating important and effective techniques for solving the problem of distributed cooperation. The monograph also includes detailed complexity analysis of algorithms, assessing their efficiency in terms of work, communication, and time.

As the aim of a theory is to codify knowledge in order for it to be transmitted (to researchers, students, engineers, practitioners, etc), the research results presented in this monograph are among the fundamental bases in distributed computing theory. When effective distributed cooperation is possible, we learn why and how it works, and where there exist inherent limitations in distributed cooperation, we learn what they are and why they exist.

Rennes, France   *Michel Raynal*
September 2007

Authors' Preface

With the advent of ubiquitous high bandwidth Internet connections, network supercomputing is increasingly becoming a popular means for harnessing the computing power of an enormous number of processes around the world. Internet supercomputing comes at a cost substantially lower than acquiring a supercomputer or building a cluster of powerful machines. Several Internet supercomputers are in existence today, for instance, Internet PrimeNet Server, a project comprised of about 30,000 servers, PCs, and laptop computers, supported by Entropia.com, Inc., is a distributed, massively parallel mathematics research Internet supercomputer. PrimeNet Server has sustained throughput of over 1 teraflop. Another popular Internet supercomputer, the SETI@home project, also reported its speed to be in teraflops.

In such distributed supercomputing settings it is often the case that a very large number of independent tasks must be performed by an equally large number of computers. Given the massive numbers of participating computers, it is invariably the case that non-trivial subsets of these machines may be faulty, disconnected, experiencing delays, or simply off-line at any given point in time. At such scales of distributed computing, failures are no longer an exception, but the norm. For example, a visitor to the network control center at Akamai Technologies, a global Internet content and application delivery company, will immediately notice that the floor-to-ceiling monitor-paneled walls of the main control room display a surprisingly large number of server icons in red, indicating server failures. Yet the services delivered by the company's 25,000 servers worldwide continue unaffected, and there is little alarm among the engineers monitoring the displays. Dealing with failures is routine business, provided the massively distributed system has built-in redundancy and is able to combine efficiency with fault-tolerance.

In another example, Internet supercomputing, such as SETI@home, involves large sets of independent tasks performed by distributed worker computers. One of the major concerns involved in such computing environments is the reliability of the results returned by the workers. While most participating computers may be reliable, a large number of the workers have been known to return incorrect results for various reasons. Workers may return incorrect results due to unintended failures caused, for example, by over-clocked processors, or they may claim to have performed assigned work so as to obtain incentives, such as getting higher rank on the SETI@home list of contributed units of work. This problem already exists in the setting where the task allocation is centralized, and assumed to be reliable. The problem becomes substantially more difficult when the task allocation also has to be implemented in a highly-distributed fashion to provide the much needed parallelism for computation speed-up and redundancy for fault tolerance. In such settings it is extremely important to develop distributed algorithms that can be used to ensure dependable and efficient execution of the very large numbers of tasks.

In this monograph we abstract the problem of distributed cooperation in terms of the *Do-All* problem, defined as the problem of p processors in the network, cooperatively performing n independent tasks, in the presence of adversity. In solving this problem, we pursue the goal of combining the reliability potential that comes with replicated processors in distributed computation, with the speed-up potential of performing the large number of tasks in parallel. The difficulty associated with combining fault-tolerance with efficiency is that the two have conflicting means: fault-tolerance is achieved by *introducing redundancy*, while efficiency is achieved by *removing redundancy*. We present several significant advances in algorithms designed to solve the *Do-All* problem in distributed message-passing settings under various models of adversity, such as processor crashes, asynchrony, message delays, network partitions, and malicious processor behaviors. The efficiency of algorithms for *Do-All* is most commonly assessed in terms of *work* and *communication* complexity, depending on the specific model of computation. Work is defined either as the total number of computational steps taken by all available processors during the computation or as the total number of *task-oriented* computational steps taken by the processors. A computational step taken by a processor is said to be task-oriented, if during that step the processor performs a *Do-All* task. We refer to the first variation of work as *total-work* and the second variation of work as *task-oriented work*. We develop corresponding complexity analyses that show to what extent efficiency can be combined with fault-tolerance. We also present lower bounds that capture theoretical limitations on the possibility of combining fault-tolerance and efficiency. In this work we ultimately aim to provide robust, i.e., efficient and fault-tolerant, algorithms that will help bridge the gap between abstract models of dependable network computing and realistic distributed systems.

Monograph Roadmap

In Chapter 1 we provide motivation, introduce the distributed cooperation problem *Do-All* and discuss several variants of the problem in different models of computation.

In Chapter 2 we formal the basic message-passing model of computation used in this monograph, and present several models of adversarial settings studied in subsequent chapters. We define the nature of the tasks – the input to the distributed cooperation problem. We define the *Do-All* problem, and its counterpart for partitionable networks, the *Omni-Do* problem. We conclude the chapter with the definitions of main complexity measures used in the sequel: total-work, task-oriented work, and message complexity.

In Chapter 3 we study the *Do-All* problem for distributed settings with processor crashes. We provide upper and lower bounds on work for solving *Do-All* under the assumption of perfect knowledge, e.g., when an algorithm is aided by an omniscient oracle. We put these result to use by developing an efficient and fault-tolerant algorithm for *Do-All* where processors communicate by means of reliable broadcasts.

In Chapter 4 we develop a solution for the *Do-All* problem for the setting with processor crashes, where processors communicate using point-to-point messaging. This algorithm uses a gossip algorithm as a building block, also presented in the chapter.

In Chapter 5 we give lower bounds on work for *Do-All* in the model where processors are subject to crashes and restarts, and we develop and analyze an algorithm for this model of adversity.

In Chapter 6 we study the complexity of *Do-All* in the adversarial model where processors are subject to Byzantine failures, that is, where faulty processors may behave arbitrarily and even maliciously. We provide several algorithms and lower bound results under this model of adversity.

In Chapter 7 we study the upper and lower bounds of solving *Do-All* in the setting where an adversary introduces processor asynchrony and message delays. We present several algorithm for this model and provide their delay-sensitive analysis.

In Chapter 8 we switch our attention to partitionable networks and the *Omni-Do* problem. We give an efficient algorithm that solves *Omni-Do* in the presence of network fragmentation and merges.

In Chapter 9 we study the *Omni-Do* problem in the model where the network can undergo arbitrary reconfigurations. We assess upper and lower bounds for the problem using competitive analysis.

In Chapter 10 we study *Do-All* in the setting where the adversary initially starts processors in isolated singleton groups, and then allows the processor to rendezvous. We analyze redundant work performed by the isolated processors prior to rendezvous, and we present several scheduling strategies designed to minimize redundant task executions.

Finally, in Chapter 11 we survey related problems and models, including the problem of distributed cooperation in shared-memory models, algorithms for the model where processors communicate through broadcast channels, and we show a connection between *Do-All* and the distributed consensus problem.

The chapters of this monograph can of course be read in the sequential order from Chapter 1 to Chapter 11. In the diagram that follows we show alternative suggested paths through the monograph. Chapters 1 and 2 should be read in sequence before other chapters. It is also recommended that Chapters 8, 9, and 10 are read in sequence. The only remaining dependency is that Chapter 3 is read before Chapter 5.

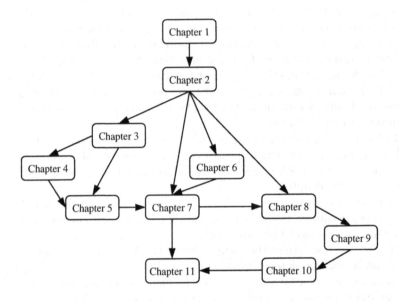

In presenting our message-passing algorithms, we aim to illustrate the most interesting algorithmic techniques and paradigms, using a clear high-level level pseudocode that is best suited to represent the nature of each algorithm.

Each chapter concludes with an overview of open problems relevant to the topics presented in the chapter, and a section containing chapter notes, including detailed bibliographic notes, and selected comparisons with and overviews of related work.

Bibliographic Notes

At the end of each chapter we provide Chapter Notes that contain bibliographic notes and overview related topics and results. The complete bibliography follows the last chapter. Here we give additional pointers to conference proceedings, archival journals, and books covering the various areas related to distributed computing and fault-tolerant algorithms. Most results in this monograph appeared as articles in journals or conference proceedings (see bibliography), additionally the main results in Chapters 3, 4, 6, 8, and 9 appear in the PhD dissertation of the first author [43].

Work on fault-tolerant distributed computation related to the content of this monograph appear in the proceedings of conferences, in journals, and in books. A reader interested in learning more about this ongoing research as well as research beyond the scope of this volume will be well served by consulting recent publication on such topics from the venues we list below.

The following conferences are examples of the most relevant fora for results related to topics in this monograph: ACM symposium on Principles of Distributed Computing (PODC), ACM symposium on Parallel Algorithms and Architectures (SPAA), ACM symposium on Theory of Computing (STOC), ACM-SIAM symposium on Discrete Algorithms (SODA), IEEE symposium on Foundations of Computer Science (FOCS), IEEE sponsored conference on Distributed Computing Systems (ICDCS), EATCS sponsored symposium on Distributed Computing (DISC), the conference on the Principles on Distributed Systems (OPODIS) and the colloquium on Structural Information and Communication Complexity (SIROCCO). The most relevant journals include: Springer Distributed Computing, SIAM Journal on Computing, Theoretical Computer Science, Information and Computation, Information Processing Letters, Parallel Processing Letters, Journal of the ACM, Journal of Algorithms, Journal of Discrete Algorithms, and Journal of Parallel and Distributed Computing.

The 1997 book by Kanellakis and Shvartsman [67] presents research results for fault-tolerant cooperative computing in the parallel model of computation. In particular, it studies the *Do-All* problem in the shared-memory model, where it is referred to as the *Write-All* problem. The current monograph deals with the message-passing models of computation and considers broader adversarial settings inherent to these distributed models. The two monographs follow similar presentation philosophies and it is reasonable to consider them as complementary volumes. The current volume includes in Chapter 11 several recent results on the *Write-All* problem that appeared since the publication of the first monograph [67].

The book by Lynch [79] provides a wealth of information on distributed computing issues, such as computational models, algorithms, fault-tolerance, lower bounds and impossibility results. This include the consensus problem, which is related to *Do-All*, and we discuss this relation in Chapter 11. Additionally, information on the Input/Output Automata used in our Chapter 8 can be found there. The book by Attiya and Welch [6] is another excellent source of information on distributed computing issues, including cooperation. The book of Guerraoui and Rodrigues [52] presents numerous important abstractions for reliable distributed computing and includes detailed examples of how these abstractions can be implemented and used in practice.

Acknowledgements

Our research on robust distributed cooperation continues to be inspired by the earlier work on fault-tolerant parallel computing of the late Paris Christos Kanellakis (1953-1995). Paris is survived by his parents, General Eleftherios and Roula Kanellakis, who have enthusiastically encouraged us to continue his work through the long years following the tragic death of Paris, his wife Maria-Teresa, and their children Alexandra and Stephanos. We warmly thank General and Mrs. Kanellakis for their inspiration and support.

The material presented in this monograph includes results obtained by the authors in collaboration with Bogdan Chlebus, Roberto De Prisco, Antonio Fernandez, Dariusz Kowalski, Greg Malewicz and Alexander Russell. We thank them for the wonderful and fruitful collaborations—without their contributions this monograph would not exist.

Our work on robust distributed cooperation also benefited from prior collaboration with several colleagues, and we gratefully acknowledge the contributions of Jonathan Buss, Shlomi Dolev, Leszek Gasieniec, Dimitrios Michailidis, Prabhakar Ragde, and Roberto Segala.

Special thanks are due to Nancy Lynch for reviewing an earlier version of this work. Her insight and valuable feedback are greatly appreciated.

In undertaking the research that ultimately resulted in this monograph, we were motivated by the work of other researchers who have also contributed to the field of fault-tolerant cooperative computing. We will be remiss without mentioning the names of Richard Anderson, Richard Cole, Cynthia Dwork, Zvi Galil, Phillip Gibbons, Joe Halpern, Maurice Herlihy, Zvi Kedem, Andrzej Lingas, Chip Martel, Keith Marzullo, Alan Mayer, Naomi Nishimura, Krishna Palem, Arvin Park, Michael Rabin, Arvind Raghunathan, Nir Shavit, Paul Spirakis, Ramesh Subramonian, Orli Waarts, Heather Woll, Moti Yung, Ofer Zajicek, and Asaph Zemach.

This work was in part supported by the National Science Foundation (NSF) Grants 9984778, 9988304, 0121277, 0311368, and by the NSF-NATO Award 0209588. The work of the first author has also been partially supported by research funds from the University of Cyprus.

We thank our Springer editor, Susan Lagerstrom-Fife, for her encouragement and support, and Sharon Palleschi, editorial assistant at Springer, for her valuable assistance during the preparation of this monograph.

Our warmest thanks go to Michel Raynal for writing the foreword of this monograph; thank you for this honor, Michel.

Finally, we would like to thank our families.

CG: I thank my wife, Agni, for the emotional support she has given me and the patience she has shown during the endless nights I spent working on this monograph, while she took care of our angel, 21 months old son Yiorgo. You both bring joy and meaning to my life and you are my source of strength and inspiration. Agni, you are the *love* of my life. Yiorgo, you *are* my life.

AAS: My wife Sana gave me more affection, care, and happiness, than I could have dreamed of. She spent many lonely nights being an epitome of patience, while sustaining herself only by my assurances that I'll belong to her yet again. Thank you, my love. I thank my children, Ginger and Ted, for being there for me when I needed you most. This time around you are grown-ups and I am proud of you. I thank my step-son Arnold for his encouragement and interest. I never thought that daily questions from a freshman "Are you done with the book yet?" would do so much to energize the work of this professor. I am glad to report: "We are done."

Nicosia, Cyprus and Storrs, CT, USA   *Chryssis Georgiou*
September 2007   *Alexander A. Shvartsman*

1

Introduction

THE ability to cooperatively perform a collection of tasks in a distributed setting is key to solving a broad range of computation problems ranging from distributed search, such as SETI@home, to distributed simulation, and multi-agent collaboration. Target distributed platforms for such applications consist of hundreds or even thousands of processing units, and encompass multiprocessor machines, clusters of workstations, wide-area networks, and network supercomputers, all in wide use today. The benefits of solving cooperation problems consisting of large numbers of tasks on multiple processors can only be realized if one is able to effectively marshal the available computing resources in order to achieve substantial speed-up relative to the time necessary to solve the problem using a single fast computer or a few of such computers in a tightly-coupled multiprocessor. In order to achieve high efficiency in using distributed computing platforms comprised of large numbers of processors it is necessary to eliminate redundant computation done by the processors. This is challenging because the availability of distributed computing resources may fluctuate due to failures and asynchrony of the involved processors, and due to delays and connectivity failures in the underlying network. Such perturbations in the computing medium may degrade the efficiency of algorithms designed to solve computational problems on these systems, and even cause the algorithms to produce incorrect results. Thus a system containing unreliable and asynchronous components must dedicate resources both to solving the computational problem, and to coordinating the fluctuating resources in the presence of adversity.

Chapter structure.

In Section 1.1 we overview the *Do-All* computing paradigm and provide examples of application domains. In Section 1.2 we discuss the *Do-All* problem in the context of adversarial settings. In Section 1.3 we discuss the goal of combining fault-tolerance and efficiency in *Do-All* algorithms and we overview the complexity measures we use to evaluate the efficiency of algorithmic solutions and to establish lower bound results.

1.1 Do-All Computing

To study the efficiency of distributed cooperative computing in the presence of adversity and the trade-offs between efficiency and fault-tolerance, we focus on the abstract problem of performing a set of tasks in a decentralized setting, known as the *Do-All* problem.

> *Do-All*: *p processors must cooperatively perform n tasks in the presence of adversity.*

In the *Do-All* problem we deal with abstract *tasks* as primitive units of work performed by the individual processors. The tasks are assumed to be *similar*, *independent*, and *idempotent*, which means the following in our context.

Similarity: The task executions on any individual processor consume equal or comparable local resources.

Independence: The completion of any task does not affect any other task, and any task can be executed concurrently with any other task.

Idempotence: Each task can be executed one or more times to produce the same final result; in other words, tasks admit at-least-once execution semantics.

We have already mentioned that distributed search and distributed simulation applications can be naturally abstracted in terms of *Do-All*. We now overview several technical areas that give rise to computational problems that can also be abstracted in terms of the *Do-All* problem.

- In image processing and computer graphics, a significant amount of data processing (e.g., operations on large data structures, computing complicated partial and ordinary differential equations) is required, especially in visualization (achieving graphical visual realism of real world objects). When the data to be computed can be decomposed into smaller independent "chunks", a usual approach is to load-balance the chunks among the different processing units of a parallel machine or a cluster of machines. The data chunks can be abstracted as *Do-All* tasks and the processing units can be abstracted as *Do-All* processors.
- In databases, when querying a large (unsorted) data space, it is often desirable to use multiple machines to search distinct records or sets of records in the database in order to decrease the search time.
- In fluid dynamics, researchers study the behavior of fluids in different settings by running simulations that involve solving numerically complicated differential equations over very large data spaces. Again, when the data can be decomposed into smaller independent chunks, the chunks are assigned on different multiprocessing units to achieve faster and reliable computation.

- Airborne radar systems are used to detect and track objects in the presence of natural and hostile interference. Such radars employ multi-element antenna arrays and require that large amount of data from each antenna element is processed in a very short time. Several processing stages in such settings involve large independent data sets that can be abstracted in terms of *Do-All*.
- Another example can be found in Cryptography. In particular, in breaking cryptographic schemes. The goal is to search and find a user's private key. A key may be a string of 128 bits, meaning that there are 2^{128} different strings that a user could choose as his private key. Among the various techniques available, the most frequently used is exhaustive search where multiple processing units search simultaneously for the key, each unit searching different sets of bit permutations. Each set of bit permutation can be abstracted as a *Do-All* task and each processing unit can be abstracted as a *Do-All* processor.

In general, any problem that involves performing a number of similar independent calculations can be abstracted in terms of the *Do-All* problem.

In the absence of adversity, the problem can be easily solved without any coordination by load-balancing the n tasks among the p processors (here $p \leq n$ is the normal setting where there are at least as many tasks as processors). For example, if the processors and the tasks are uniquely identified, and the tasks are initially known to all processors, each processor simply performs $\lceil n/p \rceil$ tasks, which are assigned based on processor identifiers PID, with padding used to include "dummy" tasks when p does not divide n. The pseudocode for such an algorithm is given below.

```
for each processor PID = 1..p begin
    Task[1..n]                    %  Globally known n tasks
    for i = 1 to ⌈n/p⌉ do
        perform Task[(PID − 1) · ⌈n/p⌉ + i]
    end for
end
```

In any such algorithm the overall number of tasks performed is $p\lceil n/p \rceil = \Theta(n)$. This is clearly an optimal solution in terms of tasks, since n tasks must be performed. Given that there is no adversity to interfere with the computation, we are guaranteed that each task is performed exactly once. Furthermore, assuming that the processors progress at about the same pace through the tasks, it takes $\Theta(n/p)$ time for the problem to be solved (this is the number of iterations in the inner loop above).

Even when the tasks are not initially known to all processors, such a solution can be extended in a way that involves minimal communication and coordination. For example, if the tasks are initially known to all processors, then no communication is required to solve *Do-All*, as shown in the algorithm above. If the subsets of tasks are initially known only to some processors and if a single task can be communicated to a processor in a fixed-size message, then the total number of messages is $n + p\lceil n/p \rceil = \Theta(n)$. This can be done by communicating all tasks to a chosen master process (e.g., based on the processor ids), which takes n messages. Then the master delivers "chunks" of tasks of size $\lceil n/p \rceil$ to individual processors in a load-balanced fashion, which takes $p\lceil n/p \rceil$ messages.

However, when adversity is introduced, developing efficient solutions for the *Do-All* problem becomes challenging.

1.2 Do-All and Adversity

Given the scale and complexity of realistic distributed platforms where the *Do-All* problem needs to be solved, any algorithm solving *Do-All* must be able to deal with adverse conditions inherent in such distributed platforms that are caused by failures of processors, network disconnections, unpredictable delays, etc. Adversity may manifest itself in several ways.

- When a processor experiences a benign failure, such as a crash, then some tasks assigned to the faulty machine may remain unperformed.
- When a processor fails in a malicious way, it can mislead the system into thinking that the tasks assigned to it have been performed, or it may even return incorrect results.
- If a processor is able to restart following a failure, it can be completely unaware of the overall computation progress.
- If processors are subjected unbounded asynchrony, and their relative processing speeds become arbitrarily large, the tasks assigned to slow processors remain undone for a very long time, while the faster processors may idle.

In all such cases, processors must not only perform their assigned tasks, but also coordinate their activity with other processors in an attempt to detect processor failures and to identify remaining tasks that they can perform should they become idle. In the *Do-All* computing setting, this is facilitate by means of communication. However the underlying network can also experience adverse conditions.

- Processors may experience intermittent connectivity, making coordination difficult or impossible.
- Network may fragment, in which case communication between processors in different partitions is impossible.
- In general, the network can undergo arbitrary reconfigurations, making it difficult to share information about the performed tasks.
- Message delays can be unpredictable, causing processors to idle during the attempts to coordinate their activities.

All such examples of adversity may cause substantial degradation in the efficiency of the computation. For example, in Chapter 3 we study the *Do-All* problem for distributed settings with processor crashes and we show that any synchronous message-passing algorithm may need to perform in the worst case $\Omega(n \log n / \log \log n)$ tasks for $p = n$, which is a $n / \log \log n$ fold degradation relative to the optimal number of tasks $\Theta(n)$.

If the adversity manifests itself in network fragmentations, such as considered in Chapter 8, and the network is partitioned into g groups (where $g \leq p$), then processors in each group may have to perform all n tasks, the result being that the overall systems performs $\Theta(g \cdot n)$ tasks, which is a g-fold degradation relative to the optimal number of tasks $\Theta(n)$.

Note that in a partitionable network it may not be sufficient for a processor to learn that all n tasks have been performed. In particular, it may also be necessary to learn the results of the computation for each task. In partitionable settings it may be impossible to obtain the results of the computation if it was performed in a (currently) disconnected group. Therefore, in these settings, we require that each processor is performing tasks until it learns the results of all tasks. We call this specialization of *Do-All* for partitionable networks the *Omni-Do* problem.

> *Omni-Do: p processors must cooperatively perform n tasks*
> *and each processor must learn the results of all tasks*
> *in the presence of adversity.*

Solving the *Do-All* and *Omni-Do* problems is always possible for the initial settings where the tasks to be performed are known to each processor, provided at least one processor does not fail. Here each processor can obliviously perform each task locally, without any coordination. This results in $\Theta(p \cdot n)$ tasks being executed, which is quite inefficient and essentially requires only a sequential algorithm at each processor. Thus the challenge of the *Do-All* computing is to develop algorithms for specific models of adversity that can tolerate adverse conditions, e.g., be fault-tolerant, while achieving efficient task execution by performing substantial fewer tasks than done by an oblivious solution, e.g., performing $o(p \cdot n)$ tasks. To further assess the efficiency of algorithms for *Do-All*, lower bounds need to develop that establish the inherent costs associated with each adversarial setting.

Do-All algorithms have also been used in developing simulations of failure-free algorithms on failure-prone processors. This is done by iteratively using a *Do-All* algorithm to simulate the steps of ideal virtual processors in adversarial settings. Thus it is also important to assess the complexity of solving *Do-All* when it is used iteratively, especially if it can be shown that the complexity of r iterations of a particular algorithm is better than the complexity of a single iteration times r. We abstract the iterative use of *Do-All* algorithms as the *r-iterative Do-All* problem: *using p processors, solve r instances of n-task Do-All with the added restriction that every task of the ith instance must be* *completed before any task of the $(i + 1)$st instance is begun.* The *r-iterative Omni-Do* problem is defined similarly.

1.3 Solving Do-All: Fault-Tolerance with Efficiency

Solving the *Do-All* problem in distributed settings is a source of both challenge and opportunity. It is challenging to develop algorithms that achieve high efficiency in solving *Do-All*, while tolerating adversarial conditions. However the fact that we are solving *Do-All* using multiple processors provides us with both the source of parallelism needed to achieve high-performance and the source of redundancy that is necessary in achieving fault-tolerance. We elaborate on this below.

Consider a fault-tolerant system with ρ-fold redundancy in processors designed to tolerate up to $\rho - 1$ processor failures. A worthwhile objective for such system is to achieve ρ-fold increase in performance in the absence of adversity. When there are indeed $\rho - 1$ failures, then the system's performance should approximate the performance of an efficient computation a uniprocessor.

Similarly, consider a decentralized system consisting of p processors designed to achieve up to p-fold speed-up. Such a system has an inherent redundancy, and there is no reason why we should not expect the system to tolerate up to $p - 1$ processor failures with graceful degradation in performance as the number of faulty processors increases.

(Of course impossibility results for some models and problems may prevent solutions that tolerate $p - 1$ failures. In such cases the algorithms should tolerate the maximum possible number of failures.)

With these observations in mind, our goal in developing algorithmic solutions for the *Do-All* problem is to combine:

- *Fault-tolerance* potential that comes with replicated processors, with
- *Efficiency* (e.g., speed-up) potential of computing with multiple processors.

The benefits of such a combination are of course obvious, yet its feasibility is far from obvious. In order to achieve this combination, we need to resolve an inherent conflict present in the means of achieving fault-tolerance and efficiency:

- *Fault-tolerance* is achieved by *introducing redundancy* in the computation in order to deal with adversity and to reassign resources, whereas
- *Efficiency* is achieved by *removing redundancy* from the computation to fully utilize each processor.

In this monograph we present algorithmic techniques for reconciling this conflict in the presence of several types of adversity. Formulating suitable models of cooperative distributed computation and models of adversity goes hand in hand with the study of algorithms and their efficiency. In the conclusion of Section 1.1 we illustrated a simple solution for the *Do-All* problem in the absence of adversity. We reasoned about the efficiency of that solution in terms of the number of tasks performed by the algorithm and the number of messages sent by the algorithm. In this monograph we use several different complexity measures to evaluate the efficiency of the algorithms presented here, and to establish the corresponding lower bounds that capture inherent limitations on the efficiency achievable for particular models of computation and adversity.

We now preview the main complexity measures used in this monograph.

Task-oriented work measures the number of tasks, including multiplicity, performed by p cooperating processors in solving the *Do-All* or *Omni-Do* problem with n tasks. This complexity measure is denoted as W, it is defined in Chapter 2, and used in the analyses in Chapters 8, 9, and 10. Task-oriented work measure is useful for establishing lower bounds on the number of task executions, and is relevant in the settings where the cost of locally executing a task dominates any local computation spent on coordination, bookkeeping, and waiting, or where the local resources can be assigned to other (not necessarily related) activities.

Total-work measures the total number of local computation steps, e.g., machine instructions, executed by p processors during the computation, in particular in performing n tasks. This includes all local steps, whether spent performing tasks, doing local bookkeeping, waiting, and idling. This complexity measure generalizes the notion of time complexity of sequential computation. This complexity measure is denoted as S, it is defined in Chapter 2, and used in the analyses in Chapters 3 through 7. Note that total-work S is always an upper bound for task-oriented work W, because it includes all step dedicated by the processors to performing the tasks, and so we have $W = O(S)$.

Message complexity measures the total number of messages sent during a computation. When processors communicate using multicasts, say to m recipients, this is accounted for as sending m distinct point-to-point messages. This complexity measure is denoted as M, it is defined in Chapter 2, and used in the analyses in Chapters 3 through 8.

Work-competitiveness establishes a bound α on the multiplicative overhead of task-oriented work W_D of a specific algorithm D relative the task-oriented work W_{OPT} of the optimal algorithm OPT in the presence of particular adversity. This measure is defined and used formally in Chapter 9. Informally, algorithm D is α-competitive if we have $W_D \leq \alpha \cdot W_{OPT}$, where each of the three involved quantities may depend on the specific adversarial behavior.

Waste measures the number of tasks executed redundantly by a set of k isolated processors up to the instant when these processors rendezvous. This notion of k-wise waste is defined and used in Chapter 10.

Time (local or global) is used to measure the number of steps (e.g., machine instructions) executed locally by a processor in performing activities of interest, or, for synchronous models, to measure the time in the conventional sense, for example in establishing the number of synchronous algorithm iterations. We use time in several analyses. We also define it formally for the analysis in Chapter 4. Note that time does not play a central role in the analysis of work-performing algorithms in the presence of adversity as it does in the analysis of sequential algorithms. This is because time, in the worst case, can either be the task-oriented work W or the total-work S, if adversity results in at most one processor executing a local computation step for each global time step.

Developing upper and lower bounds for specific models of computation and adversity is the main theme of this monograph. The development focuses on the work-oriented complexity measures, that is, task-oriented work, total-work, work-competitiveness, and waste. As we illustrated earlier, the immediate lower bound on work for *Do-All* is $\Omega(n)$, since each task has to be performed at least once. A trivial solution to *Do-All* is obtained by having each processor obliviously perform each of the n tasks. This solution has work $\Theta(n \cdot p)$ and requires no communication. Thus an important overall goal is to develop *Do-All* algorithm that are work-efficient, which means they achieve work substantially better than the oblivious algorithm, to the maximum extent allowed by the nature of adversity. Optimizing message complexity is of secondary concern. In the rest of this monograph, we present the models of computation and adversity, algorithmic solutions for distributed cooperation problems designed to work in each model and their analysis, and the corresponding lower bounds. In presenting our message-passing algorithms, our goal is to illustrate the most interesting algorithmic techniques and paradigms, using a clear high-level level pseudocode that is best suited to represent the nature of each algorithm. Most results we present in this volume are accompanied by detailed proofs that, in addition to proving the result, provide insight into behaviors of algorithms and adversaries, and serve as illustrations of the relevant proof techniques.

Each chapter includes detailed bibliographic notes, and selected comparisons with and overviews of related work. In chapters following the main definitions in Chapter 2, we also include an overview of selected open problems relevant to the topics presented in each chapter.

1.4 Chapter Notes

The *Do-All* problem has been studied in a variety of settings, e.g., in *shared-memory* models [67, 88, 51, 5], in *message-passing* models [30, 25, 20, 38] and in *partitionable networks* [29, 83]. Dwork, Halpern, and Waarts [30] defined and studied the *Do-All* problem for message-passing models; they also defined the task-oriented work measure. Dolev, Segala, and Shvartsman [29] studied the problem of distributed cooperation in the setting of processor groups in partitionable networks, and they introduced the *Omni-Do* problem for that context. In shared-memory models, the *Do-All* problem is known as the *Write-All* problem: *given a zero-valued array of n elements and p processors, write value 1 into each array location.* This problem was introduced by Kanellakis and Shvartsman [66], who also defined the total-work measure (available processor steps).

Do-All algorithms have been used in developing simulations of failure-free algorithms on failure-prone processors, e.g., as in the works of Kedem, Palem, and Spirakis [70], Martel, Park, and Subramonian [87], and Kanellakis and Shvartsman [67, 104]. This is done by iteratively using a *Do-All* algorithm to simulate the steps of failure-free processors on failure-prone processors.

Examples of cooperation problems that can be abstracted in terms of the *Do-All* computing include distributed search, e.g., SETI@home [73], distributed simulation, e.g., [24], multi-agent collaboration, e.g., [2, 107], image processing [109], computer graphics [37], visualization [91, 101, 50], databases querying [1, 31], fluid dynamics simulations [49, 63], airborne radar applications [94], and cryptography [106].

Distributed Cooperation Problems:
Models and Definitions

$\mathbf{F}$ORMULATING suitable models of cooperative computation goes hand in hand with the study of algorithms and their efficiency. In this chapter we formalize the modeling framework used in the sequel to study problems of cooperative task execution in distributed environments under several adversarial settings. The framework includes abstract models of computation, definitions of adversity, the problem of distributed cooperation, viz. the *Do-All* problem, and the complexity measures used to evaluate the efficiency of algorithms solving the *Do-All* problems in various settings and to establish the corresponding lower bounds.

2.1 Model of Computation

2.1.1 Distributed Setting

We consider a distributed system consisting of p processors; each processor has a unique identifier (PID) from the set $\mathcal{P} = [p] = \{1, 2, \ldots, p\}$. We assume that p is known to all processors.

Each processor's activity is governed by a local clock. When the processor clocks are globally synchronized, the distributed setting is *synchronous* and we say that the processors are synchronous. In this case, processor activities are structured in terms of synchronous *steps* (constant units of time). When the processors take local steps at arbitrary relative speeds, the distributed setting is *asynchronous* and we say that the processors are asynchronous.

2.1.2 Communication

We consider the message-passing model where processors communicate by sending messages. We assume that messages are neither lost nor corrupted in transit. We consider two settings regarding the connectivity of the underlying communication network:

- *Fully Connected Network*: any processor in $\mathcal{P}$ can send messages to any other processor in $\mathcal{P}$.
- *Partitionable Network*: the processors may be partitioned into *groups* of communicating processors. We assume that communication within groups is reliable but communication across groups is not possible, as there are no communication paths linking processors in different groups (messages sent by a processor from one group to a processor to another group are simply not delivered). Partitions may change over time.

In *synchronous* message-passing systems we assume that message delivery has fixed latency known to the processors. Specifically, within a step, a processor can send messages to other processors and receive messages from other processors sent to it in the previous step, if any.

In *asynchronous* systems, we assume no bounds on the message delivery latency. To establish specific upper and lower complexity bounds for such systems we may assume upper bounds on message latency; this is done for analysis purposes only and the processors are never aware of these latency bounds, and operate under the assumption of unbounded latency.

2.2 Models of Adversity

We now proceed with the definitions of the adversarial settings that abstract realistic situations occurring in distributed systems where the *Do-All* problem needs to be solved. The adversity manifests itself in terms of processor and network failures. Additionally, for asynchronous systems the adversity may manifest itself through unpredictable message delays. We first present the failure types and then introduce the notion of an adversary and of an adversarial model.

2.2.1 Processor Failure Types

We consider the following processor failure types.

Processor stop-failures/crashes. We consider *crash* failures, where a processor may crash at any moment during the computation and once crashed it does not restart, and does not perform any further actions. Messages are not delivered to crashed processors. We also define the notion of a *fail-stop* failure to be a crash failure (whether in synchronous or asynchronous settings) that can be detected. In synchronous settings, crash failures can be detected (e.g., by timeouts) and hence in such settings the two terms have the same meaning.

Processor crashes and restarts. Here, following a crash, a processor may *restart* at any point in the computation. For synchronous settings a crashed processor can restart at most once during a single local step. For example, a processor can restart once in response to a local clock tick. Upon a crash, the processor loses its state, and upon a restart, its state is reset to some known initial state. Thus the processor can be made aware of the restart.

Byzantine processor failures. A faulty processor can behave arbitrarily. In particular, following a Byzantine failure, the processor can do nothing, do something not directed by its protocol, send arbitrary messages, or behave normally. A faulty processor controls only its own messages and its own actions, and it cannot control other processors' messages and actions. Specifically, a faulty processor cannot corrupt another processor's state, modify or replace another processor's messages, and cannot impersonate other processors (i.e., create and send messages that appear to have been sent by another processor). A faulty processor cannot "undo" a part of the computation (e.g., a computation task) that was previously successfully executed.

2.2.2 Network Partitions

In some settings we consider networks that are subject to *partitions*. Partitionable networks may undergo dynamic changes in the network topology that partition the processors into non-overlapping *groups*, where communication is only possible for processors within a single group. A crashed processor is modeled by the creation of a singleton group that remains forever disconnected from the rest of the network.

When a network reconfigures from one partition to another, we refer to this as a *regrouping*. We also consider special types of regroupings: when a single group partitions into a collection of new disjoint groups, we call this a *fragmentation*. When a collection of groups merge and form a new group that contains all the processors from the collection of groups, we call this a *merge*. We also use the term *rendezvous* to denote a merge that involves only the singleton groups, i.e., groups consisting of single processors. Note that some regroupings are neither fragmentations nor merges, for example, if due to a regrouping event two initial groups are reconfigured into two different groups, this cannot be modeled as a single fragmentation or a merge event.

2.2.3 Adversaries and their Behavior

In order to model an adversarial setting we define the concept of the *adversary* that allows us to abstract and formalize the interference with a computation that is not under the control of the computation. An event caused by the adversary, such as a processor crash and group fragmentation, interferes with the computation and typically degrades the efficiency of the computation. The concept of the adversary is used in the analysis of algorithms and for obtaining lower bound results for specific problems. An adversary interferes with a computation based on its knowledge about the computation. We consider two *adversary types*:

(a) *omniscient or on-line*: the adversary has complete knowledge of the computation that it is affecting, and it makes instant dynamic decisions on how to affect the computation.

(b) *oblivious or off-line*: the adversary determines the sequence of events it will cause before the start of the computation and without having any *a priori* knowledge on how the computation will be affected under this sequence.

The distinction between the two adversary types is only significant for randomized algorithms, where the knowledge of the random "coin tosses" may be used by the adversary to its advantage. For deterministic algorithms the two adversary types are the same, since the adversary knows exactly, before the beginning of the computation, how a specific deterministic algorithm is affected by a specific event caused by the adversary.

Consider an adversary $\mathcal{A}$ and an algorithm A that solves a specific problem in the presence of adversary $\mathcal{A}$. We denote by $\mathcal{E}(A, \mathcal{A})$ the set of all executions of algorithm A for adversary $\mathcal{A}$. Let ξ be an execution in $\mathcal{E}(A, \mathcal{A})$. We denote by $\xi|_{\mathcal{A}}$ the set (or the sequence) of events caused by $\mathcal{A}$ in ξ and we refer to it as the *adversarial pattern* of ξ.

We represent an adversarial model as adversary $\mathcal{A}$ consisting of the set of all possible adversarial patterns (for all algorithms). This allows us to consider inclusion relations among adversaries. If adversary $\mathcal{A}_1$ is defined as a certain set of patterns, and adversary $\mathcal{A}_2$ is defined as a larger set of patterns, then it naturally follows that $\mathcal{A}_1 \subset \mathcal{A}_2$, capturing the fact that $\mathcal{A}_2$ is a stronger adversary.

For the adversarial pattern $\xi|_{\mathcal{A}}$ of an execution ξ, we denote by $\|\xi|_{\mathcal{A}}\|$ the *weight* of $\xi|_{\mathcal{A}}$. The value of $\|\xi|_{\mathcal{A}}\|$ depends on the specific adversary $\mathcal{A}$ considered, and we will define weights of adversarial patterns where needed in the sequel. For example, if adversary $\mathcal{A}$ causes processor crashes, then we define $\|\xi|_{\mathcal{A}}\|$ to be the number of crashes caused by the adversary; if the adversary causes fragmentations, then $\|\xi|_{\mathcal{A}}\|$ is the number of new groups created due to the fragmentations. Unless otherwise stated, the processors know neither $\xi|_{\mathcal{A}}$ nor any bounds on $\|\xi|_{\mathcal{A}}\|$.

Following the above general definition of adversaries, specific adversaries are presented in the chapters where they are used.

2.3 Tasks and Do-All Computing

We define a *task* to be any computation that can be performed by a single processor in constant time. The tasks are assumed to be *similar, independent*, and *idempotent*. By the similarity of the tasks we mean that the task executions consume equal or comparable resources. By the independence of the tasks we mean that the tasks can be executed in any order, that is, the execution of a task is independent of the execution of any of the other tasks. By the idempotence of the tasks we mean that the tasks admit *at-least-once* execution semantics. We define the *result* of a task to be the outcome of the task execution.

For a problem requiring that some n tasks, comprising the input, are performed, we assume that each task has a unique identifier (TID) from the set $T = [n] = \{1, 2, \ldots, n\}$, and that n is fixed and known to all processors.

We also consider sequences of task-sets $T_1, T_2, \ldots, T_r$, where each T_i, for $1 \leq i \leq r$, is a set of n tasks and the execution of any task in T_i must be delayed until all tasks in T_{i-1} are performed. This models the situation where the execution of the tasks in T_i depends on the execution of the tasks in T_{i-1}, for $2 \leq i \leq r$. Within each T_i the tasks are independent, similar, and idempotent. We also assume that each task in T_i, $1 \leq i \leq r$, has a unique TID. For example, each task in T_i may have a TID from the set $\{(i-1)n+1, (i-1)n+2, \ldots, in\}$.

We always assume that the tasks are known to the processors.

2.3.1 The Do-All Problem

We now define the abstract problem of having p processors cooperatively perform n tasks in the presence of adversity.

Definition 2.1. Do-All: *Given a set T of n tasks, perform all tasks using p processors, under adversary $\mathcal{A}$.*

We let $Do\text{-}All_{\mathcal{A}}(n, p, f)$ stand for the *Do-All* problem for n tasks, p processors and adversary $\mathcal{A}$ constrained to adversarial patterns of weight less or equal to f (the definition of weight is specific to the adversary). We consider $Do\text{-}All_{\mathcal{A}}(n, p, f)$ to be solved when all n tasks are completed and at least one operational processor knows this.

Algorithms for the *Do-All* problem, among other applications, have been used in developing *simulations* of failure-free algorithms on failure prone processors. done by iteratively using a *Do-All* algorithm to simulate the steps of the n failure-free "virtual" processors on p failure-prone "physical" processors (here the usual case is that the number of physical processors does not exceed the number of virtual processors, i.e., $p \leq n$). We abstract this idea as the *iterative Do-All* problem:

Definition 2.2. r-Iterative Do-All: *Given any sequence $T_1, \ldots, T_r$ of r sets of n tasks, perform all $r \cdot n$ tasks using p processors by doing one set at a time, under adversary $\mathcal{A}$.*

We let $r\text{-}Do\text{-}All_{\mathcal{A}}(n, p, f)$ stand for the *iterative Do-All* problem for r sets of n tasks, p processors, and adversary $\mathcal{A}$ constrained to adversarial patterns of weight less or equal to f. We consider $r\text{-}Do\text{-}All_{\mathcal{A}}(n, p, f)$ to be solved, when all $r \cdot n$ tasks are completed and at least one operational processor knows this.

Consider an algorithm A solving the $Do\text{-}All_{\mathcal{A}}(n, p, f)$ problem with cost $O(x)$. It is trivial to observe that algorithm A can solve the $r\text{-}Do\text{-}All_{\mathcal{A}}(n, p, f)$ problem with cost $r \cdot O(x)$. We show in the next chapter that at least for some models of computation and adversity, e.g., for synchrony and processor crashes, we can obtain better results. This is done by understanding how the adversarial behavior is spread over several iterations of *Do-All*. (It is also an open question to understand whether complexity improvements can be obtained in other models.)

2.3.2 The Omni-Do Problem

When solving *Do-All* in partitionable networks, our goal is to utilize the resources of every group of the system during the entire computation. This is so for two reasons: (1) A client, at any point of the computation, may request for a result of a task from a certain group, for example, this might be the only group that the client can communicate with. Hence, we would like all groups to be able to provide the results of all tasks. (2) If different groups happen to perform different tasks and a regrouping merges these two groups, then more computational progress can be achieved with less computation waste. Hence, we would like processors in all groups to be computing in anticipation of regroupings.

Therefore, in partitionable networks, we require that each processor is performing tasks until it learns the results of all tasks. We call this variation of the *Do-All* problem *Omni-Do*.

Definition 2.3. *Omni-Do: Given a set $\mathcal{T}$ of n tasks and p message-passing processors, each processor must learn the results of all tasks, under adversary $\mathcal{A}$.*

We let *Omni-Do*$_\mathcal{A}(n, p, f)$ stand for the *Omni-Do* problem for n tasks, p processors, and adversary $\mathcal{A}$ constrained to adversarial patterns of weight less or equal to f (the definition of the weight of a pattern depends on the adversary). We consider *Omni-Do*$_\mathcal{A}(n, p, f)$ to be solved when all operational processors know the results of all n tasks.

Finally, unless otherwise stated, we assume that the number of processors p is no more than the number of tasks n ($p \leq n$). Studying *Do-All* or *Omni-Do* in the case of $p > n$ is not as interesting. This is so because the most interesting challenge is to consider the settings where maximum parallelism can be extracted for the case when each processor can initially have at least one distinct task to work on. Additionally the algorithms solving our cooperation problems can be used for simulation where a fault-free computation for n processors is simulated in a fault-prone model consisting of p processors; here the most interesting case is when the number of simulating processors does not exceed the number of simulated processors.

2.4 Measures of Efficiency

We now define the complexity measures that are used to evaluate the efficiency of algorithms and to establish lower bounds for cooperative computation.

Work complexity. We first define the notion of *work*. We are considering two definitions. The first, called *total-work*, accounts for all computation steps performed by the available processors; this is also called the *available processor steps* measure. The second, called *task-oriented work*, accounts only for the tasks performed by the available processors, discounting all other computation steps performed by the available processors. We note that the second definition is meaningful only for task-performing algorithms, while the total-work measure is more general. We also make an immediate observation that total-work is never less than the task-oriented work (this is elaborated on following the formal definitions of work).

We assume that it takes a unit of time for a processor to perform a unit of work, according to its local clock. Let A be an algorithm that solves a problem of size n with p processors under adversary $\mathcal{A}$. For an execution $\xi \in \mathcal{E}(A, \mathcal{A})$ denote by $S_i(\xi)$ the number of processors completing a unit of work at time i of the execution, according to some external global clock (not available to the processors).

Definition 2.4 (*total-work* or *available processor steps*). *Let A be an algorithm that solves a problem of size n with p processors under adversary $\mathcal{A}$. For execution $\xi \in \mathcal{E}(A, \mathcal{A})$, where $\|\xi|_{\mathcal{A}}\| \leq f$, let time $\tau(\xi)$ be the time (according to the external clock) by which A solves the problem. Then* total-work complexity S *of algorithm A is:*

$$
S = S_{\mathcal{A}}(n, p, f) = \max_{\xi \in \mathcal{E}(A, \mathcal{A}),\ \|\xi|_{\mathcal{A}}\| \leq f} \left\{ \sum_{i=1}^{\tau(\xi)} S_i(\xi) \right\}.
$$

Note that in Definition 2.4 the idling processors consume a unit of work per idling step even though they do not execute tasks. In the cases where we deal with randomized algorithms, we assess *expected total-work* $ES_{\mathcal{A}}(n, p, f)$ computed as the expectation of the sum $\sum_{i=1}^{\tau(\xi)} S_i(\xi)$ from Definition 2.4.

Let A be a task-performing algorithm that solves a problem with n tasks and p processors under adversary $\mathcal{A}$. For an execution $\xi \in \mathcal{E}(A, \mathcal{A})$ denote by $W_i(\xi)$ the number of processors completing a task at time i of the execution, according to some external global clock (not available to the processors).

Definition 2.5 (*task-oriented work*). *Let A be a task-performing algorithm that solves a problem with n tasks and p processors under adversary $\mathcal{A}$. For execution $\xi \in \mathcal{E}(A, \mathcal{A})$, where $\|\xi|_{\mathcal{A}}\| \leq f$, let time $\tau(\xi)$ be the time (according to the external clock) by which A solves the problem. Then* task-oriented work complexity W *of algorithm A is:*

$$W = W_{\mathcal{A}}(n, p, f) = \max_{\xi \in \mathcal{E}(A, \mathcal{A}),\ \|\xi|_{\mathcal{A}}\| \leq f} \left\{ \sum_{i=1}^{\tau(\xi)} W_i(\xi) \right\}.$$

Note that in Definition 2.5 the idling processors are not charged for work (since we count only task-oriented units of work). When dealing with randomized algorithms, expected *expected task-oriented work* $EW_{\mathcal{A}}(n, p, f)$ is assessed as the expectation of the sum $\sum_{i=1}^{\tau(\xi)} W_i(\xi)$ from Definition 2.5.

Observe from the above definitions that the *total-work* measure is more "conservative" than the *task-oriented work* measure. Given an algorithm A that solves *Do-All* under adversary $\mathcal{A}$ then $W_{\mathcal{A}}(n, p, f) = O(S_{\mathcal{A}}(n, p, f))$, since $S_{\mathcal{A}}(n, p, f)$ counts the idle/wait steps, which are not included in $W_{\mathcal{A}}(n, p, f)$. This if an upper bound is established for total-work, it is automatically the upper bound for task-oriented work. The equality $W_{\mathcal{A}}(n, p, f) = S_{\mathcal{A}}(n, p, f)$ can be achieved, for example, by algorithms that perform at least one task during any fixed time period. It also follows that $S_{\mathcal{A}}(n, p, f) = \Omega(W_{\mathcal{A}}(n, p, f))$. This if a lower bound is established for task-oriented work, it is automatically the lower bound for total-work.

Also note that Definitions 2.4 and 2.5 do not depend on the specifics of the target model of computation, e.g., whether it is message-passing or shared-memory. When presenting algorithmic solutions or lower/upper bounds, we explicitly state which work measure is assumed.

We also use two additional work-oriented complexity measures in latter chapters. In Chapter 9 we define the notion of *work-competitiveness* that relates the work of a particular algorithm to that of an optimal algorithm. In Chapter 10 we define the notion of *waste* that measures the number of tasks executed redundantly by a set of isolated processors up to the instant when these processors rendezvous.

Message complexity. The efficiency of message-passing algorithms is additionally characterized in terms of their *message complexity*. Let A be an algorithm that solves a problem of size n with p processors under adversary $\mathcal{A}$. For an execution $\xi \in \mathcal{E}(A, \mathcal{A})$ denote by $M_i(\xi)$ the number of point-to-point messages sent at time i of the execution, according to some external global clock.

Definition 2.6 (message complexity). *Let* A *be an algorithm that solves a problem of size* n *with* p *processors under adversary* $\mathcal{A}$. *For execution* $\xi \in \mathcal{E}(A, \mathcal{A})$, *where* $\|\xi|_{\mathcal{A}}\| \leq f$, *let time* $\tau(\xi)$ *be the time (according to the external clock) by which* A *solves the problem. Then* message complexity M *of algorithm* A *is:*

$$M = M_{\mathcal{A}}(n, p, f) = \max_{\xi \in \mathcal{E}(A, \mathcal{A}),\ \|\xi|_{\mathcal{A}}\| \leq f} \left\{ \sum_{i=1}^{\tau(\xi)} M_i(\xi) \right\}.$$

Note that when processors communicate using broadcasts or multicasts, each broadcast / multicast is counted as the number of point-to-point messages from the sender to each receiver. In the cases where we deal with randomized algorithms, we assess *expected message complexity* $EM_{\mathcal{A}}(n, p, f)$ computed as the expectation of the sum $\sum_{i=1}^{\tau(\xi)} M_i(\xi)$ from Definition 2.6.

Measuring time. In the analysis of work-performing algorithms in the presence of adversity the time complexity does not play a central role as compared to the role it plays in the analysis of sequential algorithms. This is because, in the worst case, time can either be the task-oriented work W or the total-work S, if adversity results in at most one processor executing a local computation step for each global time step. We use the conventional notion of *time* (local or global) to measure the number of steps (e.g., machine instructions) executed locally by a processor in performing activities of interest, or, for synchronous models, to measure the time in the conventional sense, for example in establishing the number of synchronous algorithm iterations. We use time in several analyses. We also define it formally for the analysis in Chapter 4.

2.5 Chapter Notes

The distributed cooperation problem that we call *Do-All* here was first studied in message-passing systems by Dwork, Halpern, and Waarts in [30], who defined the task-oriented work measure and who provided several algorithms solving the problem. De Prisco, Mayer, and Yung were first to study the *Do-All* problem under the total-work complexity measure. The distributed cooperation problem was first called "*Do-All*" by Chlebus, De Prisco, and Shvartsman [15], who studied it for the model with processor crashes and restarts. The *Omni-Do* problem was first studied by Dolev, Segala and Shvartsman in [29]. The problem was subsequently called "*Omni-Do*" by Georgiou and Shvartsman in [48], who studied it in the settings with network fragmentation and merges.

The problem of cooperative computing in the presence of adversity in shared-memory settings was first considered by Kanellakis and Shvartsman [66]. They referred to the problem as "*Write-All*". Algorithms solving the *Write-All* problem have been used in developing simulations of failure-free algorithms on failure-prone processors, e.g., [70, 104, 87, 67]. This is done by iteratively using a *Write-All* algorithm to simulate the steps of failure-free processors on failure-prone processors. Motivated by such algorithm simulations, Georgiou, Russell and Shvartsman [45] formulated the *iterative Do-All* problem and studied it in message-passing and shared-memory models.

Definition 2.4 of total-work, denoted by S, is based on the *available processor steps* measure, introduced by Kanellakis and Shvartsman in [66]. Definition 2.5 of task-oriented work, denoted by W, is based on the *number of tasks performed* measure, introduced by Dwork, Halpern and Waarts in [30].

The definition of the fail-stop model (with or without restarts) is taken from the work of Schlichting and Schneider [102]. Byzantine processor failures were introduced by Lamport, Shostak and Pease in [78]. Group-oriented algorithms for partitionable networks are typically studied in conjunction with Group Communication Services [97]. The adversarial classifications oblivious/off-line and omniscient/on-line are taken from [12].

3

Synchronous Do-All with Crashes: Using Perfect Knowledge and Reliable Multicast

WE start the study of the *Do-All* problem by considering a synchronous distributed environment and under the adversary that can cause processor crashes, the more benign type of adversity. In order to understand better the inherent limitations and difficulties of solving the *Do-All* and *iterative Do-All* problems in the presence of crashes, we first abstract away any communication issues by assuming an oracle that provides load-balancing and computational progress information to the processors. Such and oracle provides, what we call, *perfect knowledge* to the algorithms solving the problem. We present matching upper and lower bounds on total-work for models with perfect knowledge. These bounds are *failure-sensitive*, which means we give bounds that carefully incorporate the (maximum) number of processor crashes. We then present an algorithm that efficiently solves the *Do-All* and *iterative Do-All* problems assuming a message-passing environment where *reliable multicast* is available. If a processor crashes after starting a multicast of a message, then this message is either received by all non-faulty targeted processors or by none. In this setting the availability of reliable multicast effectively approximates the availability of perfect knowledge, making it possible to use the complexity results for perfect knowledge in the analysis of the algorithm.

Chapter structure.

In Section 3.1 we define the adversary considered in this chapter, called $\mathcal{A}_C$. In Section 3.2 the upper and lower bound on total-work for *Do-All* and *iterative Do-All* are presented. In Section 3.3 we present an algorithm, called algorithm AN, that solves *Do-All* using reliable multicast. We give its correctness and its complexity analysis. Also a non-trivial result for *iterative Do-All* for message-passing systems is given. We discuss open problems in Section 3.4.

3.1 Adversarial Model

We denote by $\mathcal{A}_C$ the omniscient (on-line) adversary that can cause processor crashes, as defined in Section 2.2.1. Once a processor is crashed, it does not restart. Consider an algorithm A that performs a computation in the presence of adversary $\mathcal{A}_C$. Let ξ be an execution in $\mathcal{E}(A, \mathcal{A}_C)$. We represent the adversarial pattern $\xi|_{\mathcal{A}_C}$ as a set of triples $(crash, \text{PID}, t)$, where $crash$ is the event caused by the adversary, PID is the identifier of the processor that crashes, and t is the time of the execution (according to some external global clock not available to the processors) when the adversary crashes processor PID. Any adversarial pattern contains at most one triple $(crash, \text{PID}, t)$ for any PID, viz., if processor PID crashes, the time t when it crashes is uniquely defined.

For an adversarial pattern $\xi|_{\mathcal{A}_C}$ we define $f_c(\xi|_{\mathcal{A}_C}) = \|\xi|_{\mathcal{A}_C}\|$ to be the number of processors that crash. It is only interesting to consider the executions ξ where $f_c(\xi|_{\mathcal{A}_C}) < p$, that is the executions in which at least one processor remains operational.

3.2 Lower and Upper Bounds for Abstract Models

In this section we consider computations where the processors, instead of communicating with each other, communicate with some deterministic omniscient *oracle*, call it oracle $\mathcal{O}$, to obtain information regarding the status of the computation.

The assumption of perfect knowledge (or the oracle assumption) abstracts away any concerns about communication that normally dominate specific message-passing and shared-memory models. This allows for the most general results to be established and it enables us to use these results in the context of specific models by understanding how the information provided by an oracle is simulated in specific algorithms. Also, any lower bound developed under the assumption of perfect knowledge, applies equally well to other models where means of communication between processors are specified, for example, message-passing and shared-memory models.

3.2.1 Modeling Knowledge

Knowledge is modeled via Oracle $\mathcal{O}$ that provides termination and load-balancing information to the processors. In particular, the oracle informs the processors whether the computation is completed and if not, what task to perform next. We assume that the oracle performs perfect load-balancing, that is, the live processors are only allocated to unperformed tasks, and all such tasks are allocated a balanced number of live processors. We also assume that a processor can obtain load-balancing and termination information from the oracle in $O(1)$ time and that it can consult the oracle only once per local clock-tick.

Note that from the above assumptions all processor steps are in fact task-oriented steps, and hence in this setting the work and task-oriented work complexities measures are equivalent metrics for evaluating *Do-All* algorithms. Furthermore, we let *Do-All*$^{\mathcal{O}}_{\mathcal{A}_C}(n, p, f)$ and *r-Do-All*$^{\mathcal{O}}_{\mathcal{A}_C}(n, p, f)$ stand for the *Do-All*$_{\mathcal{A}_C}(n, p, f)$ and *r-Do-All*$_{\mathcal{A}_C}(n, p, f)$ problems, respectively, when the processors are assisted by oracle $\mathcal{O}$.

We present *matching* upper and lower bound results on work for these problems.

3.2.2 Lower Bounds

We begin by developing lower bounds for *Do-All*$^{\mathcal{O}}_{\mathcal{A}_C}(n, p, f)$ and *r-Do-All*$^{\mathcal{O}}_{\mathcal{A}_C}(n, p, f)$. Note that the results in this section hold also for the *Do-All*$_{\mathcal{A}_C}(n, p, f)$ and *r-Do-All*$_{\mathcal{A}_C}(n, p, f)$ problems (without the oracle), as well as for *Do-All*$_{\mathcal{A}}(n, p, f)$ and *r-Do-All*$_{\mathcal{A}}(n, p, f)$, where $\mathcal{A}_C \subseteq \mathcal{A}$. (e.g., processor crashes and restarts).

The following mathematical facts are used in the proofs.

Fact 3.1 *If $a_1, a_2, \ldots, a_m$ ($m > 1$) is a sorted list of nonnegative integers, then for all j ($1 \leq j < m$) we have $\left(1 - \frac{j}{m}\right) \sum_{i=1}^{m} a_i \leq \sum_{i=j+1}^{m} a_i$.*

Fact 3.2 *Given $n \in \mathbb{N}$, $\kappa \in \mathbb{R}$, such that $n \cdot \kappa > 1$, $\kappa \leq \frac{1}{2}$, and $\sigma \in \mathbb{N}$ such that $\sigma < \frac{\log n}{\log(\kappa^{-1})} - 1$, then the following inequality holds: $\underbrace{\lfloor \ldots \lfloor \lfloor n \cdot \kappa \rfloor \cdot \kappa \rfloor \ldots \cdot \kappa \rfloor}_{\sigma \ times} > 0$.*

Proof. To show the result it suffices to show that, after dropping one floor and strengthening the inequality: $(\underbrace{\lfloor \ldots \lfloor \lfloor n \cdot \kappa \rfloor \cdot \kappa \rfloor \ldots \cdot \kappa \rfloor}_{\sigma-1 \ times} \cdot \kappa) - 1 > 0$, or that

$$\underbrace{\lfloor \ldots \lfloor \lfloor n \cdot \kappa \rfloor \cdot \kappa \rfloor \ldots \cdot \kappa \rfloor}_{\sigma-1 \ times} > \frac{1}{\kappa}.$$

Applying this transformation for $\sigma - 1$ more steps, we see that it suffices to show that $n > \frac{1}{\kappa^{\sigma}} + \frac{1}{\kappa^{\sigma-1}} + \ldots + \frac{1}{\kappa}$, or, using geometric progression summation, that $n > \frac{(\kappa^{-1})^{\sigma+1} - (\kappa^{-1})}{(\kappa^{-1}) - 1}$.

We observe that $(\kappa^{-1})^{\sigma+1} > \frac{(\kappa^{-1})^{\sigma+1} - (\kappa^{-1})}{(\kappa^{-1}) - 1}$ for $\kappa \leq \frac{1}{2}$, thus it is enough to show that $n > (\kappa^{-1})^{\sigma+1}$. After taking logarithms of both sides of the inequality, $\log n > (\sigma + 1) \log(\kappa^{-1})$, and so it suffices to have $\sigma < \frac{\log n}{\log(\kappa^{-1})} - 1$. □

We now define a specific adversarial strategy of adversary $\mathcal{A}_C$ used to derive our lower bounds. Let A be an iterative algorithm that solves the *Do-All* problem. Let p_i be the number of processors remaining at the end of the ith iteration of an execution of A and let u_i denote the number of tasks that remain to be done at the end of iteration i. Initially, $p_0 = p$ and $u_0 = n$. The adversarial strategy is defined assuming the same initial number of tasks and processors, that is, $p_0 = n_0$. The strategy of the adversary is defined for each iteration of the algorithm. Based on a variable κ, defined in the interval $(0, 1/2)$, the adversary determines which processors will be allowed to work and which will be stopped in a given iteration. We call this adversarial strategy $\mathfrak{A}$.

Adversarial strategy $\mathfrak{A}$:

Iteration 1: The adversary chooses $u_1 = \lfloor \kappa u_0 \rfloor$ tasks with the least number of processors assigned to them. This can be done since the adversary is omniscient; it knows all the actions to be performed by A (as well as any advice provided by the oracle). The adversary then crashes the processors assigned to these tasks, if any.

Iteration i: Among u_{i-1} tasks remaining after the iteration $i - 1$, the adversary chooses $u_i = \lfloor \kappa u_{i-1} \rfloor$ tasks with the least number of processors assigned to them and crashes these processors.

Termination: The adversary continues for as long as $u_i > 1$. As soon as $u_i = 1$, the adversary allows all remaining processors to perform the single remaining task, and A terminates.

We now study the adversarial strategy $\mathfrak{A}$ and derive lower bound results.

Remark 3.3. Relationship between n and κ: If κ is chosen so that $\kappa \cdot n \leq 1$ then by the adversarial strategy $\mathfrak{A}$, an algorithm solving *Do-All* may be able to solve it in a constant number of iterations (namely two) with work $O(p)$. This is because $u_1 = \lfloor \kappa u_0 \rfloor \leq \kappa n \leq 1$. Henceforth we consider κ to be such that $\kappa \cdot n > 1$.

Lemma 3.4. *For adversarial strategy $\mathfrak{A}$, if at iteration i the number of remaining tasks is $u_{i-1} > 1$, then*

(a) $u_i = \lfloor \ldots \lfloor \lfloor \underbrace{n \cdot \kappa \rfloor \cdot \kappa \rfloor \ldots \cdot \kappa}_{i\ times} \rfloor$, *and*

(b) $p_i \geq (1 - \kappa)^i p_0$.

Proof. Part (a) is immediate from the definition of $\mathfrak{A}$. To express the number of surviving processors p_i for part (b), we use Fact 3.1 with the following definitions:

Let $m = u_{i-1}$, and let $a_1, \ldots, a_m$ be the quantities of processors assigned to each task, sorted in ascending order. Let a_m also include the quantity of any un-assigned processors, i.e., a_1 is the least number of processors assigned to a task, a_2 is the next least quantity of processors, etc. (In other words, $a_1 \leq a_2 \leq \ldots \leq a_m$.) Let $j = u_i$. Thus the adversary stops exactly $\sum_{i=1}^{j} a_i$ processors. At the beginning of iteration i, the number of processors $p_{i-1} = \sum_{i=1}^{m} a_i$, therefore, the number of surviving processors $p_i = \sum_{i=j+1}^{m} a_i$.

Using Fact 3.1, we have $p_i \geq (1 - \frac{u_i}{u_{i-1}})p_{i-1}$, and after substituting for $u_i = \lfloor \kappa u_{i-1} \rfloor$ we have

$$p_i \geq \left(1 - \frac{\lfloor \kappa u_{i-1} \rfloor}{u_{i-1}}\right) p_{i-1} \geq (1 - \kappa) p_{i-1} \geq (1 - \kappa)^i p_0,$$

as desired.   □

Lemma 3.5. *Given any algorithm solving the Do-All$^{\mathcal{O}}_{\mathcal{A_C}}(p, p, f)$ problem ($p = n$), the adversarial strategy $\mathfrak{A}$ will cause the algorithm to cycle through at least $\frac{\log p}{\log(\kappa^{-1})} - 1$ iterations.*

Proof. Let τ be the earliest iteration when the last task is performed. We use Fact 3.2 with σ the largest integer such that $\sigma < \log p / \log(\kappa^{-1}) - 1$. Then $u_\sigma = \underbrace{\lfloor \ldots \lfloor \lfloor p \cdot \kappa \rfloor \cdot \kappa \rfloor \ldots \cdot \kappa \rfloor}_{\sigma \; times} > 0$, and so τ must be greater than σ because $u_\tau = 0$. Thus, $\tau \geq \frac{\log p}{\log(\kappa^{-1})} - 1 > \sigma$.   □

Lemma 3.6. *Given any algorithm A that solves the Do-All$^{\mathcal{O}}_{\mathcal{A_C}}(p, p, f)$ problem ($p = n$) with $f < p$, the adversarial strategy $\mathfrak{A}$ with $\kappa = \frac{1}{\log p}$ causes work $S = \Omega\left(p\frac{\log p}{\log \log p}\right).$*

Proof. We first assume that $p > 4$ (we aim to establish an asymptotic result, and this eliminates uninteresting cases). Since $\kappa = 1/\log p$, we have that $\kappa \in (0, 1/2)$ when $p > 4$. From Lemma 3.4(a) and Lemma 3.5 we see that $\mathfrak{A}$ will cause algorithm A to iterate at least $\tau = (\log p / \log \log p) - 1$ times. Now observe that the work must be at least $p_\tau \cdot \tau$, where p_τ is the number of surviving processors after A terminates. From Lemma 3.4(b) we have that $p_\tau \geq (1 - \kappa)^\tau p_0 = (1 - \frac{1}{\log p})^\tau p$. Therefore,

$$p_\tau \geq p\left(1 - \frac{1}{\log p}\right)^{\frac{\log p}{\log \log p} - 1} \geq p\left(1 - \frac{1}{\log p}\right)^{\frac{\log p}{\log \log p}}$$
$$\geq p\left(1 - \left(\frac{1}{\log p}\right) \cdot \left(\frac{\log p}{\log \log p}\right)\right) = p - \frac{p}{\log \log p}.$$

Let f_τ denote the actual number of crashes caused by the adversary. Then, $f_\tau = p - p_\tau \leq p - p + \frac{p}{\log \log p} = \frac{p}{\log \log p} < p$. Hence, $\mathfrak{A}$ when using this specific κ does not exceed the allowed number of crashes. Now, the work caused by $\mathfrak{A}$ is:

$$S = \Omega(p_\tau \cdot \tau) = \Omega\left(\left(p - \frac{p}{\log \log p}\right) \cdot \left(\frac{\log p}{\log \log p} - 1\right)\right) = \Omega\left(p\frac{\log p}{\log \log p}\right).$$

This completes the proof.   □

Corollary 3.7. *Given any algorithm* A *that solves the Do-All$_{\mathcal{AC}}^{\mathcal{O}}(n, p, f)$ prob-lem ($p \leq n$) there exists an adversarial strategy that causes work* $S = \Omega\left(n + p\dfrac{\log p}{\log \log p}\right)$.

Proof. Note that $S = \Omega(n)$ because all tasks must be performed. From Lemma 3.6 we know that Do-All$_{\mathcal{AC}}^{\mathcal{O}}(p, p, f)$ requires $\Omega(p \log p / \log \log p)$ work. Given that work is nondecreasing in n (as follows from Definition 2.4) we obtain the desired result by combining the two bounds. $\square$

Observe that Lemma 3.6 and Corollary 3.7 do not show how work depends on f. We now give lower bounds considering moderate number of crashes ($f \leq p / \log p$).

Lemma 3.8. *Given any algorithm* A *that solves the Do-All$_{\mathcal{AC}}^{\mathcal{O}}(p, p, f)$ problem* ($p = n$), *the adversarial strategy* $\mathfrak{A}$ *with* $(\kappa^{-1}) \log(\kappa^{-1}) = \dfrac{p \log p}{f}$ *and* $f \leq \dfrac{p}{\log p}$ *causes work* $S = \Omega\left(p \log_{\frac{p}{f}} p\right)$.

Proof. We assume that $p > 4$ (we aim to establish an asymptotic result, and this eliminates uninteresting cases). From $(\kappa^{-1}) \log(\kappa^{-1}) = \frac{p \log p}{f}$, $f \leq \frac{p}{\log p}$, and $p > 4$ we see that $\log(\kappa^{-1}) > 4\kappa$. This implies that $\kappa \in (0, 1/2)$. Hence, from Lemma 3.5 we have that $\mathfrak{A}$ will cause algorithm A to iterate at least $\tau = (\log p / \log(\kappa^{-1})) - 1$ times.

Now observe that the work must be at least $p_\tau \cdot \tau$, where p_τ is the number of surviving processors after A terminates. Recall from Lemma 3.4(b) that $p_\tau \geq (1 - \kappa)^\tau p_0$. Therefore,

$$
\begin{aligned}
p_\tau &\geq p(1 - \kappa)^\tau & &\geq p(1 - \kappa)^{\frac{\log p}{\log(\kappa^{-1})} - 1} \\
&\geq p(1 - \kappa)^{\frac{\log p}{\log(\kappa^{-1})}} & &\geq p\left(1 - \kappa \cdot \frac{\log p}{\log(\kappa^{-1})}\right) \\
&= p\left(1 - \left(\frac{\kappa}{\log(\kappa^{-1})}\right)\log p\right) &= p&\left(1 - \left(\frac{f}{p \log p}\right)\log p\right) \\
&= p - f.
\end{aligned}
$$

Let f_τ denote the actual number of crashes caused by the adversary. Then, $f_\tau = p - p_\tau \leq p - (p - f) = f$. Hence, $\mathfrak{A}$ when using this specific κ does not exceed the allowed number of crashes ($f \leq p / \log p$).

Recall that $(\kappa^{-1}) \log(\kappa^{-1}) = \frac{p \log p}{f}$, therefore, $(\kappa^{-1}) = \Theta\left(\dfrac{\frac{p \log p}{f}}{\log\left(\frac{p \log p}{f}\right)}\right)$. Thus,

$$
\log(\kappa^{-1}) = \Theta\left(\log\left(\frac{p \log p}{f}\right) - \log \log\left(\frac{p \log p}{f}\right)\right) = \Theta\left(\log\left(\frac{p \log p}{f}\right)\right).
$$

Then, noting that $p_\tau \geq p - f \geq p - p / \log p = \Theta(p)$ and that $\kappa \cdot p > 1$ (see Remark 3.3), we assess the work S caused by $\mathfrak{A}$ as follows:

$$S = \Omega(p_\tau \cdot \tau) = \Omega\left(p \cdot \frac{\log p}{\log(\kappa^{-1})}\right) = \Omega\left(p + p\frac{\log p}{\log(\frac{p\log p}{f})}\right).$$

Now recall that $p/f \geq \log p$. Hence, for any $p > 4$ we have that $p/f > 2$ and that $\log((p\log p)/f) = \log(p/f) + \log\log p = \Theta(\log(p/f))$. From the above,

$$S = \Omega\left(p + p\frac{\log p}{\log(\frac{p}{f})}\right) = \Omega\left(p\log_{\frac{p}{f}} p\right).$$

This completes the proof.   □

Corollary 3.9. *Given any algorithm* A *that solves the Do-All$^{\mathcal{O}}_{\mathcal{A_C}}(n, p, f)$ problem ($p \leq n$), there exists an adversarial strategy that causes $f \leq \frac{p}{\log p}$ crashes, and work $S = \Omega\left(n + p\log_{\frac{p}{f}} p\right)$.*

Proof. Note that $S = \Omega(n)$ because all tasks must be performed. From Lemma 3.8 we know that Do-All$^{\mathcal{O}}_{\mathcal{A_C}}(p, p, f)$ requires $\Omega(p\log_{\frac{p}{f}} p)$ work, for $f \leq p/\log p$. Given that work is nondecreasing in n we obtain the desired result by combining the two bounds.   □

We now give the main (failure-sensitive) lower-bound result.

Theorem 3.10. *Given any algorithm* A *that solves the Do-All$^{\mathcal{O}}_{\mathcal{A_C}}(n, p, f)$ problem there exists an adversarial strategy that causes work*

$$S = \Omega\left(n + p\frac{\log p}{\log(p/f)}\right) \text{ when } f \leq \frac{p}{\log p}, \text{ and}$$

$$S = \Omega\left(n + p\frac{\log p}{\log\log p}\right) \text{ when } \frac{p}{\log p} < f < p.$$

Proof. For the range of failures $f \leq p/\log p$, per Corollary 3.9, the work is $\Omega(n + p\log_{p/f} p)$.

From Corollary 3.9 we also obtain the fact that when $f = p/\log p$ then work must be $\Omega(n + p\log p/\log\log p)$. Note that this is the worst case work for any f (see Corollary 3.7). Therefore, for the range $p/\log p < f < p$, the adversary establishes this worst case work using the initial $p/\log p$ failures. □

The above theorem yields a lower bound result for the r-Do-All$^{\mathcal{O}}_{\mathcal{A_C}}(n, p, f)$ problem.

Theorem 3.11. *Given any algorithm that solves the r-Do-All$^{\mathcal{O}}_{\mathcal{A_C}}(n, p, f)$ problem, there exists an adversarial strategy that causes work*

$$S = \Omega\left(r \cdot \left(n + p\frac{\log p}{\log(pr/f)}\right)\right) \text{ when } f \leq \frac{pr}{\log p}, \text{ and}$$

$$S = \Omega\left(r \cdot \left(n + p\frac{\log p}{\log\log p}\right)\right) \text{ when } \frac{pr}{\log p} < f < p.$$

Proof. Consider two cases:

Case 1: $f > \frac{pr}{\log p}$. In this case the adversary may crash $p/\log p$ processors in every round of r-*Do-All*$^{\mathcal{O}}_{\mathcal{A}_C}(n, p, f)$. Note that for this adversary $\Omega(p)$ processors remain alive during the first $\lceil r/2 \rceil$ rounds. Per Theorem 3.10 this results in $\lceil r/2 \rceil \cdot \Omega (n + p \log p / \log \log p) = \Omega (nr + pr \log p / \log \log p)$ work.

Case 2: $f \le \frac{pr}{\log p}$. In this case the adversary ideally would crash f/r processors in every round. It can do that in the case where r divides f. If this is not the case, then the adversary crashes $\lceil f/r \rceil$ processors in r_A rounds and $\lfloor f/r \rfloor$ in r_B rounds in such a way that $r = r_A + r_B$. Again considering the first half of the rounds and appealing to Theorem 3.10 results in a $\Omega \left(nr + pr \log_{pr/f} p \right)$ lower bound for work. Note that we consider only the case where $r \le f$; otherwise the work is trivially $\Omega(rn)$.

The result then follows by combining the two cases.   □

3.2.3 Upper Bounds

To study the upper bounds for *Do-All* we give an oracle-based algorithm in Figure 3.1. The algorithm uses oracle $\mathcal{O}$ that performs the termination and load-balancing computation on behalf of the processors. In particular, during each synchronous iteration of an execution of the algorithm, the oracle $\mathcal{O}$ makes available to each processor i two values: *Oracle-complete*, a Boolean which takes the value true if and only if all tasks are complete at the beginning of this iteration, and *Oracle-task*(i), a natural number from $[n]$, whose value is a task identifier. *Oracle-task* is a function from processor identifiers to task identifiers, with the property that processors are only allocated to undone tasks, and that all such tasks are allocated a balanced number of processors. For example, if processors $i_1, \ldots, i_k \in [p]$ are alive and tasks $j_1, \ldots, j_\ell \in [n]$ are undone at the beginning of a given iteration of the algorithm, then *Oracle-task*$(i_s) = j_t$, where $t = (s - 1 \bmod \ell) + 1$.

---

for each processor PID $= 1..p$ **begin**
    while not *Oracle-complete*
        perform task with TID $=$ *Oracle-task*(PID)
end

Fig. 3.1. Oracle-based algorithm.

We begin with the following result:

Lemma 3.12. *The Do-All*$^{\mathcal{O}}_{\mathcal{A}_C}(n, p, f)$ *problem can be solved with* $f < p$ *using work*

$$S = O \left(n + p \frac{\log p}{\log \log p} \right).$$

Note that Lemma 3.12 does not show how, if at all, work depends on f. We now present an upper bound considering moderate number of crashes ($f \leq p/\log p$).

Lemma 3.13. *The Do-All$^\mathcal{O}_{\mathcal{AC}}(n, p, f)$ problem can be solved with $f \leq p/\log p$ using work*

$$S = O\left(n + p \log_{\frac{p}{f}} p\right).$$

Proof. For an iteration of the algorithm in Figure 3.1, let Δf denote the number of processor crashes in this iteration. (Δf can be different for each iteration, though the sum of these for all iterations cannot exceed f.) We set $b = b(p, f) = \frac{p}{2f}$, and we define $S(n, p, f)$ to be the work required to solve Do-All$^\mathcal{O}_{\mathcal{AC}}(n, p, f)$. Our goal is to show that for all u, p and f, the work $S(u, p, f)$ is no more than $16p + u + p \log_{\frac{p}{2f}}(\min(u, p))$, where $u \leq n$ denotes the number of undone tasks. The proof proceeds by induction on u.

Base Case: Observe that when $u \leq 16$, $S(u, p, f) \leq 16p < 16p + u + p \log_b(\min(u, p))$, for all p and f.

Inductive Hypothesis: Assume that we have proved the theorem for all $u < \hat{u}$ ($\hat{u} \leq n$) and all p and f.

Inductive Step: Consider $u = \hat{u}$. We investigate two cases:

Case 1: $p \leq \hat{u}$ (in particular, $\min(\hat{u}, p) = p$). In this case each processor is assigned to a unique task, hence

$$S(\hat{u}, p, f) \leq p + \max_{0 \leq \Delta f \leq f} S(\hat{u} - p + \Delta f, p - \Delta f, f - \Delta f).$$

As $p - \Delta f > 0$, $\hat{u} - p + \Delta f < \hat{u}$ and, by the induction hypothesis,

$$S(\hat{u}, p, f) \leq p + \max_{0 \leq \Delta f \leq f} \Big[16(p - \Delta f) + (\hat{u} - p + \Delta f)$$
$$+ (p - \Delta f) \log_{b(p - \Delta f, f - \Delta f)}(\min(\hat{u} - p + \Delta f, p - \Delta f) \Big]$$

Now, $b(p - \Delta f, f - \Delta f) \geq b(p, f)$, and

$$\log_{b(p,f)}(\min(\hat{u} - p + \Delta f, p - \Delta f) \leq \log_{b(p,f)}(p - \Delta f),$$

so that

$$S(\hat{u}, p, f) \leq 16p + \hat{u} + p \log_{b(p,f)} p = 16p + \hat{u} + p \log_{b(p,f)}(\min(\hat{u}, p)),$$

as desired.

Case 2: $p > \hat{u}$ (in particular, $\min(\hat{u}, p) = \hat{u}$). In this case, by assumption we have

$$S(\hat{u}, p, f) \leq p + \max_{0 \leq \Delta f \leq f} S(\gamma \hat{u}, p - \Delta f, f - \Delta f),$$

where $\gamma = \gamma(\hat{u}, p, \Delta f)$ is the ratio of the number of the remaining tasks to $\hat{u}$ $(0 \leq \gamma < 1)$.

Let $\phi = \Delta f / p \leq f / p < 1$, the fraction of processors which fail during this iteration; then $\phi/2 < \gamma < 2\phi$. (To see this, observe that

$$\frac{\phi p}{\lceil p/\hat{u} \rceil \hat{u}} = \frac{\phi p / \lceil p/\hat{u} \rceil}{\hat{u}} \leq \gamma \leq \frac{\phi p / \lfloor p/\hat{u} \rfloor}{\hat{u}} = \frac{\phi p}{\lfloor p/\hat{u} \rfloor \hat{u}}.$$

Let $p = c\hat{u}$, $c > 1$. Then

$$\frac{c}{\lceil c \rceil} \phi = \frac{\phi c \hat{u}}{\lceil c \rceil \hat{u}} \leq \gamma \leq \frac{\phi c \hat{u}}{\lfloor c \rfloor \hat{u}} = \frac{c}{\lfloor c \rfloor} \phi.$$

Now observe that $1 \leq \frac{c}{\lfloor c \rfloor} < 2$ and $1/2 < \frac{c}{\lceil c \rceil} \leq 1$, $\forall c > 1$, and hence, $\phi/2 < \gamma < 2\phi$, as desired.) Then,

$$S(\hat{u}, p, f) \leq p + \max_{\phi \in [0, f/p]} S(\gamma \hat{u}, (1 - \phi)p, f - \phi p).$$

As $\gamma \hat{u} < \hat{u}$, we may apply the induction hypothesis:

$$S(\hat{u}, p, f) \leq p + \max_{\phi \in [0, f/p]} \left[16(1 - \phi)p + \gamma \hat{u} + (1 - \phi)p \log_{b'} (\min(\gamma \hat{u}, (1 - \phi)p)) \right],$$

where $b' = b(p - \phi p, f - \phi p)$. As above, $b' \geq b(p, f)$ and $\min(\gamma \hat{u}, (1-\phi)p)) \leq \gamma \hat{u}$, so that

$$S(\hat{u}, p, f) \leq p + \max_{\phi \in [0, f/p]} \left[16(1 - \phi)p + \gamma \hat{u} + (1 - \phi)p \log_{b(p,f)}(\gamma \hat{u}) \right].$$

To complete the proof, it suffices to show that for all $\phi \in [0, f/p]$,

$$15p + p \log_{b(p,f)} \hat{u} - (1 - \phi)p \log_{b(p,f)}(\gamma \hat{u}) \geq 16(1 - \phi)p - \hat{u}(1 - \gamma).$$

Upper bounding $16(1 - \phi)p - \hat{u}(1 - \gamma)$ with $16(1 - \phi)p$ and dividing through by p, it is sufficient to show that

$$15 + \log_{b(p,f)} \hat{u} - (1 - \phi) \log_{b(p,f)}(\gamma \hat{u}) \geq 16(1 - \phi),$$

or, equivalently,

$$\log_{b(p,f)} \hat{u} - (1 - \phi) \log_{b(p,f)}(\gamma \hat{u}) \geq 1 - 16\phi.$$

We now focus on the left hand side of the above equation:

$$\log_{b(p,f)} \hat{u} - (1 - \phi) \left[\log_{b(p,f)} \gamma + \log_{b(p,f)} \hat{u} \right]$$
$$= \phi \log_{b(p,f)} \hat{u} + (1 - \phi) \log_{b(p,f)} \gamma^{-1}.$$

Since $f \leq \frac{p}{\log(\min(\hat{u},p))} = \frac{p}{\log\hat{u}}$, for any $\hat{u} > 16$ we have that $\frac{p}{2f} > 2$. Observe that,

$$\phi \log_{b(p,f)} \hat{u} + (1 - \phi) \log_{b(p,f)} \gamma^{-1} \geq (1 - \phi) \log_{b(p,f)} \gamma^{-1}$$

since $\hat{u} \geq p/f > p/2f$. (Note that if $\hat{u} < p/f$, then all tasks are completed in this iteration.)

Recall that $\gamma^{-1} \geq (2\phi)^{-1}$ and $\phi < f/p$. Therefore,

$$(1 - \phi) \log_{b(p,f)} \gamma^{-1} \geq (1 - \phi) \log_{b(p,f)} (2\phi)^{-1} \geq 1 - 16\phi.$$

Evidently,

$$S = O\left(n + p + p \log_{\frac{p}{f}}(\min(n,p))\right) = O\left(n + p \log_{\frac{p}{f}} p\right),$$

as desired. $\qquad\qquad\square$

We now give the main (failure-sensitive) upper-bound result.

Theorem 3.14. *The Do-All$_{\mathcal{A}_C}^{\mathcal{O}}(n,p,f)$ problem can be solved using work*

$$S = O\left(n + p \frac{\log p}{\log(p/f)}\right) \quad \text{when } f \leq \frac{p}{\log p}, \text{ and}$$

$$S = O\left(n + p \frac{\log p}{\log \log p}\right) \quad \text{when } \frac{p}{\log p} < f < p.$$

Proof. This follows from Lemmas 3.12 and 3.13. $\qquad\qquad\square$

Remark 3.15. Theorems 3.10 and 3.14 show matching lower and upper on total-work for the *Do-All* problem with crash-prone processors under the perfect knowledge assumption. In the analyses of both bounds we essentially account for the tasks performed by the processors. It is not difficult to see that the same bounds apply also to the task-oriented work in this setting.

Upper bounds for iterative *Do-All*. We continue to show an upper bound result for the *iterative Do-All* problem. In principle r-Do-All$_{\mathcal{A}_C}(n,p,f)$ can be solved by running an algorithm for Do-All$_{\mathcal{A}_C}(n,p,f)$ for r iterations. For example, r-Do-All$_{\mathcal{A}_C}^{\mathcal{O}}(n,p,f)$ can be solved by running the oracle-based algorithm in Figure 3.1 for r iterations. If the work of a *Do-All* solution is S, then the work of the *r-iterative Do-All* is at most $r \cdot S$. However we show that it is possible to obtain a finer result that takes into account the diminishing number of failures "available" to the adversary. In particular we obtain the following (failure-sensitive) upper bound on work.

Theorem 3.16. *The r-Do-All$^{\mathcal{O}}_{\mathcal{AC}}(n, p, f)$ problem can be solved using work*

$$S = O\left(r \cdot \left(n + p\frac{\log p}{\log(pr/f)}\right)\right) \quad when \ f \leq \frac{pr}{\log p}, \ and$$

$$S = O\left(r \cdot \left(n + p\frac{\log p}{\log\log p}\right)\right) \quad when \ \frac{pr}{\log p} < f < p.$$

Proof. Let r_i denote the ith round of the iterative Do-All. Let p_i be the number of active processors at the beginning of r_i and f_i be the number of crashes during r_i. Note that $p_1 = p$, where r_1 is the first round of r-Do-All$^{\mathcal{O}}_{\mathcal{AC}}(n, p, f)$ and that $p_i \leq p$. We consider two cases:

Case 1: $f > \frac{pr}{\log p}$. Consider a round r_i. From Theorem 3.14 we see that the work for this round is $O\left(n + p_i \log_{p_i/f_i} p_i\right)$ when $f_i \leq p_i/\log p_i$ and $O\left(n + p_i \log p_i/\log\log p_i\right)$ otherwise. However in this case, we can have $f_i = \Theta(p/\log p)$ for all r_i without "running out" of processors. Thus,

$$S_1 = O\left(r \cdot \left(n + p\frac{\log p}{\log\log p}\right)\right).$$

Case 2: $f \leq \frac{pr}{\log p}$. First observe that any reasonable adversarial strategy would not kill more that $p_i/\log p_i$ processors in round r_i, since it would not cause more work than $O(n + p_i \log p_i/\log\log p_i)$ (which is achieved when $f_i \geq p_i/\log p_i$). Therefore, we consider $f_i \leq p_i/\log p_i$ for all rounds r_i. Hence, the work in every round r_i (per Theorem 3.14) is $O\left(n + p_i \log p_i/\log(p_i/f_i)\right) = O\left(n + p \log p/\log(p/f_i)\right)$.

Let $S(n, p, f)$ be this one-round upper bound. As $f = \sum f_i$, an upper bound on r-Do-All$^{\mathcal{O}}_{\mathcal{AC}}(n, p, f)$ can be given by maximizing $\sum_i S(n, p_i, f_i)$ over all such adversarial patterns. As $S(\cdot, \cdot, \cdot)$ is monotone in p, we may assume that $p_i = p$ for the purposes of the upper bound. We show that this maximum is attained at $f_1 = f_2 = \ldots = f_r$. For simplicity, treat f_i as a continuous parameter and consider the factor in the single round work expression (given above) that depends on f_i: $c/\log(\frac{p}{f_i})$, where c is the constant hidden by the $O(\cdot)$ notation.

The first derivative over f_i is $\frac{\partial}{\partial f_i}\left(c/\log\left(\frac{p}{f_i}\right)\right) = c/f_i(\log p - \log f_i)^2$, and its second derivative is $\frac{\partial^2}{\partial f_i^2}\left(c/\log\left(\frac{p}{f_i}\right)\right) = 2c/f_i^2(\log p - \log f_i)^3 - c/f_i^2(\log p - \log f_i)^2$. Observe that the second derivative is negative in the domain considered (assuming $p > 16$). Hence the first derivative is decreasing (with f_i). In this case, given any two f_i, f_j where $f_i > f_j$, the adversarial pattern obtained by replacing f_i with $f_i - \epsilon$ and f_j by $f_j + \epsilon$ (where $\epsilon < (f_i - f_j)/2$) results in increased work. This implies that the sum maximized when all f_is are equal, specifically when $f_i = f/r$.

As the above upper bound on the sum $\sum_i S(n, p_i, f_i)$ is valid over *all* f_i in this range, it holds in particular for the choices made by the adversary that must, of course, cause an integer number of faults in each round. Therefore,

$$S_2 = O\left(r \cdot \left(n + p \frac{\log p}{\log(\frac{pr}{f})}\right)\right).$$

The result then follows by combining the two cases.   □

3.3 Solving Do-All Using Reliable Multicast

In this section we present and analyze a synchronous deterministic algorithm for $Do\text{-}All_{\mathcal{AC}}(n, p, f)$ that uses crash-prone message-passing processors. We also establish complexity results for the iterative $Do\text{-}All$ in this message-passing model.

In the algorithm, called algorithm AN (Algorithm crash-No-restart), we implement the idea of an oracle (as used in the previous section) by using *coordinators* that accumulate the knowledge about the progress of the algorithm thus approximating the perfect knowledge of the oracle. The algorithm is analyzed with the help of the techniques developed in this chapter. This is done by separately assessing the cost of tolerating failures and the cost of achieving perfect knowledge. The first analysis is derived from the results obtained under the assumption of perfect knowledge (previous section). The latter is derived from the structure of the algorithm.

Algorithm AN uses a multiple-coordinator approach to solve $Do\text{-}All_{\mathcal{AC}}(n, p, f)$ on crash-prone synchronous message-passing processors ($p \leq n$). The model assumes that messages incur a known bounded delay and that *reliable multicast* is available: when a processor multicasts a message to a collection of processors, either all messages are delivered to non-faulty processors or no messages are delivered.

The algorithmic technique uses an aggressive coordination paradigm that permits multiple processors to act as coordinators concurrently. The number of coordinators is managed adaptively. When failures of coordinators disrupt the progress of the computation, the number of coordinators is increased; when the failures subside, a single coordinator is appointed.

The algorithm is tolerant of f crash-failures ($f < p$). It has total-work (available processor steps) complexity[1] $S = O((n + p \log p / \log \log p) \log f)$ and message complexity $M = O(n + p \log p / \log \log p + fp)$. (Algorithm AN also forms the basis for another algorithm for crash-prone processors that are able to restart that we present in Chapter 5.)

The algorithm assumes that the communication is reliable. If a processor sends a message to another operational processor and when the message arrives at the destination the processor is still operational, then the message is

---

[1] The expression "log f" stands for 1 when $f < 2$ and $\log_2 f$ otherwise.

received. Moreover, if an operational processor sends a multicast message and then fails, then either the message is sent to all destinations or to none at all. Such multicast is received by all operational processors. There are several reasons for considering solutions with such reliable multicast. First of all, in a distributed setting where processors cooperate closely, it becomes increasingly important to assume the ability to perform efficient and reliable broadcast or multicast. This assumption might not hold for extant WANs, but broadcast LANs (e.g., Ethernet and bypass rings) have the property that if the sender is transmitting a multicast message, then the message is sent to all destination. Of course this does not guarantee that such multicast will be received, however when a processor is unable to receive or process a message, e.g., due to unavailable buffer space or failure of the network interface hardware at the destination, this can be interpreted as a failure of the receiver.

By separating the concerns between the reliability of processors and the underlying communication medium, we are able to formulate solutions at a higher level of modularity so that one can take advantage of efficient reliable broadcast algorithms overall algorithmic approach.

3.3.1 Algorithm AN

We first overview the algorithmic techniques, then present algorithm AN in detail.

Algorithm AN proceeds in a *loop* that is repeated until all the tasks are executed. A single iteration of the loop is called a *phase*. A phase consists of three consecutive *stages*. Each stage consists of three steps (thus a phase consists of 9 steps). In each stage processors use the first step to receive messages sent in the previous stage, the second step to perform local computation, and the third step to send messages. We refer to these three step as the *receive* substage, the *compute* substage and the *send* substage.

Coordinators and workers. A processor can be a *coordinator* of a given phase. All processors (including coordinators) are *workers* in a given phase. Coordinators are responsible for recording progress, while workers perform tasks and report on that to the coordinators. In the first phase one processor acts as the coordinator. There may be multiple coordinators in subsequent phases.

The number of processors that assume the coordinator role is determined by the *martingale principle*: if none of the expected coordinators survive through the entire phase, then the number of coordinators for the next phase is doubled. Whenever at least one coordinator survives a given phase, the number of coordinators for the next phase is reduced to one.

If at least one processor acts as a coordinator during a phase and it completes the phase without failing, we say that the phase is *attended*, the phase is *unattended* otherwise.

Local views. Processors assume the role of coordinator based on their local knowledge. During the computation each processor w maintains a list $L_w = \langle q_1, q_2, ..., q_k \rangle$ of supposed live processors. We call such list a *local view*. The processors in L_w are partitioned into *layers* consisting of consecutive sublists of L_w: $L_w = \langle \Lambda^0, \Lambda^1, ..., \Lambda^j \rangle^2$. The number of processors in layer Λ^{i+1}, for $i = 0, 1, ..., j-1$, is the double of the number of processors in layer Λ^i. Layer Λ^j may contain less processors. When $\Lambda^0 = \langle q_1 \rangle$ the local view can be visualized as a binary tree rooted at processor q_1, where nodes are placed from left to right with respect to the linear order given by L_w. Thus, in a tree-like local view, layer Λ^0 consists of processor q_1, layer Λ^i consists of 2^i consecutive processors starting at processor q_{2^i} and ending at processor $q_{2^{i+1}-1}$, with the exception of the very last layer that may contain a smaller number of processors.

Example 3.17. Suppose that we have a system of $p = 31$ processors. Assume that for a phase ℓ all processors are in the local view of a worker w, in order of processor identifier, and that the view is a tree-like view (e.g., at the beginning of the computation, for $\ell = 0$). If in phase ℓ processors $1, 5, 7, 18, 20, 21, 22, 23, 24, 31$ fail (hence phase ℓ is unattended) and in phase $\ell + 1$, processors $2, 9, 15, 25, 26, 27, 28, 29, 30$ fail (phase $\ell + 1$ is attended by processor 3), then the view of processor w for phase $\ell + 2$ is the one in Figure 3.2.

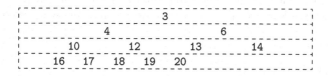

Fig. 3.2. A local view for phase $\ell + 2$.

The local view is used to implement the martingale principle of appointing coordinators as follows. Let $L_{\ell,w} = \langle \Lambda^0, \Lambda^1, ..., \Lambda^j \rangle$ be the local view of worker w at the beginning of phase ℓ. Processor w expects processors in layer Λ^0 to coordinate phase ℓ; if no processor in layer Λ^0 completes phase ℓ, then processor w expects processors in layer Λ^1 to coordinate phase $\ell+1$; in general processor w expects processors in layer Λ^i to coordinate phase $\ell+i$ if processors in all previous layers Λ^k, $\ell \leq k < \ell + i$, did not complete phase $\ell + k$. The local view is updated at the end of each phase.

Phase structure and task allocation. The structure of a phase of the algorithm is as follows. Each processor w keeps its local information about

---

[2] For sequences $L = \langle e_1, ..., e_n \rangle$ and $K = \langle d_1, ..., d_m \rangle$ we define $\langle L, K \rangle$ to be the sequence $\langle e_1, ..., e_n, d_1, ..., d_m \rangle$.

the set of tasks already performed, denoted D_w, and the set of live processors, denoted P_w, as known by processor w. Set D_w is always an underestimate of the set of tasks actually done and P_w is always an overestimate of the set of processors that are "available" from the start of the phase We denote by U_w the set of *unaccounted* tasks, i.e., whose done status is unknown to w. Sets U_w and D_w are related by $U_w = \mathcal{T} \setminus D_w$, where $\mathcal{T}$ is the set of all the tasks. Given a phase ℓ we use $P_{\ell,w}$, $U_{\ell,w}$ and $D_{\ell,w}$ to denote the values of the corresponding sets at the beginning of phase ℓ.

Computation starts with phase 0 and any processor q has all processors in $L_{0,q}$ and has $D_{0,q}$ empty. At the beginning of phase ℓ each worker (that is, each processor) w performs one task according to its local view $L_{\ell,w}$ and its knowledge of the set $U_{\ell,w}$ of unaccounted tasks, using the following *load balancing rule*. Worker w executes the task whose rank is $(i \bmod |U_{\ell,w}|)^{th}$ in the set $U_{\ell,w}$ of unaccounted tasks, where i is the rank of processor w in the local view $L_{\ell,w}$. Then the worker reports the execution of the task to all the processors that, according to the worker's local view, are supposed to be coordinators of phase ℓ. For simplicity we assume that a processor sends a message to itself when it is both worker and coordinator. Any processor c that, according to its local view, is supposed to be coordinator, gathers reports from the workers, updates its information about $P_{\ell,c}$ and $U_{\ell,c}$ and broadcasts this new information causing the local views to be reorganized.

We will see that at the beginning of any phase ℓ all live processors have the same local view L_ℓ and the same set U_ℓ of unaccounted tasks and that accounted tasks have been actually executed. A new phase starts if U_ℓ is not empty.

Details of algorithm AN

We now present algorithm AN in detail. The algorithm follows the algorithmic structure described in the previous section. The computation starts with phase number 0 and proceeds in a loop until all tasks are known to have been executed. The detailed description of a phase is given in Figure 3.3.

Local view update rule. In phase 0 the local view $L_{0,w}$ of any processor w is a tree-like view containing all the processors in $\mathcal{P}$ ordered by their PIDs. Let $L_{\ell,w} = \langle \Lambda^0, \Lambda^1, ..., \Lambda^j \rangle$ be the local view of processor w for phase ℓ. We distinguish two possible cases.

Case 1: Phase ℓ is unattended. Then the local view of processor w for phase $\ell + 1$ is $L_{\ell+1,w} = \langle \Lambda^1, ..., \Lambda^j \rangle$.

Case 2: Phase ℓ is attended. Then processor w receives **summary** messages from some coordinator in Λ^0. Processor w computes its set P_w as described in stage 3 (we will see that all processors compute the same set P_w). The local view $L_{\ell+1,w}$ of w for phase $\ell + 1$ is a tree-like local view containing the processors in P_w ordered by their PIDs.

Phase ℓ of algorithm AN:

STAGE 1.

RECEIVE: The receive substage is not used.

COMPUTE: In the compute substage, any processor w performs a specific task z according to the load balancing rule.

SEND: In the send substage processor w sends a report(z) to any coordinator, that is, to any processor in the first layer of the local view $L_{\ell,w}$.

STAGE 2.

RECEIVE: : In the receive substage the coordinators gather report messages. For any coordinator c, let $z_c^1, \ldots, z_c^{k_c}$ be the set of TIDs received.

COMPUTE: In the compute substage c sets $D_c \leftarrow D_c \cup \bigcup_{i=1}^{k_c} \{z_c^i\}$, and P_c to the set of processors from which c received report messages.

SEND: In the send substage, coordinator c multicasts the message summary(D_c, P_c) to processors in P_c.

STAGE 3.

RECEIVE: During the receive substage summary messages are received by live processors. For any processor w, let $(D_w^1, P_w^1), \ldots, (D_w^{k_w}, P_w^{k_w})$ be the sets received in summary messages (we will see in the analysis that these messages are in fact identical).

COMPUTE: In the compute substage w sets $D_w \leftarrow D_w^i$ and $P_w \leftarrow P_w^i$ for an arbitrary $i \in \{1, \ldots, k_w\}$ and updates its local view L_w (the update rule is described in detail in the text below).

SEND: The send substage is not used.

Fig. 3.3. Phase ℓ of algorithm AN

Figure 3.4 gives a pictorial description of a single phase of algorithm AN with its three stages, each consisting of receive, compute, and send substages.

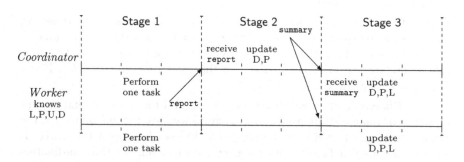

Fig. 3.4. A phase of algorithm AN.

3.3.2 Correctness of algorithm AN

We now show that algorithm AN solves the *Do-All* problem under adversary $\mathcal{A}_C$. We consider only the executions with at at least one non-crashed processor (i.e., $f < p$).

Given an execution of the algorithm, we enumerate the phases. We denote the attended phases of the execution by $\alpha_1, \alpha_2, \ldots$, etc. We denote by π_i the sequence of unattended phases between the attended phases α_i and α_{i+1}. We refer to π_i as the ith (unattended) period; an unattended period can be empty. Hence the computation proceeds as follows: unattended period π_0, attended phase α_1, unattended period π_1, attended phase α_2, and so on. We will show that after a finite number of attended phases the algorithm terminates. If the algorithm correctly solves the problem, it must be the case that there are no tasks left unaccounted after a certain phase α_τ.

Next we show that at the beginning of each phase every live processor has consistent knowledge of the ongoing computation. Then we prove safety (accurate processor and task accounting) and progress (task execution) properties, which imply the correctness of the algorithm.

Lemma 3.18. *In any execution of algorithm AN, for any two processors w, v alive at the beginning of phase ℓ, we have that $L_{\ell,w} = L_{\ell,v}$ and that $U_{\ell,w} = U_{\ell,v}$.*

Proof. By induction on the number of phases. For the base case we need to prove that the lemma is true for the first phase. Initially we have that $L_{0,w} = L_{0,v} = \langle \mathcal{P} \rangle$ and $U_w = U_v = \mathcal{T}$. Hence the base case is true.

Assume that the lemma is true for phase ℓ. We need to prove that it is true for phase $\ell + 1$. Let w and v be two processors alive at the beginning of phase $\ell + 1$. Since there are no restarts, processors w and v are alive also at the beginning of phase ℓ. By the inductive hypothesis we have that $L_{\ell,w} = L_{\ell,v}$ and $U_{\ell,w} = U_{\ell,v}$. We now distinguish two possible cases: phase ℓ is unattended and phase ℓ is attended.

Case 1: Phase ℓ is unattended. Then there are no coordinators and no summary messages are received by w and v during phase ℓ. Thus the sets U_w and U_v are not modified during phase ℓ. Moreover processors w and v use the same rule to update the local view (case 1 of the local view update rule). Hence $L_{\ell+1,w} = L_{\ell+1,v}$ and $U_{\ell+1,w} = U_{\ell+1,v}$.

Case 2: Phase ℓ is attended. Since $L_{\ell,w} = L_{\ell,v}$ all the workers send report messages to some coordinators $c_1, \ldots, c_k$. Since we have reliable multicast, the report message of each worker reaches all the coordinators if the worker is alive, or no one if it failed. Thus summary messages sent by the coordinators are all equal. Let summary(D, P) be one such a message. Since the phase is attended and broadcast is reliable both processors w and v receive the summary(D, P) message from at least one coordinator. Hence in stage 3 of phase ℓ, workers w and v set $D_{\ell+1,w} = D_{\ell+1,v} = D$ and consequently we have $U_{\ell+1,w} = U_{\ell+1,v}$. They also set $P_{\ell+1,w} = P_{\ell+1,v} = P$ and use the same rule (case 2 of the local view update rule) to update the local view. Hence $L_{\ell+1,w} = L_{\ell+1,v}$. □

Because of Lemma 3.18, we can define $L_\ell = L_{\ell,w}$ for any live processor w as the view at the beginning of phase ℓ, $P_\ell = P_{\ell,w}$ as the set of live processors, $D_\ell = D_{\ell,w}$ as the set of done tasks and $U_\ell = U_{\ell,w}$ as the set of unaccounted tasks at the beginning of phase ℓ.

We denote by p_ℓ the cardinality of the set of live processors computed for phase ℓ, i.e., $p_\ell = |P_\ell|$, and by u_ℓ the cardinality of the set of unaccounted tasks for phase ℓ, i.e., $u_\ell = |U_\ell|$. We have $p_1 = p$ and $u_0 = t$.

Lemma 3.19. *In any execution of algorithm AN, if a processor w is alive during the first two stages of phase ℓ then processor w belongs to P_ℓ.*

Proof. Let w be a processor alive at the beginning of phase ℓ. Processor w (whether it is a coordinator or not) is taken out of the set P_ℓ only if a coordinator does not receive a `report` message from w in phase $\ell - 1$. If w is a coordinator and all coordinators are dead, then w would be removed by the local view update rule. This is possible only if w fails during phase $\ell - 1$. Since w is alive at the beginning of phase ℓ, processor w does not fail in phase $\ell - 1$. □

Lemma 3.20. *In any execution of algorithm AN, if a task z does not belong to U_ℓ then it has been executed in one of the phases $1, 2, ..., \ell - 1$.*

Proof. Task z is taken out of the set U_ℓ by a coordinator c when c receives a `report`(z) message in a phase prior to ℓ. However a worker sends such a message only after executing task z. Task z is taken out of the set U_ℓ by a worker w when w receives a `summary`(D_c, P_c) message from some coordinator c in phase prior to ℓ, and $z \in D_c$. Again this means that z must have been reported as done to c. □

Lemma 3.21. *In any execution of algorithm AN, for any phase ℓ we have that $u_{\ell+1} \leq u_\ell$.*

Proof. By the code of the algorithm, no task is added to U_ℓ. □

Lemma 3.22. *In any execution of algorithm AN, for any attended phase ℓ we have that $u_{\ell+1} < u_\ell$.*

Proof. Since phase ℓ is attended, there is at least one coordinator c alive in phase ℓ. By Lemma 3.19 processor c belongs to P_ℓ and thus it executes one task. Hence at least one task is executed and consequently at least one task is taken out of U_ℓ. By Lemma 3.21, no task is added to U_ℓ during phase ℓ. □

Lemma 3.23. *In any execution of algorithm AN, any unattended period consists of at most $\log f$ phases.*

Proof. Consider the unattended period π_i and let ℓ be its first phase. First we claim that the first layer of view L_ℓ consists of a single processor. This is so because (a) either $i = 0$ and $\ell = 0$, in which case L_0 is the initial local view, or (b) $i > 0$ and π_i is preceded by attended phase α_i, in which case L_ℓ is constructed by the local update rule to have a single processor in its first layer. By Lemma 3.19 any processor alive at the beginning of phase ℓ belongs to P_ℓ and thus to L_ℓ. By the local view update rule for unattended phases, we have that eventually all processors in L_ℓ are supposed to be coordinators. Since $f < p$, at least one processor is alive and thus eventually there is an attended phase. The $\log f$ upper bound follows from the the martingale principle governing the sizes of consecutive layers of view. The number of processors accommodated in the layers of the view doubles for each successive layer. Hence, denoting by f_i the number of failures in π_i, we have that the number of phases in π_i is at most $\log f_i$. Obviously $f_i < f$.   □

Finally we show the correctness of algorithm AN.

Theorem 3.24. *In any execution of algorithm* AN, *the algorithm terminates with all tasks performed.*

Proof. By Lemma 3.19 no live processor leaves the computation and since $f < p$ the computation ends only when U_ℓ is empty. By Lemma 3.20, when the computation ends, all tasks are performed. It remains to prove that the algorithm actually terminates. By Lemma 3.23 for every $1 + \log f$ phases there is at least one attended phase. Hence, by Lemmas 3.21 and 3.22, the number of unaccounted tasks decreases by at least one in every $1 + \log f$ phases. Thus, the algorithm terminates after at most $O(n \log f)$ phases.   □

Since the algorithm terminates after a finite number of attended phases with all tasks performed, we let τ be such that $U_{\alpha_{\tau+1}} = \emptyset$, and consequently $u_{\alpha_{\tau+1}} = 0$.

3.3.3 Analysis of Algorithm AN

We now analyze the performance of algorithm AN in terms of total-work (available processor steps) S and the message complexity M (recall that each multicast costs as much as sending point-to-point messages to each destination).

To assess work S we consider separately all the attended phases and all the unattended phases of the execution. Let S_a be the part of S spent during all the attended phases and S_u be the part of S spent during all the unattended phases. Hence we have $S = S_a + S_u$.

Lemma 3.25. *In any execution of algorithm* AN *with* $f < p$ *we have* $S_a = O(n + p \log p / \log \log p)$.

Proof. We consider all the attended phases $\alpha_1, \alpha_2, ..., \alpha_\tau$ by subdividing them into two cases.

Case 1: All attended phases α_i such that $p_{\alpha_i} \leq u_{\alpha_i}$. The load balancing rule assures that at most one processor is assigned to a task. Hence the available processor steps used in this case can be charged to the number of tasks executed which is at most $n + f \leq n + p$. Hence $S_1 = O(n + p)$.

Case 2: All attended phases in which $p_{\alpha_i} > u_{\alpha_i}$. We let $d(p)$ stand for $\log p / \log \log p$. We consider the following two subcases.

Subcase 2.1: All attended phases α_i after which $u_{\alpha_{i+1}} < u_{\alpha_i} / d(p)$. Since $u_{\alpha_{i+1}} < u_{\alpha_i} < p_{\alpha_i} < p$ and phase α_τ is the last phase for which $u_\tau > 0$, it follows that subcase 2.1 occurs $O(\log_{d(p)} p)$ times. The quantity $O(\log_{d(p)} p)$ is $O(d(p))$ because $d(p)^{d(p)} = \Theta(p)$. No more than p processors complete such phases, therefore the part $S_{2.1}$ of S_a spent in this case is

$$S_{2.1} = O\left(p \frac{\log p}{\log \log p}\right).$$

Subcase 2.2: All attended phases α_i after which $u_{\alpha_{i+1}} \geq u_{\alpha_i} / d(p)$. Consider a particular phase α_i. Since in this case $p_{\alpha_i} > u_{\alpha_i}$, by the load balancing rule at least $\lfloor \frac{p_{\alpha_i}}{u_{\alpha_i}} \rfloor$ but no more than $\lceil \frac{p_{\alpha_i}}{u_{\alpha_i}} \rceil$ processors are assigned to each of the u_{α_i} unaccounted tasks. Since $u_{\alpha_{i+1}}$ tasks remain unaccounted after phase α_i, the number of processors that failed during this phase is at least

$$u_{\alpha_{i+1}} \left\lfloor \frac{p_{\alpha_i}}{u_{\alpha_i}} \right\rfloor \geq \frac{u_{\alpha_i}}{d(p)} \cdot \frac{p_{\alpha_i}}{2 u_{\alpha_i}}$$
$$= \frac{p_{\alpha_i}}{2 d(p)} .$$

Hence, the number of processors that proceed to phase α_{i+1} is no more than

$$p_{\alpha_i} - \frac{p_{\alpha_i}}{2 d(p)} = p_{\alpha_i} \left(1 - \frac{1}{2 d(p)}\right) .$$

Let $\alpha_{i_0}, \alpha_{i_1}, ..., \alpha_{i_k}$ be the attended phases in this subcase. Since the number of processor in phase α_{i_0} is at most p, the number of processors alive in phase α_{i_j} for $j > 0$ is at most $p(1 - \frac{1}{2 d(p)})^j$. Therefore the part $S_{2.2}$ of S_a spent in this case is bounded as follows:

$$S_{2.2} \leq \sum_{j=0}^{k} p \left(1 - \frac{1}{2 d(p)}\right)^j$$
$$\leq \frac{p}{1 - (1 - \frac{1}{2 d(p)})}$$
$$= p \cdot 2 d(p)$$
$$= O(p \cdot d(p)) .$$

Summing up the contributions of all the cases considered we get S_a:

$$S_a = S_1 + S_{2.1} + S_{2.2} = O\left(n + p\frac{\log p}{\log\log p}\right),$$

as desired.   □

Lemma 3.26. *In any execution of algorithm* AN *with* $f < p$ *we have* $S_u = O(S_a \log f)$.

Proof. The number of processors alive in a phase of the unattended period π_i is at most p_{α_i}, that is the number of processors alive in the attended phase immediately preceding π_i. To cover the case when π_0 is not empty, we let $\alpha_0 = 0$ and $p_{\alpha_0} = |\mathcal{P}| = p$. By Lemma 3.23 the number of phases in period π_i is at most $\log f$. Hence the part of S_u spent in period π_i is at most $p_{\alpha_i} \log f$. We have

$$S_u \leq \sum_{i=0}^{\tau}(p_{\alpha_i} \log f)$$

$$= \log f \cdot \sum_{i=1}^{\tau} p_{\alpha_i}$$

$$\leq (p + S_a)\log f = O(S_a \log f) .$$

    □

We now consider the analysis of algorithm AN for the range of crashes $f \leq \frac{p}{\log p}$.

Lemma 3.27. *In any execution of algorithm* AN *with* $f \leq \frac{p}{\log p}$ *we have* $S_a = O\left(n + p\log_{\frac{p}{f}} p\right)$.

Proof. Let $\alpha_1, \alpha_2, \ldots \alpha_\tau$, denote all the attended phases of this execution (α_τ is the last phase of the execution). Given a phase α of an execution of algorithm AN, we define p_α to be the number of live processors and u_α to be the number of undone tasks at the beginning of the phase; here $p_{\alpha_1} \leq p$ (at most p processor are alive) and $u_{\alpha_1} \leq n$ (at most n tasks remain).

Observe that for all α_i, $1 \leq i \leq \tau - 1$ it holds that (a) $u_{a_i} > u_{a_{i+1}}$ (by Lemma 3.22), and (b) $p_{a_i} \geq p_{a_{i+1}}$ (the number of processors can only decrease due to crashes).

In the correctness analysis we have shown that if at the beginning of phase α_i the processors have consistent information on the identities and the number of surviving processors p_{α_i} and the identities and the number of remaining tasks u_{α_i} (Lemma 3.18). Hence, the processors in attended phases can perform perfect load balancing, as in the case where the processors are assisted by the oracle $\mathcal{O}$, in the oracle model. Therefore, focusing only on the attended phases (and assuming that in the worst case no progress is made in unattended phases), we obtain the desired result by induction on the number of remaining tasks, as in the proof of Lemma 3.13.   □

We now combine the results of the key lemmas to obtain the work complexity of algorithm AN.

Theorem 3.28. *In any execution of algorithm* AN *its work complexity is*

$$S = O\left(\log f\left(n + p\frac{\log p}{\log(p/f)}\right)\right) \quad when \ f \le \frac{p}{\log p}, \ and$$

$$S = O\left(\log f\left(n + p\frac{\log p}{\log\log p}\right)\right) \quad when \ \frac{p}{\log p} < f < p.$$

Proof. The total work S is given by $S = S_a + S_u$. The theorem follows from Lemmas 3.25 and 3.26 for $f < p$, and from Lemma 3.27 for $\frac{p}{\log p} < f < p$. $\square$

Remark 3.29. We have shown a lower bound of $\Omega(n + p\log p/\log\log p)$ for any algorithm that performs tasks by balancing loads of surviving processors in each time step. The work of algorithm AN comes within a factor of $\log f$ (and thus also $\log p$) relative to that lower bound. This suggests that improving the work result is difficult and that better solutions may have to involve a trade-off between the work and message complexities.

We now assess the message complexity. First remember that the computation proceeds as follows: $\pi_0, \alpha_1, \pi_1, \alpha_2, ..., \pi_{\tau-1}, \alpha_\tau$. In order to count the total number of messages we distinguish between the attended phases preceded by a nonempty unattended period and the attended phases which are not preceded by unattended periods. Formally, we let M_u be the number of messages sent in $\pi_{i-1}\alpha_i$, for all those i's such that π_{i-1} is nonempty and we let M_a be the number of messages sent in $\pi_{i-1}\alpha_i$, for all those i's such that π_{i-1} is empty (clearly in these cases we have $\pi_{i-1}\alpha_i = \alpha_i$). Next we estimate M_a and M_u and thus the message complexity M of algorithm AN.

Lemma 3.30. *In any execution of algorithm* AN *with* $f < p$ *we have* $M_a = O(S_a)$.

Proof. First notice that in a phase ℓ where there is a unique coordinator the number of messages sent is $2p_\ell$. By the definition of M_a, messages counted in M_a are messages sent in a phase α_i such that π_{i-1} is empty. This means that the phase previous to α_i is α_{i-1} which, by definition, is attended. Hence by the local view update rule of attended phases we have that α_i has a unique coordinator. Thus phase α_i gives a contribution of at most $2p_{\alpha_i}$ messages to M_a. It is possible that some of the attended phases do not contribute to M_a, however counting all the attended phases as contributing to M_a we have that $M_a \le \sum_{i=1}^{\tau} 2p_{\alpha_i} = 2S_a$. $\square$

Lemma 3.31. *In any execution of algorithm* AN *with* $f < p$ *we have* $M_u = O(fp)$.

Proof. First we notice that in any phase the number of messages sent is $O(cp)$ where c is the number of coordinators for that phase. Hence to estimate M_u we simple count all the supposed coordinators in the phases included in $\pi_{i-1}\alpha_i$, where π_{i-1} is nonempty.

Let i be such that π_{i-1} is not empty. Since the number of processors doubles in each consecutive layer of the local view according to the martingale principle, we have that the total number of supposed coordinators in all the phases of $\pi_{i-1}\alpha_i$ is $2f_{i-1} + 1 = O(f_{i-1})$, where f_{i-1} is the number of failures during π_{i-1}. Hence the total number of supposed coordinators, in all of the phases contributing to M_u, is $\sum_{i=1}^{\tau} O(f_{i-1}) = O(f)$.
Hence the total number of messages counted in M_u is $O(fp)$. $\square$

We assess the message complexity of algorithm AN as $M = M_a + M_u$.

Theorem 3.32. *In any execution of algorithm AN we have*

$$M = O\left(n + p\frac{\log p}{\log(p/f)} + fp\right) \ \text{when} \ f \leq \frac{p}{\log p}, \ \text{and}$$

$$M = O\left(n + p\frac{\log p}{\log\log p} + fp\right) \ \text{when} \ \frac{p}{\log p} < f < p.$$

Proof. The total number of messages sent is $M = M_a + M_u$. The theorem follows from Lemmas 3.30 and 3.31, and Lemmas 3.25 and 3.27. $\square$

3.3.4 Analysis of Message-Passing Iterative Do-All

We now consider the r-Do-All$_{A_C}(n, p, f)$ problem for synchronous message-passing crash-prone processors under the assumption of reliable multicast. For this purpose, we use Algorithm AN iteratively.

Theorem 3.33. *The r-Do-All$_{A_C}(n, p, f)$ problem can be solved on synchronous message-passing crash-prone processors with*

$$S = O\left(r \cdot \log\frac{f}{r} \cdot \left(n + p\frac{\log p}{\log(pr/f)}\right)\right) \ \text{and} \ M = O\left(r \cdot \left(n + p\frac{\log p}{\log(pr/f)}\right) + fp\right)$$

when $f \leq \frac{pr}{\log p}$, and with

$$S = O\left(r \cdot \log\frac{f}{r} \cdot \left(n + p\frac{\log p}{\log\log p}\right)\right) \ \text{and} \ M = O\left(r \cdot \left(n + p\frac{\log p}{\log\log p}\right) + fp\right)$$

when $\frac{pr}{\log p} < f < p$.

Proof. The iterative *Do-All* can be solved by running algorithm AN on r instances, each of size n, in sequence. We call this algorithm AN*. To analyze the efficiency of AN* we use the same approach as in the proof of Theorem 3.16. In the current context we base our work complexity arguments on the result of Theorem 3.28, and we base our message complexity arguments on the result of Theorem 3.32. $\square$

Note that we achieve better complexity results in this case than those that can be obtained by merely multiplying the complexity results for algorithm AN times r, the number of task-sets.

3.4 Open Problems

The results in this chapter on work with perfect knowledge give matching upper and lower bounds. However the perfect knowledge oracle is a strong assumption, and the adversary causing crashes is relatively weak. It is very interesting to produce analogous lower (and upper) bounds, where the knowledge of the oracle is progressively weakened (and the adversary itself is strengthened as we do in several other chapters).

As we pointed out in Remark 3.29, the work of algorithm AN comes within a factor of $\log f$ (and thus also $\log p$) relative to the corresponding that lower bound. Closing the remaining gap, given that it is small, is a difficult open problem. This is in part due that $\log f$ overhead is associated with the cost of approximating the perfect knowledge oracle. Finally, in algorithm AN we aim to optimize work first, then assess the message efficiency. For the settings where communication is very expensive, efficiency considerations may require that solutions involve a trade-off between the work and message complexities, and perhaps using a complexity analysis that integrates work and messaging into a single measure.

3.5 Chapter Notes

Kanellakis and Shvartsman [67] showed that $Do\text{-}All^{\mathcal{O}}_{\mathcal{A}_C}(n, p, f)$ can be solved with synchronous crash-prone processors using total-work $S = O(n + p \log p / \log \log p)$ for $f < p \leq n$. This is the result stated in Lemma 3.12 (its proof appears in [67]). They also showed that this bound is tight, by giving a matching lower bound; this result is stated in Corollary 3.7 (we recreate a proof for this result). Note that the bounds in [67] were given for the shared-memory model under the assumption that processors can read all memory in constant time (memory snapshots). It is not difficult to see that the memory snapshot assumption in shared-memory is equivalent to the assumption of perfect knowledge, where a deterministic omniscient oracle provides load-balancing and termination information to the processors in constant time.

The presentation in Section 3.2 and the failure-sensitive analysis of algorithm AN is based on a paper by Georgiou, Russell, and Shvartsman [45]. The presentation of Section 3.3 follows that of Chlebus, De Prisco, and Shvartsman in [15].

There are several algorithms for implementing reliable multicast, for example see the presentation by Hadzilacos and Toueg in [53].

This chapter focuses on the deterministic models of computation and worst case analysis. Randomization can yield better expected work complexity. A randomized solution for the synchronous *Do-All* problem with crashes assuming reliable multicast is presented by Chlebus and Kowalski [17]. They assume a *weakly-adaptive linearly bounded* adversary: the adversary selects

$f < c \cdot p$ $(0 < c < 1)$ crash-prone processors prior to the start of the computation, then any of these processors may crash at any time during the computation. The randomized algorithm has expected combined total-work complexity and message complexity $S + M = O(n + p(1 + \log^* p - \log^*(p/n)))$, where $\log^*$ is the number of times the log function has to be applied to its argument to yield the result that is no larger than 1. This is in contrast with the lower bound $\Omega(n + p \cdot \log n / \log \log n)$ on total-work required in the worst case by any deterministic algorithm in the same setting (Lemma 3.7).

In this chapter we have demonstrated that by separating the concerns between the reliability of processors and the underlying communication medium, we are able to formulate solutions at a higher level of modularity. One benefit of this is that such algorithms can use other distributed system services, such as reliable multicast, to implement communication among processors without altering the overall algorithmic approach. Lastly, the presented multi-coordinator approach presents a venue for optimizing *Do-All* solutions and for beating the $\Omega(n + (f + 1)p)$ lower bound of stage-checkpointing algorithms, such as that presented by De Prisco, Mayer, and Yung [25].

4

Synchronous Do-All with Crashes and Point-to-Point Messaging

WE now study the *Do-All* problem assuming that only point-to-point messaging is available for processors to communicate. This in contrast with the assumptions in the previous chapter, we considered the *Do-All* problem assuming that processors where assisted by an oracle or that reliable multicast was available. As one would expect, in the point-to-point messaging setting the problem becomes more challenging and different techniques need to be employed in order to obtain efficient (deterministic) algorithms for *Do-All*.

We consider $Do\text{-}All_{\mathcal{A}_C}(n, p, f)$, that is the *Do-All* problem for n tasks, p processors, up to f crashes, as determined by the adversary $\mathcal{A}_C$. The key in developing efficient deterministic algorithms for *Do-All* in this setting lies in the ability to share knowledge among processors efficiently. Algorithms that rely on unique coordinators or checkpointing mechanisms incur a work overhead penalty of $\Omega(n + fp)$ for f crashes; this overhead is particularly large, for large f, for example, when $f = \omega(\log^{\Theta(1)} p)$. Algorithm AN (from the previous chapter) beats this lower bound by using multiple coordinators, however it uses reliable multicast, which can be viewed as a strong assumption in some distributed settings. Therefore, we are interested in developing algorithms that do not use checkpointing or reliable multicast and that are efficient, especially for large f.

In this chapter we present a synchronous, message-passing, deterministic algorithm for $Do\text{-}All_{\mathcal{A}_C}(n, p, f)$. This algorithm has total-work complexity $O(n + p \log^3 p)$ and message complexity $M(p^{1+2\varepsilon})$, for any $\varepsilon > 0$. Thus, the work complexity of this algorithm beats the above mentioned lower bound (for $f = \omega(\log^3 p)$) and it is comparable to that of algorithm AN–however it uses simple point-to-point messaging. The algorithm does not use coordinator or checkpointing strategies to implement information sharing among processors. Instead, it uses an approach where processors share information using an algorithm developed to solve the *gossip problem* in synchronous message-passing systems with processor crashes. To achieve messaging efficiency, the point-to-point messaging is constrained by means of a communication graph that represents a certain subset of the edges in a complete communication network. Processors send messages based on permutations with certain properties.

Chapter structure.

In Section 4.1 we define the gossip problem and relevant measures of efficiency. In Section 4.2 we present combinatorial tools that are used in the analysis of the gossip and *Do-All* algorithms. In Section 4.3 we present a gossip algorithm, show its correctness, and perform its complexity analysis. In Section 4.4 we present the *Do-All* algorithm itself, show its correctness, and give complexity analysis. We discuss open problems in Section 4.5.

4.1 The Gossip Problem

The *Gossip* problem is considered one of the fundamental problems in distributed computing and it is normally stated as follows: each processor has a distinct piece of information, called a *rumor*, and the goal is for each processor to learn all rumors. In our setting, where we consider processor crashes, it might not always be possible to learn the rumor of a processor that crashed, since all the processors that have learned the rumor of that processor might have also crashed in the course of the computation. Hence, we consider a variation of the traditional gossip problem. We require that every non-faulty processor learns the following about each processor v: either the rumor of v or that v has crashed. It is important to note that we do not require for the non-faulty processors to reach agreement: if a processor crashes then some of the non-faulty processors may get to learn its rumor while others may only learn that it has crashed.

Formally, we define the *Gossip* problem with crash-prone processors, as follows:

Definition 4.1. *The Gossip problem: Given a set of p processors, where initially each processor has a distinct piece of information, called a* rumor, *the goal is for each processor to learn all the rumors in the presence of processor crashes. The following conditions must be satisfied:*

(1) Correctness: (a) All non-faulty processors learn the rumors of all nonfaulty processors, (b) For every failed processor v, non-faulty processor w either knows that v has failed, or w knows v's rumor.

(2) Termination: Every non-faulty processor terminates its protocol.

We let $Gossip_{\mathcal{A}_C}(p, f)$ stand for the *Gossip* problem for p processors (and p rumors) and adversary $\mathcal{A}_C$ constrained to adversarial patterns of weight less or equal to f.

We now define the measures of efficiency we use in studying the complexity of the *Gossip* problem. We measure the efficiency of a *Gossip* algorithm in terms of its *time complexity* and *message complexity*. Time complexity is measured as the number of parallel steps taken by the processors until the *Gossip* problem is *solved*. The *Gossip* problem is said to be solved at step τ, if τ is the first step where the correctness condition is satisfied and at least one (non-faulty) processor terminates its protocol. More formally:

Definition 4.2 (time complexity). *Let* A *be an algorithm that solves a problem with p processors under adversary* $\mathcal{A}$*. If execution* $\xi \in \mathcal{E}(A, \mathcal{A})$*, where* $\|\xi|_{\mathcal{A}}\| \leq f$*, solves the problem by time* $\tau(\xi)$*, then the* time complexity T *of algorithm* A *is:*

$$T = T_{\mathcal{A}}(p, f) = \max_{\xi \in \mathcal{E}(A, \mathcal{A}),\ \|\xi|_{\mathcal{A}}\| \leq f} \{\tau(\xi)\}.$$

The message complexity is defined as in Definition 2.6 where the size of the problem is p: it is measured as the total number of point-to-point messages sent by the processors until the problem is solved. As before, when a processor communicates using a multicast, its cost is the total number of point-to-point messages.

4.2 Combinatorial Tools

We present tools used to control the message complexity of the gossip algorithm presented in the next section.

4.2.1 Communication Graphs

We first describe *communication graphs* — conceptual data structures that constrain communication patterns.

Informally speaking, the computation begins with a communication graph that contains all nodes, where each node represents a processor. Each processor v can send a message to any other processor w that v considers to be non-faulty and that is a neighbor of v according to the communication graph. As processors crash, meaning that nodes are "removed" from the graph, the neighborhood of the non-faulty processors changes dynamically such that the graph induced by the remaining nodes guarantees "progress in communication": progress in communication according to a graph is achieved if there is at least one "good" connected component, which evolves suitably with time and satisfies the following properties: (i) the component contains "sufficiently many" nodes so that collectively they have learned "suitably many" rumors, (ii) it has "sufficiently small" diameter so that information can be shared among the nodes of the component without "undue delay", and (iii) the set of nodes of each successive good component is a subset of the set of nodes of the previous good component.

We use the following terminology and notation. Let $G = (V, E)$ be a (undirected) graph, with V the set of nodes (representing processors, $|V| = p$) and E the set of edges (representing communication links). For a subgraph G_Q of G induced by Q ($Q \subseteq V$), we define $N_G(Q)$ to be the subset of V consisting of all the nodes in Q and their neighbors in G. The maximum node degree of graph G is denoted by Δ.

Let G_{V_i} be the subgraph of G induced by the sets V_i of nodes. Each set V_i corresponds to the set of processors that haven't crashed by step i of a given execution. Hence $V_{i+1} \subseteq V_i$ (since processor do not restart). Also, each $|V_i| \geq p - f$, since no more than $f < p$ processors may crash in a given execution. Let G_{Q_i} denote a component of G_{V_i} where $Q_i \subseteq V_i$.

To formulate the the notion of a "good" component G_{Q_i} we define a property, called *Compact Chain Property* (CCP):

Definition 4.3. *Graph* $G = (V, E)$ *has the* Compact Chain Property *$CCP(p, f, \varepsilon)$, if:*

I. *The maximum degree of* G *is at most* $\left(\frac{p}{p-f}\right)^{1+\varepsilon}$,

II. *For a given sequence* $V_1 \supseteq \ldots \supseteq V_k$ *($V = V_1$), where* $|V_k| \geq p - f$, *there is a sequence* $Q_1 \supseteq \ldots \supseteq Q_k$ *such that for every* $i = 1, \ldots, k$:

    (a) $Q_i \subseteq V_i$,
    (b) $|Q_i| \geq |V_i|/7$, *and*
    (c) *the diameter of* G_{Q_i} *is at most* $31 \log p$.

The following shows existence of graphs satisfying *CCP* for some parameters.

Lemma 4.4. *For* $p > 2$, *every* $f < p$, *and constant* $\varepsilon > 0$, *there is a graph* G *of* $O(p)$ *nodes satisfying property* $CCP(p, f, \varepsilon)$.

4.2.2 Sets of Permutations

We now deal with *sets of permutations* that satisfy *certain properties*. These permutations are used by the processors in the gossip algorithm to decide to what subset of processors they send their rumor in each step of a given execution. Consider the symmetric group $\mathcal{S}_t$ of all permutations on set $\{1, \ldots, t\}$, with the composition operation $\circ$, and identity $\mathbf{e}_t$ (t is a positive integer). For permutation $\pi = \langle \pi(1), \ldots, \pi(t) \rangle$ in $\mathcal{S}_t$, we say that $\pi(i)$ is a d-left-to-right maximum (d-lrm in short), if there are less than d previous elements in π of value greater than $\pi(i)$, i.e., $|\{\pi(j) : \pi(j) > \pi(i) \land j < i\}| < d$. For a given permutation π, let (d)-LRM(π) denote the number of d-left-to-right maxima in π.

Let Υ and Ψ, $\Upsilon \subseteq \Psi$, be two sets containing permutations from $\mathcal{S}_t$. For every σ in $\mathcal{S}_t$, let $\sigma \circ \Upsilon$ denote the set of permutations $\{\sigma \circ \pi : \pi \in \Upsilon\}$. Now we define the notion of *surfeit*. (We will show that *surfeit* relates to the redundant activity in our algorithms, i.e., "overdone" activity, or literally "surfeit".) For a given Υ and permutation $\sigma \in \mathcal{S}_t$, let $(d, |\Upsilon|)$-Surf(Υ, σ) be equal to $\sum_{\pi \in \Upsilon}(d)$-LRM$(\sigma^{-1} \circ \pi)$. We then define the (d, q)-surfeit of set Ψ as (d, q)-Surf$(\Psi) = \max\{(d, q)$-Surf$(\Upsilon, \sigma) : \Upsilon \subseteq \Psi \wedge |\Upsilon| = q \wedge \sigma \in \mathcal{S}_t\}$.

The following results are known for (d, q)-surfeit.

Lemma 4.5. *Let Υ be a set of q random permutations on set $\{1, \ldots, t\}$. For every fixed positive integer d, the probability that (d, q)-Surf$(\Upsilon, \mathbf{e}_t) > t \ln t + 10qd \ln(t + p)$ is at most $e^{-[t \ln t + 9qdH_{t+p}] \ln(9/e)}$.*

Theorem 4.6. *For a random set of p permutations Ψ from $\mathcal{S}_t$, the event "for every positive integers d and $q \leq p$, (d, q)-Surf$(\Psi) > t \ln t + 10qd \ln(t + p)$" holds with probability at most $e^{-t \ln t \cdot \ln(9/e^2)}$.*

Using the probabilistic method we obtain the following result.

Corollary 4.7. *There is a set of p permutations Ψ from $\mathcal{S}_t$ such that, for every positive integers d and $q \leq p$, (d, q)-Surf$(\Psi) \leq t \ln t + 10qd \ln(t + p)$.*

The efficiency of the gossip algorithm (and hence the efficiency of a *Do-All* algorithm that uses such gossip) relies on the existence of the permutations in the thesis of the corollary (however the algorithm is correct for any permutations). These permutations can be efficiently constructed.

4.3 The Gossip Algorithm

We now present the gossip algorithm, called GOSSIP$_\varepsilon$.

4.3.1 Description of Algorithm GOSSIP$_\varepsilon$

Suppose constant $0 < \varepsilon < 1/3$ is given. The algorithm proceeds in a loop that is repeated until each non-faulty processor v learns either the rumor of every processor w or that w has failed. A single iteration of the loop is called an *epoch*. The algorithm terminates after $\lceil 1/\varepsilon \rceil - 1$ epochs. Each of the first $\lceil 1/\varepsilon \rceil - 2$ epochs consists of $\alpha \log^2 p$ *phases*, where α is such that $\alpha \log^2 p$ is the smallest integer that is larger than $341 \log^2 p$. Each phase is divided into two *stages*, the *update* stage, and the *communication* stage. In the update stage processors update their local knowledge regarding other processors' rumor (known/unknown) and condition (failed/operational) and in the communication stage processors exchange their local knowledge (more momentarily). We say that processor v *heard about processor w* if either v knows the rumor of w or it knows that w has failed. Epoch $\lceil 1/\varepsilon \rceil - 1$ is the terminating epoch where each processor sends a message to all the processors that it haven't heard about, requesting their rumor.

The pseudocode of the algorithm is given in Figure 4.1 (we assume, where needed, that every *if-then* has an implicit *else* clause containing the necessary number of no-ops to match the length of the code in the *then* clause; this is used to ensure the synchrony of the system). The details of the algorithm are explained in the rest of this section.

Initialization

  $status_v$ = collector;
  ACTIVE$_v$ = $\langle 1, 2, \ldots, p \rangle$;
  BUSY$_v$ = $\langle \pi_v(1), \pi_v(2), \ldots, \pi_v(p) \rangle$;
  WAITING$_v$ = $\langle \pi_v(1), \pi_v(2), \ldots, \pi_v(p) \rangle \setminus \langle v \rangle$;
  RUMORS$_v$ = $\langle (v, rumor_v) \rangle$;
  NEIGHB$_v$ = $N_{G_1}(v) \setminus \{v\}$;
  CALLING$_v$ = $\{\}$;
  ANSWER$_v$ = $\{\}$;

Iterating epochs

  for $\ell = 1$ **to** $\lceil 1/\varepsilon \rceil - 2$ **do**
    if BUSY$_v$ is empty **then** set $status_v$ to idle;
    NEIGHB$_v$ = $\{w : w \in$ ACTIVE$_v \wedge w \in N_{G_\ell}(v) \setminus \{v\}\}$;

    repeat $\alpha \log^2 p$ times   *% iterating phases*
    update stage;
    communication stage;

Terminating epoch ($\lceil 1/\varepsilon \rceil - 1$)

  update stage;
  if $status_v$ = collector **then**
    send $\langle$ACTIVE$_v$, BUSY$_v$, RUMORS$_v$, call$\rangle$ to each processor in WAITING$_v$;
  receive messages;
  send $\langle$ACTIVE$_v$, BUSY$_v$, RUMORS$_v$, reply$\rangle$ to each processor in ANSWER$_v$;
  receive messages;
  update RUMORS$_v$;

Fig. 4.1. Algorithm GOSSIP$_\varepsilon$, stated for processor v; $\pi_v(i)$ denotes the ith element of permutation π_v.

Local knowledge and messages.

Initially each processor v has its $rumor_v$ and permutation π_v from a set Ψ of permutations on $[p]$, such that Ψ satisfies the thesis of Corollary 4.7. Moreover, each processor v is associated with the variable $status_v$. Initially $status_v$ = collector (and we say that v is a collector), meaning that v has not heard from all processors yet. Once v hears from all other processors, then $status_v$ is set to informer (and we say that v is an informer), meaning that now v will inform the other processors of its status and knowledge. When processor v learns that all non-faulty processors w also have $status_w$ = informer then at the beginning of the next epoch, $status_v$ becomes idle (and we say that v idles), meaning that v idles until termination, but it might send responses to messages (see call-messages below).

Each processor maintains several lists and sets. We now describe the lists maintained by processor v:

- List ACTIVE$_v$: it contains the pids of the processors that v considers to be non-faulty. Initially, list ACTIVE$_v$ contains all p pids.
- List BUSY$_v$: it contains the pids of the processors that v consider as collectors. Initially list BUSY$_v$ contains all pids, *permuted according to* π_v.
- List WAITING$_v$: it contains the pids of the processors that v did not hear from. Initially list WAITING$_v$ contains all pids except from v, *permuted according to* π_v.
- List RUMORS$_v$: it contains pairs of the form $(w, rumor_w)$ or $(w, \perp)$. The pair $(w, rumor_w)$ denotes the fact that processor v knows processor w's rumor and the pair $(w, \perp)$ means that v does not know w's rumor, but it knows that w has failed. Initially list RUMORS$_v$ contains the pair $(v, rumor_v)$.

A processor can send a message to any other processor, but to lower the message complexity, in some cases (see communication stage) we require processors to communicate according to a conceptual communication graph G_ℓ, $\ell \leq \lceil 1/\varepsilon \rceil - 2$, that satisfies property $CCP(p, p - p^{1-\ell\varepsilon}, \varepsilon)$ (see Definition 4.3 and Lemma 4.4). When processor v sends a message m to another processor w, m contains lists ACTIVE$_v$, BUSY$_v$ RUMORS$_v$, and the variable *type*. When *type* = call, processor v requires an answer from processor w and we refer to such message as a *call-message*. When *type* = reply, no answer is required—this message is sent as a response to a call-message.

We now present the sets maintained by processor v.

- Set ANSWER$_v$: it contains the pids of the processors that v received a call-message. Initially set ANSWER$_v$ is empty.
- Set CALLING$_v$: it contains the pids of the processors that v will send a call-message. Initially CALLING$_v$ is empty.
- Set NEIGHB$_v$: it contains the pids of the processors that are in ACTIVE$_v$ and that according to the communication graph G_ℓ, for a given epoch ℓ, are neighbors of v (NEIGHB$_v$ = $\{w : w \in$ ACTIVE$_v \wedge w \in N_{G_\ell}(v)\}$). Initially, NEIGHB$_v$ contains all neighbors of v (all nodes in $N_{G_1}(v)$).

Communication stage.

In this stage the processors communicate in an attempt to obtain information from other processors. This stage contains *four sub-stages*:

- First sub-stage: every processor v that is either a collector or an informer (i.e., *status$_v$* $\neq$ idle) sends message $\langle$ACTIVE$_v$, BUSY$_v$, RUMORS$_v$, call$\rangle$ to every processor in CALLING$_v$. The idle processors do not send any messages in this sub-stage.
- Second sub-stage: all processors (collectors, informers and idling) collect the information sent to by the other processors in the previous sub-stage. Specifically, processor v collects lists ACTIVE$_w$, BUSY$_w$ and RUMORS$_w$ of every processor w that received a call-message from and v inserts w in set ANSWER$_v$.

- Third sub-stage: every processor (regardless of its status) responds to each processor that received a call-message from. Specifically, processor v sends message $\langle \text{ACTIVE}_v, \text{BUSY}_v, \text{RUMORS}_v, \texttt{reply} \rangle$ to the processors in ANSWER_v and empties ANSWER_v.
- Fourth sub-stage: the processors receive the responses to their call-messages.

Update stage.

In this stage each processor v updates its local knowledge based on the messages it received in the *last communication stage*[1]. If $status_v = \texttt{idle}$, then v idles. We now present the six **update rules** and their processing. Note that the rules are not disjoint, but we apply them in the order from (r1) to (r6):

(r1) Updating BUSY_v or RUMORS_v: For every processor w in CALLING_v (i) if v is an informer, it removes w from BUSY_v, (ii) if v is a collector and RUMORS_w was included in one of the messages that v received, then v adds the pair $(w, rumor_w)$ in RUMORS_v and, (iii) if v is a collector but RUMORS_w was not included in one of the messages that v received, then v adds the pair $(w, \perp)$ in RUMORS_v.

(r2) Updating RUMORS_v and WAITING_v: For every processor w in $[p]$, (i) if $(w, rumor_w)$ is not in RUMORS_v and v learns the rumor of w from some other processor that received a message from, then v adds $(w, rumor_w)$ in RUMORS_v, (ii) if both $(w, rumor_w)$ and $(w, \perp)$ are in RUMORS_v, then v removes $(w, \perp)$ from RUMORS_v, and (iii) if either of $(w, rumor_w)$ or $(w, \perp)$ is in RUMORS_v and w is in WAITING_v, then v removes w from WAITING_v.

(r3) Updating BUSY_v: For every processor w in BUSY_v, if v receives a message from processor v' so that w is not in $\text{BUSY}_{v'}$, then v removes w from BUSY_v.

(r4) Updating ACTIVE_v and NEIGHB_v: For every processor w in ACTIVE_v (i) if w is not in NEIGHB_v and v received a message from processor v' so that w is not in $\text{ACTIVE}_{v'}$, then v removes w from ACTIVE_v, (ii) if w is in NEIGHB_v and v did not receive a message from w, then v removes w from ACTIVE_v and NEIGHB_v, and (iii) if w is in CALLING_v and v did not receive a message from w, then v removes w from ACTIVE_v.

(r5) Changing status: If the size of RUMORS_v is equal to p and v is a collector, then v becomes an informer.

(r6) Updating CALLING_v: Processor v empties CALLING_v and (i) if v is a collector then it updates set CALLING_v to contain the first $p^{(\ell+1)\varepsilon}$ pids of list WAITING_v (or all pids of WAITING_v if $sizeof(\text{WAITING}_v) < p^{(\ell+1)\varepsilon})$ and all pids of set NEIGHB_v, and

---

[1] In the first update stage of the first phase of epoch 1, where no communication has yet to occur, no update of the list or sets takes place.

(ii) if v is an informer then it updates set CALLING$_v$ to contain the first $p^{(\ell+1)\varepsilon}$ pids of list BUSY$_v$ (or all pids of BUSY$_v$ if $sizeof(\text{BUSY}_v) < p^{(\ell+1)\varepsilon})$ and all pids of set NEIGHB$_v$.

Terminating epoch.

Epoch $\lceil 1/\varepsilon \rceil - 1$ is the last epoch of the algorithm. In this epoch, each processor v updates its local information based on the messages it received in the last communication stage of epoch $\lceil 1/\varepsilon \rceil - 2$. If after this update processor v is still a collector, then it sends a call-message to every processor that is in WAITING$_v$ (list WAITING$_v$ contains the pids of the processors that v does not know their rumor or does not know whether they have crashed). Then every processor v receives the call-messages sent by the other processors (set ANSWER$_v$ is updated to include the senders) . Next, every processor v that received a call-message sends its local knowledge to the sender (i.e. to the members of set ANSWER$_v$). Finally each processor v updates RUMORS$_v$ based on any received information. More specifically, if a processor w responded to v's call-message (meaning that v now learns the rumor of w), then v adds $(w, rumor_w)$ in RUMORS$_v$. If w did not respond to v's call-message, and $(w, rumor_w)$ is not in RUMORS$_v$ (it is possible for processor v to learn the rumor of w from some other processor v' that learned the rumor of w before processor w crashed), then v knows that w has crashed and adds $(w, \perp)$ in RUMORS$_v$.

4.3.2 Correctness of Algorithm GOSSIP$_\varepsilon$

We show that algorithm GOSSIP$_\varepsilon$ solves the $Gossip_{\mathcal{A}_C}(p, f)$ problem correctly, meaning that by the end of epoch $\lceil 1/\varepsilon \rceil - 1$ each non-faulty processor has heard about all other $p - 1$ processors. First we show that no non-faulty processor is removed from a processor's list of active processors.

Lemma 4.8. *In any execution of algorithm GOSSIP$_\varepsilon$, if processors v and w are non-faulty by the end of any epoch $\ell < \lceil 1/\varepsilon \rceil - 1$, then w is in ACTIVE$_v$.*

Proof. Consider processors v and w that are non-faulty by the end of epoch $\ell < \lceil 1/\varepsilon \rceil - 1$. We show that w is in ACTIVE$_v$. The proof of the inverse is done similarly. The proof proceeds by induction on the number of epochs.

Initially all processors (including w) are in ACTIVE$_v$. Consider phase s of epoch 1 (for simplicity assume that s is not the last phase of epoch 1). By the update rule, a processor w is removed from ACTIVE$_v$ if v is not idle and

(a) during the communication stage of phase s, w is not in NEIGHB$_v$ and v received a message from a processor v' so that w is not in ACTIVE$_{v'}$,
(b) during the communication stage of phase s, w is in NEIGHB$_v$ and v did not receive a message from w, or
(c) v sent a call-message to w in the communication stage of phase s of epoch 1 and v did not receive a response from w in the same stage.

Case (c) is not possible: Since w is non-faulty in all phases s of epoch 1, w receives the call-message from v in the communication stage of phase s and adds v in ANSWER$_w$. Then, processor w sends a response to v in the same stage. Hence v does not remove w from ACTIVE$_v$.

Case (b) is also not possible: Since w is non-faulty and w is in NEIGHB$_v$, by the properties of the communication graph G_1, v is in NEIGHB$_w$ as well (and since v is non-faulty). From the description of the first sub-stage of the communication stage, if $status_w \neq$ idle, w sends a message to its neighbors, including v. If $status_w =$ idle, then w will not send a message to v in the first sub-stage, but it will send a reply to v' call-message in the third sub-stage. Therefore, by the end of the communication stage, v has received a message from w and hence it does not remove w from ACTIVE$_v$.

Neither Case (a) is possible: This follows inductively, using points (b) and (c): no processor will remove w from its set of active processors in a phase prior to s and hence v does not receive a message from any processor v' so that w is not in ACTIVE$_{v'}$.

Now, assuming that w is in ACTIVE$_v$ by the end of epoch $\ell - 1$, we show that w is still in ACTIVE$_v$ by the end of epoch ℓ. Since w is in ACTIVE$_v$ by the end of epoch $\ell - 1$, w is in ACTIVE$_v$ at the beginning of the first phase of epoch ℓ. Using similar arguments as in the base case of the induction and from the inductive hypothesis, it follows that w is in ACTIVE$_v$ by the end of the first phase of epoch ℓ. Inductively it follows that w is in ACTIVE$_v$ by the end of the last phase of epoch ℓ, as desired.   □

Next we show if a non-faulty processor w has not heard from all processors yet then no non-faulty processor v removes w from its list of busy processors.

Lemma 4.9. *In any execution of algorithm* GOSSIP$_\varepsilon$ *and any epoch* $\ell < \lceil 1/\varepsilon \rceil - 1$, *if processors* v *and* w *are non-faulty by the end of epoch* ℓ *and* $status_w =$ collector, *then* w *is in* BUSY$_v$.

Proof. Consider processors v and w that are non-faulty by the end of epoch $\ell < \lceil 1/\varepsilon \rceil - 1$ and $status_w =$ collector. The proof proceeds by induction on the number of epochs.

Initially all processors w have status collector and w is in BUSY$_v$ (CALLING$_v \setminus$ NEIGHB$_v$ is empty). Consider phase s of epoch 1. By the update rule, a processor w is removed from BUSY$_v$ if

(a) at the beginning of the update stage of phase s, v is an informer and w is in CALLING$_v$, or
(b) during the communication stage of phase s, v receives a message from a processor v' so that w is not in BUSY$_{v'}$.

Case (a) is not possible: Since v is an informer and w is in CALLING$_v$ at the beginning of the update stage of phase s, this means that in the communication stage of phase $s - 1$, processor v was already an informer and it sent a call-message to w. In this case, w would receive this message and it would become an informer during the update stage of phase s. This violates the assumption of the lemma.

Case (b) is also not possible: For w not being in BUSY$_{v'}$ it means that either (i) in some phase $s' < s$, processor v' became an informer and sent a call-message to w, or (ii) during the communication stage of a phase $s'' < s$, v' received a message from a processor v'' so that w was not in BUSY$_{v''}$. Case (i) implies that in phase $s' + 1$, processor w becomes an informer which violates the assumption of the lemma. Using inductively case (i) it follows that case (ii) is not possible either.

Now, assuming that by the end of epoch $\ell - 1$, w is in BUSY$_v$ we would like to show that by the end of epoch ℓ, w is still in BUSY$_v$. Since w is in BUSY$_v$ by the end of epoch $\ell - 1$, w is in BUSY$_v$ at the beginning of the first phase of epoch ℓ. Using similar arguments as in the base case of the induction and from the inductive hypothesis, it follows that w is in BUSY$_v$ by the end of the first phase of epoch ℓ. Inductively it follows that w is in BUSY$_v$ by the end of the last phase of epoch ℓ, as desired.   □

We now show that each processor's list of rumors is updated correctly.

Lemma 4.10. *In any execution of algorithm* GOSSIP$_\varepsilon$ *and any epoch* $\ell < \lceil 1/\varepsilon \rceil - 1$,
(i) *if processors v and w are non-faulty by the end of epoch ℓ and w is not in* WAITING$_v$, *then* $(w, rumor_w)$ *is in* RUMORS$_v$, *and*
(ii) *if processor v is non-faulty by the end of epoch ℓ and $(w, \perp)$ is in* RUMORS$_v$, *then w is not in* ACTIVE$_v$.

Proof. We first prove part (i) of the lemma. Consider processors v and w that are non-faulty by the end of epoch ℓ and that w is not in WAITING$_v$. The proof proceeds by induction on the number of epochs. The proof for the first epoch is done similarly as the the proof of the inductive step (that follows), since at the beginning of the computation each $w \neq v$ is in WAITING$_v$ and RUMORS$_v$ contains only the pair $(v, rumor_v)$, for every processor v.

Assume that part (i) of the lemma holds by the end of epoch $\ell - 1$, we would like to show that it also holds by the end of epoch ℓ. First note the following facts: no pair of the form $(w, rumor_w)$ is ever removed from RUMORS$_v$ and no processor identifier is ever added to WAITING$_v$. We use these facts implicitly in the remainder of the proof (cases (a) and (b)). Suppose, to the contrary, that at the end of epoch ℓ there are processors v, w which are non-faulty by the end of epoch ℓ and w is not in WAITING$_v$ and $(w, \perp)$ is in RUMORS$_v$. Take v such that v put the pair $(w, \perp)$ to its RUMORS$_v$ as the earliest node during epoch ℓ and this pair has remained in RUMORS$_v$ by the end of epoch ℓ. It follows that during epoch ℓ at least one of the following cases must have happened:
(a) Processor v sent a call-message to processor w in the communication stage of some phase and v did not receive a response from w (see update rule (r1)). But since w is not-faulty by the end of epoch ℓ it replied to v according to the third sub-stage of communication stage. This is a contradiction.

(b) During the communication stage of some phase processor v received a message from processor v' so that $(w, \perp)$ is in RUMORS$_{v'}$ (see update rule (r2)). But this contradicts the choice of v.
Hence part (i) is proved.

The proof of part (ii) of the lemma is analogous to the proof of part (i). The key argument is that the pair $(w, \perp)$ is added in RUMORS$_v$ if w does not respond to a call-message sent by v which in this case w is removed from ACTIVE$_v$ (if w was not removed from ACTIVE$_v$ earlier). □

Finally we show the correctness of algorithm GOSSIP$_\varepsilon$.

Theorem 4.11. *By the end of epoch $\lceil 1/\varepsilon \rceil - 1$ of any execution of algorithm* GOSSIP$_\varepsilon$, *every non-faulty processor v either knows the rumor of processor w or it knows that w has crashed.*

Proof. Consider a processor v that is non-faulty by the end of epoch $\lceil 1/\varepsilon \rceil - 1$. Note that the claims of Lemmas 4.8, 4.9, and 4.10 also hold after the end of the update stage of the terminating epoch. This follows from the fact that the last communication stage of epoch $\lceil 1/\varepsilon \rceil - 2$ precedes the update stage of the terminating epoch and the fact that this last update stage is no different from the update stage of prior epochs (hence the same reasoning can be applied to obtain the result).

If after this last update, processor v is still a collector, meaning that v did not hear from all processors yet, according to the description of the algorithm, processor v will send a call-message to the processors whose pid is still in WAITING$_v$ (by Lemma 4.10 and the update rule, it follows that list WAITING$_v$ contains all processors that v did not hear from yet). Then all non-faulty processors w receive the call-message of v and then they respond to v. Then v receives these responses. Finally v updates list RUMORS$_v$ accordingly: if a processor w responded to v's call-message (meaning that v now learns the rumor of w), then v adds $(w, rumor_w)$ in RUMORS$_v$. If w did not respond to v's call-message, and $(w, rumor_w)$ is not in RUMORS$_v$ (it is possible for processor v to learn the rumor of w from some other processor v' that learned the rumor of w before processor w crashed), then v knows that w has crashed and adds $(w, \perp)$ in RUMORS$_v$.

Hence the last update that each non-faulty processor v performs on RUMORS$_v$ maintains the validity that the list had from the previous epochs (guaranteed by the above three lemmas). Moreover, the size of RUMORS$_v$ becomes equal to p and v either knows the rumor of each processor w, or it knows that v has crashed, as desired. □

Note from the above that the correctness of algorithm GOSSIP$_\varepsilon$ does not depend on whether the set of permutations Ψ satisfy the conditions of Corollary 4.7. The algorithm is correct for any set of permutations of $[p]$.

4.3.3 Analysis of Algorithm GOSSIP$_\varepsilon$

Consider some set V_ℓ, $|V_\ell| \geq p^{1-\ell\varepsilon}$, of processors that are not idle at the beginning of epoch ℓ and do not fail by the end of epoch ℓ. Let $Q_\ell \subseteq V_\ell$ be such that $|Q_\ell| \geq |V_\ell|/7$ and the diameter of the subgraph induced by Q_ℓ is at most $31 \log p$. Q_ℓ exists because of Lemma 4.4 applied to graph G_ℓ and set V_ℓ.

For any processor v, let CALL$_v$ = CALLING$_v \setminus$ NEIGHB$_v$. Recall that the size of CALL is equal to $p^{(\ell+1)\varepsilon}$ (or less if list WAITING, or BUSY, is shorter than $p^{(\ell+1)\varepsilon}$) and the size of NEIGHB is at most $p^{(\ell+1)\varepsilon}$. We refer to the call-messages sent to the processors whose pids are in CALL as *progress-messages*. If processor v sends a progress-message to processor w, it will remove w from list WAITING$_v$ (or BUSY$_v$) by the end of current stage. Let $d = (31 \log p + 1)p^{(\ell+1)\varepsilon}$. Note that $d \geq (31 \log p + 1) \cdot |$CALL$|$.

We begin the analysis of the gossip algorithm by proving a bound on the number of progress-messages sent under certain conditions.

Lemma 4.12. *The total number of progress-messages sent by processors in Q_ℓ from the beginning of epoch ℓ until the first processor in Q_ℓ will have its list WAITING (or list BUSY) empty, is at most $(d, |Q_\ell|)$-Surf(Ψ).*

Proof. Fix Q_ℓ and consider some permutation $\sigma \in S_p$ that satisfies the following property: "Consider $i < j \leq p$. Let τ_i (τ_j) be the time step in epoch ℓ where some processor in Q_ℓ hears about $\sigma(i)$ ($\sigma(j)$) the first time among the processors in Q_ℓ. Then $\tau_i \leq \tau_j$." (We note that it is not difficult to see that for a given Q_ℓ we can always find $\sigma \in S_p$ that satisfies the above property.) We consider only the subset $\Upsilon \subseteq \Psi$ containing permutations of indexes from set Q_ℓ. To show the lemma we prove that the number of messages sent by processors from Q_ℓ is at most $(d, |\Upsilon|)$-Surf$(\Upsilon, \sigma) \leq (d, |Q_\ell|)$-Surf$(\Psi)$. Suppose that processor $v \in Q_\ell$ sends a progress-message to processor w. It follows from the diameter of Q_ℓ and the size of set CALL in epoch ℓ, that none of processor $v' \in Q_\ell$ had sent a progress-message to w before $31 \log p$ phases, and consequently position of processor w in permutation π_v is at most $d - |$CALL$| \leq d - p^{(\ell+1)\varepsilon}$ greater than position of w in permutation $\pi_{v'}$.

For each processor $v \in Q_\ell$, let P_v contain all pairs (v, i) such that v sends a progress-message to processor $\pi_v(i)$ by itself during the epoch ℓ. We construct function h from the set $\bigcup_{v \in Q_\ell} P_v$ to the set of all d-lrm of set $\sigma^{-1} \circ \Psi$ and show that h is one-to-one function. We run the construction independently for each processor $v \in Q_\ell$. If $\pi_v(k)$ is the first processor in the permutation π_v to whom v sends a progress-message at the beginning of epoch ℓ, we set $h(v, k) = 1$. Suppose that $(v, i) \in P_v$ and we have defined function h for all elements from P_v less than (v, i) in the lexicographic order. We define $h(v, i)$ as the first $j \leq i$ such that $(\sigma^{-1} \circ \pi_v)(j)$ is a d-lrm not assigned yet by h to any element in P_v.

Claim. *For every* $(v, i) \in P_v$, $h(v, i)$ *is well defined.*

We prove the Claim. For the first element in P_v function h is well defined. For the first d elements in P_v it is also easy to show that h is well defined, since the first d elements in permutation π_v are d-lrms. Suppose h is well defined for all elements from P_v less than (v, i) and (v, i) is at least the $(d+1)$st element in P_v. We show that $h(v, i)$ is also well defined. Suppose to the contrary, that there is no position $j \leq i$ such that $(\sigma^{-1} \circ \pi_v)(j)$ is a d-lrm and j is not assigned by h before step of construction for $(v, i) \in P_v$. Let $j_1 < \ldots < j_d < i$ be the positions such that $(v, j_1), \ldots, (v, j_d) \in P_v$ and $(\sigma^{-1} \circ \pi_v)(h(j_1)), \ldots, (\sigma^{-1} \circ \pi_v)(h(j_d))$ are greater than $(\sigma^{-1} \circ \pi_v)(i)$. They exist from the fact, that $(\sigma^{-1} \circ \pi_v)(i)$ is not d-lrm and every "previous" d-lrms in π_v are assigned by L. Obviously processor $w = \pi_v(h(j_1))$ received a first progress-message at least $\frac{d}{|\text{CALL}|} = 31 \log p + 1$ phases before it received a progress-message from v. From the choice of σ, processor $w' = \pi_v(i)$ had received a progress-message from some other processor in Q'_ℓ at least $31 \log p + 1$ phases before w' received a progress-message from v. This contradicts the remark at the beginning of the proof of the lemma. This completes the proof of the Claim.

The fact that h is a one-to-one function follows directly from the definition of h. It follows that the number of progress-messages sent by processors in Q_ℓ until the list WAITING (or list BUSY) of a processor in Q_ℓ is empty, is at most $(d, |\Upsilon|)$-Surf$(\Upsilon, \sigma) \leq (d, |Q_\ell|)$-Surf$(\Psi)$, as desired. $\qquad\square$

We now define an invariant, that we call I_ℓ, for $\ell = 1, \ldots, \lceil 1/\varepsilon \rceil - 2$:

I_ℓ: There are at most $p^{1-\ell\varepsilon}$ non-faulty processors having status collector or informer in any step after the end of epoch ℓ.

Using Lemma 4.12 and Corollary 4.7 we show the following:

Lemma 4.13. *In any execution of algorithm* GOSSIP$_\varepsilon$, *the invariant* I_ℓ *holds for any epoch* $\ell = 1, \ldots, \lceil 1/\varepsilon \rceil - 2$.

Proof. For $p = 1$ it is obvious. Assume $p > 1$. We will use Lemma 4.4 and Corollary 4.7. Consider any epoch $\ell < \lceil 1/\varepsilon \rceil - 1$. Suppose to the contrary, that there is a subset V_ℓ of non-faulty processors after the end of epoch ℓ such that each of them has status either collector or informer and $|V_\ell| > p^{1-\ell\varepsilon}$. Since G_ℓ satisfies $CCP(p, p - p^{1-\ell\varepsilon}, \varepsilon)$, there is a set $Q_\ell \subseteq V_\ell$ such that $|Q_\ell| \geq |V_\ell|/7 > p^{1-\ell\varepsilon}/7$ and the diameter of the subgraph induced by Q_ℓ is at most $31 \log p$. Applying Lemma 4.12 and Corollary 4.7 to the set Q_ℓ, epoch ℓ, $t = p$, $q = |Q_\ell|$ and $d = 31 p^{(\ell+1)\varepsilon} \log p$, we obtain that the total number of messages sent until some processor $v \in Q_\ell$ has list BUSY$_v$ empty, is at most

$$2 \cdot (31(\log p + 1)p^{(\ell+1)\varepsilon}, |Q_\ell|)\text{-Surf}(\Psi) + 31|Q_\ell|p^{(\ell+1)\varepsilon} \log p$$

$$\leq 341|Q_\ell|p^{(\ell+1)\varepsilon} \log^2 p \ .$$

More precisely, until some processor in Q_ℓ has status informer, the processors in Q_ℓ have sent at most $(31(\log p + 1)p^{(\ell+1)\varepsilon}, |Q_\ell|)$-Surf($\Psi$) messages. Then, after the processors in Q_ℓ send at most $31|Q_\ell|p^{(\ell+1)\varepsilon} \log p$ messages, every processor in Q_ℓ has status informer. Finally, after the processors in Q_ℓ send at most $(31(\log p + 1)p^{(\ell+1)\varepsilon}, |Q_\ell|)$-Surf($\Psi$) messages, some processor in $Q_\ell \subseteq V_\ell$ has its list BUSY empty.

Notice that since no processor in Q_ℓ has status idle in epoch ℓ, each of them sends in every phase of epoch ℓ at most $|\text{CALL}| \le p^{(\ell+1)\varepsilon}$ progress-messages. Consequently the total number of phases in epoch ℓ until some of the processors in Q_ℓ has its list BUSY empty, is at most

$$\frac{341|Q_\ell|p^{(\ell+1)\varepsilon} \log^2 p}{|Q_\ell|p^{(\ell+1)\varepsilon}} \le 341 \log^2 p \ .$$

Recall that $\alpha \log^2 p \ge 341 \log^2 p$. Hence if we consider the first $341 \log^2 p$ phases of epoch ℓ, the above argument implies that there is at least one processor in V_ℓ that has status idle, which is a contradiction. Hence, I_ℓ holds for epoch ℓ. □

We now show the time and message complexity of algorithm GOSSIP$_\varepsilon$.

Theorem 4.14. *Algorithm* GOSSIP$_\varepsilon$ *solves the* Gossip$_{\mathcal{A}_C}(p, f)$ *problem with time complexity* $T = O(\log^2 p)$ *and message complexity* $M = O(p^{1+3\varepsilon})$.

Proof. First we show the bound on time. Observe that each update and communication stage takes $O(1)$ time. Therefore each of the first $\lceil 1/\varepsilon \rceil - 2$ epochs takes $O(\log^2 p)$ time. The last epoch takes $O(1)$ time. From this and the fact that ε is a constant, we have that the time complexity of the algorithm is in the worse case $O(\log^2 p)$.

We now show the bound on messages. From Lemma 4.13 we have that for every $1 \le \ell < \lceil 1/\varepsilon \rceil - 2$, during epoch $\ell + 1$ there are at most $p^{1-\ell\varepsilon}$ processors sending at most $2p^{(\ell+2)\varepsilon}$ messages in every communication stage. The remaining processors are either faulty (hence they do not send any messages) or have status idle — these processors only respond to call-messages and their total impact on the message complexity in epoch $\ell + 1$ is at most as large as the others. Consequently the message complexity during epoch $\ell + 1$ is at most $4(\alpha \log^2 p) \cdot (p^{1-\ell\varepsilon}p^{(\ell+2)\varepsilon}) \le 4\alpha p^{1+2\varepsilon} \log^2 p \le 4\alpha p^{1+3\varepsilon}$. After epoch $\lceil 1/\varepsilon \rceil - 2$ there are, per $I_{\lceil 1/\varepsilon \rceil - 2}$, at most $p^{2\varepsilon}$ processors having list WAITING not empty. In epoch $\lceil 1/\varepsilon \rceil - 1$ each of these processors sends a message to at most p processors twice, hence the message complexity in this epoch is bounded by $2p \cdot p^{2\varepsilon}$. From the above and the fact that ε is a constant, we have that the message complexity of the algorithm is $O(p^{1+3\varepsilon})$. □

4.4 The Do-All Algorithm

We now put the gossip algorithm to use by constructing a robust *Do-All* algorithm, called algorithm DOALL$_\varepsilon$.

4.4.1 Description of Algorithm DOALL$_\varepsilon$

The algorithm proceeds in a loop that is repeated until all the tasks are executed and all non-faulty processors are aware of this. A single iteration of the loop is called an *epoch*. Each epoch consists of $\beta \log p + 1$ *phases*, where $\beta > 0$ is a constant integer. We show that the algorithm is correct for any integer $\beta > 0$, but the complexity analysis of the algorithm depends on specific values of β that we show to exist. Each phase is divided into two *stages*, the *work* stage and the *gossip* stage. In the work stage processors perform tasks, and in the gossip stage processors execute an instance of the GOSSIP$_{\varepsilon/3}$ algorithm to exchange information regarding completed tasks and non-faulty processors (more details momentarily). Computation starts with epoch 1. We note that (unlike in algorithm GOSSIP$_\varepsilon$) the non-faulty processors may stop executing at different steps. Hence we need to argue about the termination decision that the processors must take. This is done in the paragraph "Termination decision".

The pseudocode for a phase of epoch ℓ of the algorithm is given in Figure 4.2 (again we assume that every *if-then* has an implicit *else* containing no-ops as needed to ensure the synchrony of the system). The details are explained in the rest of this section.

Local knowledge. Each processor v maintains a list of tasks TASK$_v$ it believes not to be done, and a list of processors PROC$_v$ it believes to be non-faulty. Initially TASK$_v = \langle 1, \ldots, n \rangle$ and PROC$_v = \langle 1, \ldots, p \rangle$. The processor also has a boolean variable *done$_v$*, that describes the knowledge of v regarding the completion of the tasks. Initially *done$_v$* is set to `false`, and when processor v is assured that all tasks are completed *done$_v$* is set to `true`.

Task allocation. Each processor v is equipped with a permutation π_v from a set Ψ of permutations on $[n]$. (This is distinct from the set of permutation on $[p]$ required by the gossip algorithm.) We show that the algorithm is correct for any set of permutations on $[n]$, but its complexity analysis depends on specific set of permutations Ψ that we show to exist. These permutations can be constructed efficiently.

Initially TASK$_v$ is permuted according to π_v and then processor v performs tasks according to the ordering of the tids in TASK$_v$. In the course of the computation, when processor v learns that task z is performed (either by performing the task itself or by obtaining this information from some other processor), it removes z from TASK$_v$ while preserving the permutation order.

Work stage. For epoch ℓ, each work stage consists of $T_\ell = \left\lceil \frac{n + p \log^3 p}{\frac{p}{2^\ell} \log p} \right\rceil$ work *sub-stages*. In each sub-stage, each processor v performs a task according to TASK$_v$. Hence, in each work stage of a phase of epoch ℓ, processor v must perform the first T_ℓ tasks of TASK$_v$. However, if TASK$_v$ becomes empty at a

Initialization

$done_v$ = false;
TASK$_v = \langle \pi_v(1), \pi_v(2), \ldots, \pi_v(p) \rangle$;
PROC$_v = \langle 1, 2, \ldots, p \rangle$;

Epoch ℓ

repeat $\beta \log p + 1$ times   % *iterating phases of epoch ℓ*

   repeat $T_\ell = \lceil \frac{n + p \log^3 p}{\frac{p}{2^\ell} \log p} \rceil$ times   % *work stage begins*

   if TASK$_v$ not empty **then**
      perform task whose id is first in TASK$_v$;
      remove task's id from TASK$_v$;
   elseif TASK$_v$ empty and $done_v$ = false **then**
      set $done_v$ to true;
   if TASK$_v$ empty and $done_v$ = false **then**
      set $done_v$ to true;

   run GOSSIP$_{\varepsilon/3}$ with $rumor_v = $ (TASK$_v$,PROC$_v$,$done_v$);   % *gossip stage begins*

   if $done_v$ = true and $done_w$ = true for all w received rumor from **then**
      TERMINATE;
   else
      update TASK$_v$ and PROC$_v$;

Fig. 4.2. Algorithm DOALL$_\varepsilon$, stated for processor v; $\pi_v(i)$ denotes the ith element of permutation π_v.

sub-stage prior to sub-state T_ℓ, then v performs no-ops in the remaining sub-stages (each no-op operation takes the same time as performing a task). Once TASK$_v$ becomes empty, $done_v$ is set to **true**.

Gossip stage. Here processors execute algorithm GOSSIP$_{\varepsilon/3}$ using their local knowledge as the rumor, i.e., for processor v, $rumor_v = $ (TASK$_v$, PROC$_v$, $done_v$). At the end of the stage, each processor v updates its local knowledge based on the rumors it received. The **update rule** is as follows: (a) If v does not receive the rumor of processor w, then v learns that w has failed (guaranteed by the correctness of GOSSIP$_{\varepsilon/3}$). In this case v removes w from PROC$_v$. (b) If v receives the rumor of processor w, then it compare TASK$_v$ and PROC$_v$ with TASK$_w$ and PROC$_w$ respectively and updates its lists accordingly—it removes the tasks that w knows are already completed and the processors that w knows that have crashed. Note that if TASK$_v$ becomes empty after this update, variable $done_v$ remains **false**. It will be set to **true** in the next work stage. This is needed for the correctness of the algorithm (see Lemma 4.19).

Termination decision. We would like all non-faulty processors to learn that the tasks are done. Hence, it would not be sufficient for a processor to terminate once the value of its *done* variable is set to true. It has to be assured that all other non-faulty processors' *done* variables are set to true as well, and then terminate. This is achieved as follows: If processor v starts the gossip stage of a phase of epoch ℓ with $done_v = $ true, and all rumors it receives suggest that all other non-faulty processors know that all tasks are done (their *done* variables are set to true), then processor v terminates. If at least one processor's *done* variable is set to false, then v continues to the next phase of epoch ℓ (or to the first phase of epoch $\ell + 1$ if the previous phase was the last of epoch ℓ).

Remark 4.15. In the complexity analysis of the algorithm we first assume that $n \leq p^2$ and then we show how to extend the analysis for the case $n > p^2$. In order to do so, we assume that when $n > p^2$, before the start of algorithm DOALL$_\varepsilon$, the tasks are partitioned into $n' = p^2$ chunks, where each chunk contains at most $\lceil n/p^2 \rceil$ tasks. In this case it is understood that in the above description of the algorithm, n is actually n' and when we refer to a task we really mean a chunk of tasks.

4.4.2 Correctness of Algorithm DOALL$_\varepsilon$

We show that the algorithm DOALL$_\varepsilon$ solves the $Do\text{-}All_{A_C}(n, p, f)$ problem correctly, meaning that the algorithm terminates with all tasks performed and all non-faulty processors are aware of this. Note that this is a stronger correctness condition than the one required by the definition of *Do-All*.

First we show that no non-faulty processor is removed from a processor's list of non-faulty processors.

Lemma 4.16. *In any execution of algorithm* DOALL$_\varepsilon$, *if processors v and w are non-faulty by the end of the gossip stage of phase s of epoch ℓ, then processor w is in* PROC$_v$.

Proof. Let v be a processor that is non-faulty by the end of the gossip stage of phase s of epoch ℓ. By the correctness of algorithm GOSSIP$_{\varepsilon/3}$ (called at the gossip stage), processor v receives the rumor of every non-faulty processor w and vice-versa. Since there are no restarts, v and w were alive in all prior phases of epochs $1, 2, \ldots, \ell$, and hence, v and w received each other rumors in all these phases as well. By the update rule it follows that processor v does not remove processor w from its processor list and vice-versa. Hence w is in PROC$_v$ and w is in PROC$_v$ by the end of phase s, as desired.   □

Next we show that no undone task is removed from a processor's list of undone tasks.

Lemma 4.17. *In any execution of algorithm* DOALL$_\varepsilon$, *if a task z is not in* TASK$_v$ *of any processor v at the beginning of the first phase of epoch ℓ, then z has been performed in a phase of one of the epochs $1, 2, \ldots, \ell - 1$.*

Proof. From the description of the algorithm we have that initially any task z is in TASK_v of a processor v. We proceed by induction on the number of epochs. At the beginning of the first phase of epoch 1, z is in TASK_v. If by the end of the first phase of epoch 1, z is not in TASK_v then by the update rule either (i) v performed task z during the work stage, or (ii) during the gossip stage v received $rumor_w$ from processor w in which z was not in TASK_w. The latter suggests that processor w performed task z during the work stage. Continuing in this manner it follows that if z is not in TASK_v at the beginning of the first phase of epoch 2, then z was performed in one of the phases of epoch 1.

Assuming that the thesis of the lemma holds for any epoch ℓ, we show that it also holds for epoch $\ell + 1$. Consider two cases:

Case 1: If z is not in TASK_v at the beginning of the first phase of epoch ℓ, then since no tid is ever added in TASK_v, z is not in TASK_v neither at the beginning of the first phase of epoch $\ell + 1$. By the inductive hypothesis, z was performed in one of the phases of epochs $1, \ldots, \ell - 1$.

Case 2: If z is in TASK_v at the beginning of the first phase of epoch ℓ but it is not in TASK_v at the beginning of the second phase of epoch ℓ, then by the update rule it follows that either (i) v performed task z during the work stage of the second phase of epoch ℓ, or (ii) during the gossip stage of the second phase of epoch ℓ, v received $rumor_w$ from processor w in which z was not in TASK_w. The latter suggests that processor w performed task z during the work stage of the second phase of epoch ℓ or it learned that z was done in the gossip stage of the first phase of epoch ℓ. Either case, task z was performed. Continuing in this manner it follows that if z is not in TASK_v at the beginning of the first phase of epoch $\ell + 1$, then z was performed in one of the phases of epoch ℓ. $\qquad\square$

Next we show that under certain conditions, local progress is guaranteed. First we introduce some notation. For processor v we denote by $\text{TASK}_v^{(\ell,s)}$ the list TASK_v at the beginning of phase s of epoch ℓ. Note that if s is the last phase – $(\beta \log^2 p)$th phase – of epoch ℓ, then $\text{TASK}_v^{(\ell,s+1)} = \text{TASK}_v^{(\ell+1,1)}$, meaning that after phase s processor v enters the first phase of epoch $\ell + 1$.

Lemma 4.18. *In any execution of algorithm* DOALL_ε, *if processor v enters a work stage of a phase s of epoch ℓ with $done_w = \texttt{false}$, then* $sizeof(\text{TASK}_v^{(\ell,s+1)}) < sizeof(\text{TASK}_v^{(\ell,s)})$.

Proof. Let v be a processor that starts the work stage of phase s of epoch ℓ with $done_w = \texttt{false}$. According to the description of the algorithm, the value of variable $done_v$ is initially $\texttt{false}$ and it is set to $\texttt{true}$ only when TASK_v becomes empty. Hence, at the beginning of the work stage of phase s of epoch ℓ there is at least one task identifier in $\text{TASK}_v^{(\ell,s)}$, and therefore v performs at least one task. From this and the fact that no tid is ever added in a processor's task list, we get that $sizeof(\text{TASK}_v^{(\ell,s+1)}) < sizeof(\text{TASK}_v^{(\ell,s)})$. $\qquad\square$

We now show that when during a phase s of an epoch ℓ, a processor learns that all tasks are completed and it does not crash during this phase, then the algorithm is guaranteed to terminate by phase $s + 1$ of epoch ℓ; if s is the last phase epoch ℓ, then the algorithm is guaranteed to terminate by the first phase of epoch $\ell + 1$. For simplicity of presentation, in the following lemma we assume that s is not the last phase of epoch ℓ.

Lemma 4.19. *In any execution of algorithm* DOALL$_\varepsilon$, *for any phase s of epoch ℓ and any processor v, if $done_v$ is set to* true *during phase s and v is non-faulty by the end of phase s, then the algorithm terminates by phase $s+1$ of epoch ℓ.*

Proof. Consider phase s of epoch ℓ and processor v. According to the code of the algorithm, the value of variable $done_w$ is updated during the work stage of a phase (the value of the variable is not changed during the gossip stage). Hence, if the value of variable $done_w$ is changed during the phase s of epoch ℓ this happens before the start of the gossip stage. This means that TASK$_v$ contained in $rumor_v$ in the execution of algorithm GOSSIP$_{\varepsilon/3}$ is empty. Since v does not fail during phase s, the correctness of algorithm GOSSIP$_{\varepsilon/3}$ guarantees that all non-faulty processors learn the rumor of v, and consequently they learn that all tasks are performed. This means that all non-faulty processors w start the gossip stage of phase $s + 1$ of epoch ℓ with $done_w =$ true and all rumors they receive contain the variable $done$ set to true.

The above, in conjunction with the termination guarantees of algorithm GOSSIP$_{\varepsilon/3}$, leads to the conclusion that all non-faulty processors terminate by phase $s+1$ (and hence the algorithm terminates by phase $s+1$ of epoch ℓ). □

Finally we show the correctness of algorithm DOALL$_\varepsilon$.

Theorem 4.20. *In any execution of algorithm* DOALL$_\varepsilon$, *the algorithm terminates with all tasks performed and all non-faulty processors being aware of this.*

Proof. By Lemma 4.16, no non-faulty processor leaves the computation, and by our model at least one processor does not crash ($f < p$). Also from Lemma 4.17 we have that no undone task is removed from the computation. From the code of the algorithm we get that a processor continues performing tasks until its TASK list becomes empty and by Lemma 4.18 we have that local progress is guaranteed. The above in conjunction with the correctness of algorithm GOSSIP$_{\varepsilon/3}$ lead to the conclusion that there exist a phase s of an epoch ℓ and a processor v so that during phase s processor v sets $done_v$ to true, all tasks are indeed performed and v survives phase s. By Lemma 4.19 the algorithm terminates by phase $s + 1$ of epoch ℓ (or by the first phase of epoch $\ell + 1$ if s is the last phase of epoch ℓ). Now, from the definition of T_ℓ it follows that the algorithm terminates after at most $O(\log p)$ epochs: consider epoch $\log p$; $T_{\log p} = \lceil (n + p \log^3 p) / \log p \rceil = \lceil n / \log p + p \log^2 p \rceil$. Recall that each epoch consists of $\beta \log p + 1$ phases. Say that $\beta = 1$. Then, when a processor reaches epoch $\log p$, it can perform all n tasks in this epoch. Hence, all tasks that are not done until epoch $\log p - 1$ are guaranteed to be performed by the end of epoch $\log p$ and all non-faulty processors will know that all tasks have been performed. □

Note from the above that the correctness of algorithm DOALL_ε does not depend on the set of permutations that processors use to select what tasks to do next. The algorithm works correctly for any set of permutations on $[n]$. It also works for any integer $\beta > 0$.

4.4.3 Analysis of Algorithm DOALL_ε

We now derive the work and message complexities for algorithm DOALL_ε. The analysis is based on the following terminology. For the purpose of the analysis, we number globally all phases by positive integers starting from 1. Consider a phase i in epoch ℓ of an execution $\xi \in \mathcal{E}(\text{DOALL}_\varepsilon, \mathcal{A}_C)$. Let $V_i(\xi)$ denote the set of processors that are non-faulty at the beginning of phase i. Let $p_i(\xi) = |V_i(\xi)|$. Let $U_i(\xi)$ denote the set of tasks z such that z is in some list TASK_v, for some $v \in V_i(\xi)$, at the beginning of phase i. Let $u_i(\xi) = |U_i(\xi)|$.

Now we classify the possibilities for phase i as follows. If at the beginning of phase i, $p_i(\xi) > p/2^{\ell-1}$, we say that phase i is a *majority* phase. Otherwise, phase i is a *minority* phase. If phase i is a minority phase and at the end of i the number of surviving processors is less than $p_i(\xi)/2$, i.e., $p_{i+1}(\xi) < p_i(\xi)/2$, we say that i is an *unreliable* minority phase. If $p_{i+1}(\xi) \geq p_i(\xi)/2$, we say that i is a *reliable* minority phase. If phase i is a reliable minority phase and $u_{i+1}(\xi) \leq u_i(\xi) - \frac{1}{4}p_{i+1}(\xi)T_\ell$, then we say that i is an *optimal* reliable minority phase (the task allocation is optimal – the same task is performed only by a constant number of processors on average). If $u_{i+1}(\xi) \leq \frac{3}{4}u_i(\xi)$, then i is a *fractional* reliable minority phase (a fraction of the undone tasks is performed). Otherwise we say that i is an *unproductive* reliable minority phase (not much progress is obtained). The classification possibilities for phase i of epoch ℓ are depicted in Figure 4.3.

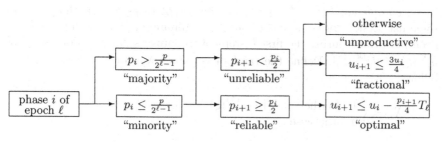

Fig. 4.3. Classification of a phase i of epoch ℓ; execution ξ is implied.

Our goal is to choose a set Ψ of permutations and a constant $\beta > 0$ such that for any execution there will be no unproductive and no majority phases. To do this we analyze sets of random permutations, prove certain properties of algorithm DOALL$_\varepsilon$ for such sets (in Lemmas 4.21 and 4.22), and finally use the probabilistic method to obtain an existential deterministic solution.

We now give the intuition why the phases, with high probability, are neither majority nor minority reliable unproductive. First, in either of such cases, the number of processors crashed during the phase is at most half of all operational processors during the phase. Consider only those majorities of processors that survive the phase and the tasks performed by them. If there are a lot of processors, then all tasks will be performed if the phase is a majority phase, or at least $\min\{u_i(\xi), |Q|T_\ell\}/4$ yet unperformed tasks are performed by the processors if the phase is a minority reliable unproductive phase, all with high probability. Hence one can derandomize the choice of suitable set of permutations such that for any execution there are neither majority nor minority reliable unproductive phases.

Lemma 4.21. *Let Q be a fixed nonempty subset of processors in phase i of epoch ℓ of algorithm DOALL$_\varepsilon$. Then the probability of event "for every execution ξ of algorithm DOALL$_\varepsilon$ such that $V_{i+1}(\xi) \supseteq Q$ and $u_i(\xi) > 0$, the following inequality holds $u_i(\xi) - u_{i+1}(\xi) \geq \min\{u_i(\xi), |Q|T_\ell\}/4$," is at least $1 - 1/e^{-|Q|T_\ell/8}$.*

Proof. Let ξ be an execution of algorithm DOALL$_\varepsilon$ such that $V_{i+1}(\xi) \supseteq Q$ and $u_i(\xi) > 0$. Let $c = \min\{u_i(\xi), |Q|T_\ell\}/4$. Let $S_i(\xi)$ be the set of tasks z such that z is in every list TASK$_v$ for $v \in Q$, at the beginning of phase i. Let $s_i(\xi) = |S_i(\xi)|$. Note that $S_i(\xi) \subseteq U_i(\xi)$, and that $S_i(\xi)$ describes some properties of set Q, while $U_i(\xi)$ describes some properties of set $V_i(\xi) \supseteq Q$. Consider the following cases:

Case 1: $s_i(\xi) \leq u_i(\xi) - c$. Then after the gossip stage of phase i we obtain the required inequality with probability 1.

Case 2: $s_i(\xi) > u_i(\xi) - c$. We focus on the work stage of phase i. Consider a conceptual process in which the processors in Q perform tasks sequentially, the next processor takes over when the previous one has performed all its T_ℓ steps during the work stage of phase i. This process takes $|Q|T_\ell$ steps to be completed. Let $U_i^{(k)}(\xi)$ denote the set of tasks z such that: z is in some list TASK$_v$, for some $v \in Q$, at the beginning of phase i and z has not been performed during the first k steps of the process, by any processor. Let $u_i^{(k)}(\xi) = |U_i^{(k)}(\xi)|$. Define the random variables X_k, for $1 \leq k \leq |Q|T_\ell$, as follows:

$$X_k = \begin{cases} 1 & \text{if either } u_i(\xi) - u_i^{(k)}(\xi) \geq c \text{ or } u_i^{(k)}(\xi) \neq u_i^{(k-1)}(\xi), \\ 0 & \text{otherwise}. \end{cases}$$

Suppose some processor $v \in Q$ is to perform the kth step. If $u_i(\xi) - u_i^{(k)}(\xi) < c$ then we also have the following:

$$s_i(\xi) - \left(u_i(\xi) - u_i^{(k)}(\xi)\right) > s_i(\xi) - c \geq u_i(\xi)/2 \geq sizeof(\text{TASK}_v)/2,$$

where TASK_v is taken at the beginning of phase i, because $3c \leq 3u_i(\xi)/4 \leq s_i(\xi)$. Thus at least a half of the tasks in TASK_v, taken at the beginning of phase i, have not been performed yet, and so $\Pr[X_k = 1] \geq 1/2$.

We need to estimate the probability $\Pr[\sum X_k \geq c]$, where the summation is over all $|Q|T_\ell$ steps of all the processors in Q in the considered process. Consider a sequence $\langle Y_k \rangle$ of independent Bernoulli trials, with $\Pr[Y_k = 1] = 1/2$. Then the sequence $\langle X_k \rangle$ statistically dominates the sequence $\langle Y_k \rangle$, in the sense that $\Pr\left[\sum X_k \geq d\right] \geq \Pr\left[\sum Y_k \geq d\right]$, for any $d > 0$. Note that $\mathbb{E}[\sum Y_k] = |Q|T_\ell/2$ and $c \leq \mathbb{E}[\sum Y_k]/2$, hence we can apply Chernoff bound to obtain

$$\Pr\left[\sum Y_k \geq c\right] \geq 1 - \Pr\left[\sum Y_k < \frac{1}{2}\mathbb{E}\left[\sum Y_k\right]\right] \geq 1 - e^{-|Q|T_\ell/8}.$$

Hence the number of tasks in $U_i(\xi)$, for any execution ξ such that $V_{i+1}(\xi) \supseteq Q$, performed by processors from Q during work stage of phase i is at least c with probability $1 - e^{-|Q|T_\ell/8}$.   □

Lemma 4.22. *Assume $n \leq p^2$ and $p \geq 2^8$. There exists a constant integer $\beta > 0$ such that for every phase i of some epoch $\ell > 1$ of any execution ξ of algorithm* DOALL$_\varepsilon$*, if there is a task unperformed by the beginning of phase i then:*

(a) the probability that phase i is a majority phase is at most $e^{-p \log p}$, and

(b) the probability that phase i is a minority reliable unproductive phase is at most $e^{-T_\ell/16}$.

Proof. We first prove clause (a). Assume that phase i belongs to epoch ℓ, for some $\ell > 1$. First we group executions ξ such that phase i is a majority phase in ξ, according to the following equivalence relation: executions ξ_1 and ξ_2 are in the same class iff $V_{i+1}(\xi_1) = V_{i+1}(\xi_2)$. Every such equivalence class is represented by some set of processors Q of size greater than $\frac{p}{2^{\ell-1}}$, such that for every execution ξ in this class we have $V_{i+1}(\xi) = Q$. In the following claim we define conditions for β for satisfying clause (a).

Claim. *For constant $\beta = 9$ and any execution ξ in the class represented by Q, where $|Q| > \frac{p}{2^{\ell-1}}$, all tasks were performed by the end of epoch $\ell - 1$ with probability at least $1 - e^{-p \log p - p}$.*

We prove the Claim. Consider an execution ξ from a class represented by Q. Consider all steps taken by processors in Q during phase j of epoch $\ell - 1$. By Lemma 4.21, since $V_{j+1}(\xi) \supseteq Q$, we have that the probability of event "if $u_j(\xi) > 0$ then $u_j(\xi) - u_{j+1}(\xi) \geq \min\{u_j(\xi), |Q|T_{\ell-1}\}/4$," is at least

$1 - 1/e^{|Q|T_{\ell-1}/8}$. If the above condition is satisfied we call phase j productive (for consistency with the names optimal and fractional; the difference is that these names are used only for minority phases–now we use it according to the progress made by processors in Q), and this happens with probability at least $1 - 1/e^{|Q|T_{\ell-1}/8}$. Since the total number of tasks is n, we have that the number of productive phases during epoch $\ell - 1$ sufficient to perform all tasks using only processors in Q is either at most

$$\frac{n}{|Q|T_{\ell-1}/4} \leq \frac{n}{n/(4\log p)} = 4\log p,$$

or, since $n \leq p^2$, is at most

$$\log_{4/3} n = 5\log p.$$

Therefore there are a total of $9\log p$ productive phases, which is sufficient to perform all tasks. Furthermore, every phase in epoch $\ell - 1$ is productive. Hence, all tasks are performed by processors in Q during $\beta\log p$ phases, for constant $\beta = 9$, of epoch $\ell - 1$ with probability at least

$$1 - 9\log p \cdot e^{-|Q|T_{\ell-1}/8} \geq 1 - e^{\ln 9 + \ln\log p - (p\log^2 p)/4} \geq 1 - e^{-p\log p - p},$$

since $p \geq 8$. Consequently all processors terminate by the end of phase $\beta\log p + 1$ with probability $1 - e^{-p\log p - p}$. This follows by the correctness of the gossip algorithm and the argument of Lemma 4.19, since epoch $\ell - 1$ lasts $\beta\log p + 1$ phases and processors in Q are non-faulty at the beginning of epoch ℓ. This completes the proof of the Claim.

There are at most 2^p of possible sets Q of processors, hence by the Claim the probability that phase i is a majority phase is at most

$$2^p \cdot e^{-p\log p - p} \leq e^{-p\log p},$$

which proves clause (a) for phase i.

Now we prove clause (b) for phase i. Consider executions such that phase i in epoch ℓ is a minority reliable phase. Similarly as above, we partitions executions according to the following equivalence relation: executions ξ_1 and ξ_2 are in the same class if there is set Q such that $H = V_{i+1}(\xi_1) = V_{i+1}(\xi_2)$. Set Q is a representative of a class. By Lemma 4.21 applied to phase i and set Q we obtain that the probability that phase i is unproductive for every execution ξ such that $V_{i+1}(\xi) = Q$ is $e^{-|Q|T_\ell/8}$. Hence the probability that for any execution ξ phase i is a minority reliable unproductive phase is at most

$$\sum_{x=1}^{p/2^{\ell-1}} \binom{p}{x} \cdot e^{-xT_\ell/8} \leq \sum_{x=1}^{p/2^{\ell-1}} 2^{x\log p} \cdot e^{-xT_\ell/8} \leq \sum_{x=1}^{p/2^{\ell-1}} e^{x\log p - xT_\ell/8}$$

$$\leq e^{\log p - T_\ell/8} \cdot \frac{1}{1 - e^{\log p - T_\ell/8}} \leq e^{-T_\ell/16},$$

(since $p \geq 2^8$), showing clause (b) for phase i. $\square$

Recall that epoch ℓ consists of $\beta \log p + 1$ phases for some $\beta > 0$ and that $T_\ell = \lceil \frac{n + p \log^3 p}{(p/2^\ell) \log p} \rceil$. Also by the correctness proof of algorithm DOALL_ε (Theorem 4.20), the algorithm terminates in at most $O(\log p)$ epochs, hence, the algorithm terminates in at most $O(\log^2 p)$ phases. Let g_ℓ be the number of steps that each gossip stage takes in epoch ℓ, i.e., $g_\ell = \Theta(\log^2 p)$.

We now show the work and message complexity of algorithm DOALL_ε.

Theorem 4.23. *There is a set of permutations Ψ and a constant integer $\beta > 0$ (e.g., $\beta = 9$) such that algorithm DOALL_ε, using permutations from Ψ, solves the Do-All$_{\mathcal{A}_C}(n, p, f)$ problem with total work $S = O(n + p \log^3 p)$ and message complexity $M = O(p^{1+2\varepsilon})$.*

Proof. We show that for any execution $\xi \in \mathcal{E}(\text{DOALL}_\varepsilon, \mathcal{A}_C)$ that solves the Do-All$_{\mathcal{A}_C}(n, p, f)$ problem there exists a set of permutations Ψ and an integer $\beta > 0$ so that the complexity bounds are as desired. Let β be from Lemma 4.22. We consider two cases:

Case 1: $n \leq p^2$. Consider phase i of epoch ℓ of execution ξ for randomly chosen set of permutations Ψ. We reason about the probability of phase i belonging to one of the classes illustrated in Figure 4.3, and about the work that phase i contributes to the total work incurred in the execution, depending on its classification. From Lemma 4.22(a) we get that phase i may be a majority phase with probability at least $e^{-p \log p}$ which is a very small probability. More precisely, the probability that for a set of permutations Ψ, in execution ξ obtained for Ψ some phase i is a majority phase, is $O(\log^2 p \cdot e^{-p \log p}) = e^{-\Omega(p \log p)}$, and consequently using the probabilistic method argument we obtain that for almost any set of permutations Ψ there is no execution in which there is a majority phase.

Therefore, we focus on minority phases that occur with high probability (per Lemma 4.22(a)). We can not say anything about the probability of a minority phase to be a reliable or unreliable, since this depends on the specific execution. Note however, that by definition, we cannot have more than $O(\log p)$ unreliable minority phases in any execution ξ (at least one processor must remain operational). Moreover, the work incurred in an unreliable minority phase i of an epoch ℓ in any execution ξ is bounded by

$$O(p_i(\xi) \cdot (T_\ell + g_\ell)) = O\left(\frac{p}{2^{\ell-1}} \cdot \left(\frac{n + p \log^3 p}{\frac{p}{2^\ell} \log p} + \log^2 p \right) \right) = O\left(\frac{n}{\log p} + p \log^2 p \right).$$

Thus, the total work incurred by all unreliable minority phases in any execution ξ is $O(n + p \log^3 p)$.

From Lemmas 4.21 and 4.22(b) we get that a reliable minority phase may be fractional or optimal with high probability $1 - e^{-T_\ell/16}$, whereas it may be unproductive with very small probability $e^{-T_\ell/16} \leq e^{-\log^2 p/16}$. Using a similar argument as for majority phases, we get that for almost all sets of permutations Ψ (probability $1 - O(\log^2 p \cdot e^{-T_\ell/16}) \geq 1 - e^{-\Omega(T_\ell)}$) and for every execution ξ, there is no minority reliable unproductive phase. The work incurred by a fractional phase i of an epoch ℓ in any execution ξ is bounded by $O(p_i(\xi) \cdot (T_\ell + g_\ell)) = O(\frac{n}{\log p} + p \log^2 p)$. Also note that by definition, there can be at most $O(\log_{3/4} n)$ $(= O(\log p)$ since $n \leq p^2)$ fractional phases in any execution ξ and hence, the total work incurred by all fractional reliable minority phases in any execution ξ is $O(n + p \log^3 p)$. We now consider the optimal reliable minority phases for any execution ξ. Here we have an optimal allocation of tasks to processors in $V_i(\xi)$. By definition of optimality, in average one task in $U_i(\xi) \setminus U_{i+1}(\xi)$ is performed by at most *four* processors from $V_{i+1}(\xi)$, and by definition of reliability, by at most *eight* processors in $V_i(\xi)$. Therefore, in optimal phases, each unit of work spent on performing a task results to a unique task completion (within a constant overhead), for any execution ξ. It therefore follows that the work incurred in all optimal reliable minority phases is bounded by $O(n)$ in any execution ξ.

Therefore, from the above we conclude that when $n \leq p^2$, for random set of permutations Ψ the work complexity of algorithm DoAll$_\varepsilon$ executed on such set Ψ is $S = O(n + p \log^3 p)$ with probability $1 - e^{-\Omega(p \log p)} - e^{-\Omega(T_\ell)} = 1 - e^{-\Omega(T_\ell)}$ (the probability appears only from analysis of majority and unproductive reliable minority phases). Consequently such set Ψ exists. Also, from Lemma 4.22 and the above discussion, $\beta > 0$ (e.g., $\beta = 9$) exists. Finally, the bound on messages using selected set Ψ and constant β is obtained as follows: there are $O(\log^2 p)$ executions of gossip stages. Each gossip stage requires $O(p^{1+\varepsilon})$ messages (message complexity of one instance of Gossip$_{\varepsilon/3}$). Thus, $M = O(p^{1+\varepsilon} \log^2 p) = O(p^{1+2\varepsilon})$.

Case 2: $n > p^2$. In this case, the tasks are partitioned into $n' = p^2$ chunks, where each chunk contains at most $\lceil n/p^2 \rceil$ tasks (see Remark 4.15). Using the result of Case 1 and selected set Ψ and constant β, we get that $S = O(n' + p \log^3 p) \cdot \Theta(n/p^2) = O(p^2 \cdot n/p^2 + n/p^2 \cdot p \log^3 p) = O(n)$. The message complexity is derived with the same way as in Case 1. $\square$

4.5 Open Problems

As demonstrated by the gossip-based *Do-All* algorithm presented in this chapter, efficient algorithms can be designed that do not rely on single coordinators or reliable multicast to disseminate knowledge between processors. Gossiping seems to be a very promising alternative. An interesting open problem is to investigate whether a more efficient gossip algorithm can be developed that could yield an even more efficient *Do-All* algorithm.

An interesting problem is to perform a failure-sensitive analysis for the *iterative Do-All* problem using point-to-point messaging. Recall that if an algorithm solves the *Do-All*$_{\mathcal{A}_C}(n, p, f)$ problem with work $O(x)$ then this algorithm can be iteratively used to solve the *r-Do-All*$_{\mathcal{A}_C}(n, p, f)$ problem with work $r \cdot O(x)$. However, it should be possible to produce an improved upper bound, for example, as we did in the previous chapter for the model with crashes and reliable multicast.

4.6 Chapter Notes

Dwork, Halpern, and Waarts [30] introduced and studied the *Do-All* in the message-passing model. They developed several deterministic algorithms that solved the problem for synchronous crash-prone processors. To evaluate the performance of their algorithms, they used the task-oriented work complexity W and the message complexity measure M. They also used the *effort* complexity measure, defined as the sum of W and M. This measure of efficiency makes sense for algorithms for which the work and message complexities are similar. However, this makes it difficult to compare relative efficiency of algorithms that exhibit varying trade-offs between the work and the communication efficiencies.

The first algorithm presented in [30], called protocol $\mathcal{B}$ has effort $O(n + p\sqrt{p})$, with work contributing the cost $O(n + p)$ and the message complexity contributing the cost $O(p\sqrt{p})$ toward the effort. The running time of the algorithm is $O(n + p)$. The algorithm uses synchrony to detect processor crashes by means of timeouts. The algorithm operates as follows. The n tasks are divided into chunks and each chunk is divided into sub-chunks. Processors checkpoint their progress by multicasting the completion information to subsets of processors after performing a subchunk, and broadcasting to all processors after completing chunks of work. Another algorithm, called protocol $\mathcal{C}$ has effort $O(n + p \log p)$. It has optimal work $W = O(n + p)$, message complexity $M = O(p \log p)$ and time $O(p^2 (n+p) 2^{n+p})$. This shows that reducing the message complexity may cause a significant increase in time. Protocol $\mathcal{D}$ is another *Do-All* algorithm that obtains work optimality and it is designed for maximum speed-up, which is achieved with a more aggressive check-pointing strategy, thus trading-off time for messages. The message complexity is quadratic in p for the fault-free case, and in the presence of $f < p$ crashes the message complexity degrades to $\Theta(fp^2)$.

De Prisco, Mayer, and Yung [25] provided an algorithmic solution for *Do-All* considering the same setting as Dwork *et al.*, (synchrony, processor crashes) but using the total-work (available processor steps) complexity measure S. They use a "lexicographic" criterion: first evaluate an algorithm according to its total-work and then according to its message complexity. This approach assumes that optimization of work is more important than optimization of communication. They present a deterministic algorithm, call it DMY, that has $S = O(n + (f + 1)p)$ and $M = O((f + 1)p)$. The algorithm operates as follows. At each step all the processors have a consistent (over)estimate of the set of all the available processors (using checkpoints). One processor is designated to be the coordinator. The coordinator allocates the undone tasks according to a certain load balancing rule and waits for notifications of the tasks which have been performed. The coordinator changes over time. To avoid a quadratic upper bound for S, substantial processor slackness is assumed $(p \ll n)$.

The authors in [25] also formally show a lower bound of $S = \Omega(n + (f + 1)p)$ for any algorithm using the stage-checkpoint strategy, this bound being quadratic in p for f comparable with p. Moreover, any protocol with at most one active coordinator (that is, a protocol that uses a single coordinator paradigm) is bound to have $S = \Omega(n+(f+1)p)$. Namely, consider the following behavior of the adversary: while there is more than one operational processor, the adversary stops each coordinator immediately after it becomes one and before it sends any messages. This creates pauses of $\Omega(1)$ steps, giving the $\Omega((f + 1)p)$ part. Eventually there remains only one processor which has to perform all the tasks, because it has never received any messages, this gives the remaining $\Omega(n)$ part. Algorithm AN (presented in Chapter 3) beats this lower bound by using a multicoordinator approach; however it makes use of reliable multicast. Algorithm DOALL_ε presented in this chapter beats this lower bound by neither using checkpointing nor single-coordinators paradigms; instead it uses a gossip algorithm for the dissemination of information.

Galil, Mayer, and Yung [38], while working in the context of Byzantine agreement [78] assuming synchronous crash-prone processors, developed an efficient algorithm, call it GMY, that has the same total-work bound as algorithm DMY $(S = O(n + (f + 1)p))$ but has better message complexity: $M = O(fp^\varepsilon + \min\{f + 1, \log p\}p)$, for any $\varepsilon > 0$. The improvement on the message complexity is mainly due to the improvement of the checkpoint strategy used by algorithm DMY by replacing the "rotating coordinator" approach with what they called the "rotating tree" (*diffusion tree*) approach.

Chlebus, Gasieniec, Kowalski, and Shvartsman [16] developed a deterministic algorithm that solves *Do-All* for synchronous crash-prone processors with combined total-work and message complexity $S + M = O(n + p^{1.77})$. This is the first algorithm that achieves subquadratic in p combined S and M for the *Do-All* problem for synchronous crash-prone processors. They present another deterministic algorithm that has total-work $S = O(n + p \log^2 p)$ against f-bounded adversaries such that $p - f = \Omega(p^\alpha)$ for a constant $0 < \alpha < 1$. They also show how to achieve $S + M = O(n + p \log^2 p)$ against a linearly-bounded adversary by carrying out communication on an underlying constant-degree network.

The presentation in this chapter is based on a paper by Georgiou, Kowalski, and Shvartsman [44]. The proofs of Lemmas 4.4, 4.5 and Theorem 4.6 appear there. For the probabilistic method and its applications see the book of Alon and Spencer [4]. The notion of the *left-to-right maximum* is due to Knuth [71] (p. 13).

The complexity results presented in this chapter involve the use of conceptual communication graphs and sets of permutations with specific combinatorial properties. Kowalski, Musial, and Shvartsman [75] showed that such combinatorial structures can be constructed efficiently.

Additionally, observe that the complexity bounds do not show how work and message complexities depend on f, the maximum number of crashes. In fact it is possible to subject the algorithm to "failure-sensitivity-training" and obtain better results. Georgiou, Kowalski, and Shvartsman show how this can be achieved in [44]. The main idea relies on the fact that checkpointing is rather efficient for a small number of failures. So, the authors use algorithm DOALL$_\varepsilon$ in conjunction with the check-pointing algorithm DMY [25], where the check-pointing and the synchronization procedures are taken from algorithm GMY [38]; in addition they use a modified version of algorithm GOSSIP$_\varepsilon$, optimized for a small number of failures. The resulting algorithm achieves total work $S = O(n + p \cdot \min\{f + 1, \log^3 p\})$ and message complexity $M = O(fp^\varepsilon + p\min\{f + 1, \log p\})$, for any $\varepsilon > 0$. More details can be found in [44].

Chlebus and Kowalski [18] were the first to define and study the *Gossip* problem for synchronous message-passing processors under an adaptive adversary that causes processor crashes (this is the version of the *Gossip* problem considered in this chapter); they developed an efficient gossip algorithm and they used it as a building block to obtain an efficient synchronous algorithm for the consensus problem with crashes. In a later work [19], the same authors developed another algorithm for the synchronous *Gossip* problem with crashes and used it to obtain an efficient early-stopping consensus algorithm for the same setting. More details on work on gossip in fault-prone distributed message-passing systems can be found in the survey of Pelc [96] and the book of Hromkovic, Klasing, Pelc, Ruzicka, and Unger [59].

5

Synchronous Do-All with Crashes and Restarts

IN general-purpose distributed computation in dynamic environments, it is important to be able to deal, and efficiently so, with processors failing, then restarting and rejoining the system.

Here we consider the *Do-All* problem of performing n tasks in a message-passing distributed environment consisting of p processors that are subject to *failures* and *restarts*. Failures are crashes, i.e., a crashed processor stops and does not perform any further actions until, and if, it restarts. Restarted processors resume computation in a predefined initial state, and no stable storage is assumed. The distributed environment is synchronous and the underlying network is fully connected, so that any processor can send a message to any other processor. Messages are not lost in transit or corrupted. Because the system is synchronous we also assume that there is a known upper bound on message delivery time. It is convenient to assume that messages sent within one step of a certain known duration are delivered before the end of the next such step. The efficiency of algorithms is evaluated in terms of total-work and message complexities.

Chapter structure.

In Section 5.1 we present the adversary, called $\mathcal{A}_{CR}$, that causes processor crashes and restarts dynamically during the computation. In Section 5.2 we present matching upper and lower bounds on the total-work of *Do-All* under adversary $\mathcal{A}_{CR}$, when the computation is assisted by an oracle providing load-balancing and computation-progress information to the processors. In Section 5.3 we present a deterministic algorithm, call AR, that efficiently solves the *Do-All*$_{\mathcal{A}_{CR}}(n, p, f)$ problem, using reliable multicast; this algorithm in an extension of algorithm AN presented in Section 3.3.1. We discuss open problems in Section 5.4.

5.1 Adversarial Model

We denote by $\mathcal{A}_{CR}$ an omniscient (on-line) adversary that can cause processor crashes *and* subsequent restarts, as defined in Section 2.2.1. Recall that crashed processors lose their local memory, and if a crashed processor restarts, it does so in a known state – thus the restarts are detectable.

Consider an algorithm A that performs a computation in the presence of adversary $\mathcal{A}_{CR}$. Let ξ be an execution in $\mathcal{E}(A, \mathcal{A}_{CR})$. We represent the adversarial pattern $\xi|_{\mathcal{A}_{CR}}$ as a set of triples (*event*, PID, t), where *event* is either a *crash* or a *restart* caused by the adversary, PID is the identifier of the processor that crashes or restarts, and t is the time of the execution (according to some external clock not available to the processors) when the adversary causes the event.

For an adversarial pattern $\xi|_{\mathcal{A}_{CR}}$, we define $f_c(\xi|_{\mathcal{A}_{CR}})$ to be the number of crashes and $f_r(\xi|_{\mathcal{A}_{CR}})$ to be the number of restarts in ξ. We then define $f_{cr} = \|\xi|_{\mathcal{A}_{CR}}\|$ to be $f_c(\xi|_{\mathcal{A}_{CR}}) + f_r(\xi|_{\mathcal{A}_{CR}})$. We observe that $f_r(\xi|_{\mathcal{A}_{CR}}) \leq f_c(\xi|_{\mathcal{A}_{CR}})$, since the number of restarts cannot exceed the number of crashes. Note that $f_{cr}(\xi|_{\mathcal{A}_{CR}})$ may not be bounded by a function of p, unless the adversary is restricted in the number of crashes or restarts that it can cause.

When analyzing the worst case asymptotic complexity of a given algorithm in $\mathcal{A}_{CR}$ it is often convenient to express the result as a function of p, the number of processors, n, the number of tasks, and $f_c(\xi|_{\mathcal{A}_{CR}})$, the number of crashes. This is possible because $f_r(\xi|_{\mathcal{A}_{CR}}) \leq f_c(\xi|_{\mathcal{A}_{CR}})$ and because $f_{cr} = f_c(\xi|_{\mathcal{A}_{CR}}) + f_r(\xi|_{\mathcal{A}_{CR}}) \leq 2f_c(\xi|_{\mathcal{A}_{CR}}) = \Theta(f_c(\xi|_{\mathcal{A}_{CR}}))$.

Adversary $\mathcal{A}_{CR}$, as defined, can generate adversarial patterns that could prevent computational progress. For example, if all processors crash and none of them restart, no computational progress is possible. More interestingly, even if processors restart, it is possible that progress can be prevented. For example, consider a scenario in which half of the processors are crashed right at the beginning of the computation. If the remaining processors, after they perform some computation, crash and then the initially crashed processors restart, then these processors may not be aware of the computation performed by the other processors (this is because no communication may have occurred between the two groups of processors – messages can be lost when processors crash). Since the processors lose their local memory upon a failure, this can be repeated forever without any progress in the computation.

To avoid such uninteresting adversarial patterns, we restrict $\mathcal{A}_{CR}$ to causing crash and restart patterns such that during any consecutive κ steps of the computation ($\kappa \geq 0$), there is *at least one* processor that is operational during all these κ steps. More formally,

Definition 5.1. *Let κ be a positive integer. An adversarial pattern of $\mathcal{A}_{CR}$ is said to be "κ-restricted" if during any consecutive κ steps $i, i+1, \ldots, i+\kappa-1$ there is at least one processor that is operational during all steps $i, i+1, \ldots, i+\kappa-1$.*

We denote the maximal subset of $\mathcal{A}_{CR}$ that contains only the κ-restricted adversarial patterns as $\mathcal{A}_{CR}^{(\kappa)}$. We also define $\mathcal{A}_{CR}^{(0)}$ to be the adversary for which no restrictions are imposed on the adversarial patterns, and thus $\mathcal{A}_{CR}^{(0)} = \mathcal{A}_{CR}$. Observe that $\mathcal{A}_{CR}^{(\kappa+1)} \subseteq \mathcal{A}_{CR}^{(\kappa)} \subseteq \ldots \subseteq \mathcal{A}_{CR}^{(1)} \subseteq \mathcal{A}_{CR}^{(0)}$ for any $\kappa \geq 1$. Thus if an algorithm solves the *Do-All* problem under adversary $\mathcal{A}_{CR}^{(\kappa)}$ it is not necessarily the case that the same algorithm solves *Do-All* under $\mathcal{A}_{CR}^{(\kappa-1)}$. This is because $\mathcal{A}_{CR}^{(\kappa-1)}$ may contain additional adversarial patterns as compared to $\mathcal{A}_{CR}^{(\kappa)}$

As we have noted above, the *Do-All* problem is not solvable under adversary $\mathcal{A}_{CR}^{(0)}$: indeed if all processors fail before executing all the tasks, then the tasks can never be completed. It is not hard to see that no solution is possible also for $\mathcal{A}_{CR}^{(1)}$. Indeed a 1-restricted adversarial pattern requires that at least one processor be alive during any step. However this is not sufficient to guarantee progress. Even if there is always one processor alive progress can be prevented (the scenario given above in which half of the processors fail while the other half of the processors restart is an example). Hence the best we can hope for is to find a solution for $\mathcal{A}_{CR}^{(2)}$, unless additional help is provided to the processors (e.g., an oracle). We notice that in a κ-restricted execution, for $\kappa \geq 2$, it is guaranteed that processors' lifetimes have some overlap and the bigger is κ the bigger is the overlap. For $\kappa = 2$ such overlap can be as small as a single step. Hence in order to not lose information about the ongoing computation (such loss, in the absence of stable storage, prevents progress), it is necessary that processors exchange state information during each step. Thus a solution that works for a small κ tends to have large message complexity.

Note also that there is a *qualitative* distinction between $\mathcal{A}_{CR}^{(1)}$ and $\mathcal{A}_{CR}^{(2)}$: processors' lifetimes may not overlap in the former while they must overlap in the latter. The difference between $\mathcal{A}_{CR}^{(\kappa)}$ and $\mathcal{A}_{CR}^{(\kappa+1)}$ when $\kappa \geq 2$ is *quantitative*: in the latter the overlap of processors' lifetimes is one step longer than in the former.

5.2 A Lower Bound on Work for Restartable Processors

As we did for the the *Do-All* problem with crashes, we provide a lower bound result assuming that processors are assisted by Oracle $\mathcal{O}$ presented in Section 3.2.1. Following the notation introduced in the same section we let *Do-All*$_{\mathcal{A}_{CR}}^{\mathcal{O}}(n, p, f)$ stand for the *Do-All*$_{\mathcal{A}_{CR}}(n, p, f)$ problem when the processors are assisted by oracle $\mathcal{O}$. Any lower bound developed for *Do-All*$_{\mathcal{A}_{CR}}^{\mathcal{O}}(n, p, f)$ trivially holds for *Do-All*$_{\mathcal{A}_{CR}}(n, p, f)$ as well as for *Do-All*$_{\mathcal{A}}(n, p, f)$ where $\mathcal{A}_{CR} \subseteq \mathcal{A}$.

Observe that with the help of the oracle makes it possible for *Write-All* to be solved under adversary $\mathcal{A}_{CR}^{(1)}$, as even if there is no overlap between the active steps of any two processors the progress can be observed and remembered by the oracle. Solutions under adversary $\mathcal{A}_{CR}^{(0)}$ are still not possible, as the adversary can crash and restart all processors at every step without allowing any processor to perform a task – and hence no progress is made at any step.

We now show a lower bound for work on solving the *Do-All* problem under adversary $\mathcal{A}_{CR}^{(1)}$. We show this with the help of the oracle, and thus the result applies to any analogous model without the oracle.

Theorem 5.2. *Given any algorithm* A *that solves the Do-All$_{\mathcal{A}_{CR}}^{\mathcal{O}}(n, p, f)$ problem* $(p \leq n)$, *there exists an adversarial strategy in* $\mathcal{A}_{CR}^{(1)}$ *that causes the algorithm to perform* $S = \Omega(n + p \log p)$ *total-work.*

Proof. The adversary $\mathcal{A}_{CR}^{(1)}$ imposes a schedule that uses the following strategy at every step of the computation: Let $u > 1$ be the number of remaining tasks. For as long as $u > p$, the adversary induces no crashes. The total-work needed to perform $n - p$ tasks when there were no failures is at least $n - p$.

As soon as a processor is about to perform some task $n - p + 1$ making $u \leq p$, the adversary crashes and then restarts all p processors but that one. For the upcoming iteration (where $u = p$), the adversary examines the algorithm to determine how the processors are assigned to remaining tasks. The adversary then lists the first $\lfloor \frac{u}{2} \rfloor$ of the remaining tasks with the least number of processors assigned to them. Assuming the oracle allows processors to perform perfect load balancing, the total number of processors assigned to these tasks does not exceed $\lceil \frac{p}{2} \rceil$. The adversary crashes these processors, allowing all others to proceed. Therefore at least $\lfloor \frac{p}{2} \rfloor$ processors will complete this iteration having together performed no more than half of the remaining tasks. Once these tasks are done, the adversary restarts all processors.

This strategy of the adversary can be continued for at least $\log p$ iterations. Therefore, the work performed by algorithm A is no less than $n - p + \lfloor \frac{p}{2} \rfloor \log p = \Omega(n + p \log p)$, as desired. $\qquad\square$

Observe that the above lower bound does not show how work depends on f, the number of crashes. It is interesting to develop failure-sensitive lower bounds in this setting that show how work depends on the number of crashes and restarts.

For completeness we show that the oracle-based algorithm given in Figure 3.1 of Section 3 can solve the $Do\text{-}All_{\mathcal{A}_{CR}}^{\mathcal{O}}(n, p, f)$ problem under adversary $\mathcal{A}_{CR}^{(1)}$. This means that the algorithm is optimal with respect to the lower bound shown in Theorem 5.2.

Theorem 5.3. *The Do-All$_{\mathcal{A}_{CR}^{(1)}}^{\mathcal{O}}(n, p, f)$ problem can be solved using total-work*

$$S = O\left(n + p \log p\right).$$

Proof. Recall that processors can obtain perfect load-balancing and termination information from the oracle in $O(1)$ time. From the discussion in Section 3.2.1 it follows that all processor steps in the presence of the oracle are in fact task-oriented steps. Hence, in order to obtain the result we only need to compute a bound on the number of tasks performed by the processors.

At each step of the execution that a processor is active, it consults the oracle of what task to perform. Say that at a given step there are u tasks that have not yet been performed. The oracle assures that no more than $\lceil p/u \rceil$ processors are assigned to each unperformed task. This strategy continues until all tasks are done.

We assess the work performed by the algorithm as follows. We list the Do-All tasks in ascending order according to the time (step) at which each task is performed (for tasks executed in the same step the order is chosen arbitrarily). We divide this list into adjacent segments numbered sequentially starting with 0, such that the segment 0 contains $\sigma_0 = n-p$ tasks, and segment $j \geq 1$ contains $\sigma_j = \lfloor \frac{p}{j(j+1)} \rfloor$ tasks, for $j = 1, \ldots, m$ for some $m \leq \sqrt{p}$.

Let u_j be the least possible number of unperformed tasks when processors were being assigned by the oracle to the tasks of the jth segment; u_j can be computed as $u_j = n - \sum_{i=0}^{j-1} \sigma_i = n - \sigma_0 - \sum_{i=1}^{j-1} \sigma_i = p - \sum_{i=1}^{j-1} \sigma_i.$
Note that u_0 if of course n. Then for $j \geq 1$ he have that

$$u_j = p - \sum_{i=1}^{j-1} \sigma_i \geq p - (p - \frac{p}{j}) = \frac{p}{j}.$$

Therefore, no more than $\lceil \frac{p}{u_j} \rceil$ processors were assigned to each task. Then, then work performed by the oracle-based algorithm is

$$S \leq \sum_{j=0}^{m} \sigma_j \left\lceil \frac{p}{u_j} \right\rceil \leq \sigma_0 + \sum_{j=1}^{m} \left\lfloor \frac{p}{j(j+1)} \right\rfloor \left\lceil \frac{p}{p/j} \right\rceil$$

$$= \sigma_0 + O\left(p \sum_{j=1}^{m} \frac{1}{j+1} \right) = O(n + p \log p),$$

as desired.   □

Remark 5.4. In the above analysis it is assumed that a processor contacts the oracle and performs the task in one local step. The accounting is done at the granularity of such local steps. If the consultation with the oracle takes place in one local step and the performance of a task in the next local step, then the result in Theorem 5.3 gives the upper bound for task-oriented work, not total-work. To assess total-work we note that a processor can crash after consulting the oracle but before performing a task. A restarted processor detects its previous crash and consults the oracle again. This incurs additional local step per each processor restart. If there are f_c crashes and f_r restarts ($f_c \geq f_r$), then total work complexity becomes $O(n + p \log p + f)$, where $f = f_c + f_r = \Theta(f_c)$. We will see that this additive work overhead f occurs in the analysis of the algorithm in the next section.

5.3 Algorithm AR for Restartable Processors

In this section we present algorithm AR that solves the *Do-All* under adversary $\mathcal{A}_{CR}^{(26)}$. The constant 26 depends on the structure of the algorithm. (With a modest effort the constant can be reduced to 17, as we explain later.)

For this algorithm we show that it has total-work (available processor steps) complexity $S = O((n + p \log p + f) \cdot \min\{\log p, \log f\})$, and its message complexity is $M = O(n + p \log p + fp)$, where f is the maximum number of crashes caused by the adversary. The algorithm is an extension of algorithm AN presented in Section 3.3.1. The difference is that there are added messages to handle the restart of processors; in the absence of restarts the two algorithms behave identically.

The algorithms assume that the communication is reliable. If a processor sends a message to another operational processor and when the message arrives at the destination the processor is still operational, then the message is received. Moreover, if an operational processor sends a multicast message and then fails, then either the message is sent to all destinations or to none at all. Such multicast is received by all operational processors.

5.3.1 Description of Algorithm AR

We first overview the algorithmic techniques, then present algorithm AR in detail.

As with algorithm AN, algorithm AR proceeds in a *loop* that is repeated until all the tasks are executed. A single iteration of the loop is called a *phase*. A phase consists of three consecutive *stages*. Each stage consists of three steps (thus a phase consists of 9 steps). We refer to these three step as the *receive* substage, the *compute* substage and the *send* substage.

As before, processors act as either *coordinators* or *workers*. If at least one processor acts as a coordinator during a phase and it completes the phase without failing, we say that the phase is *attended*, the phase is *unattended* otherwise.

Local views. Processors assume the role of coordinator based on their local knowledge. During the computation each processor w maintains a list $L_w = \langle q_1, q_2, ..., q_k \rangle$ of supposed live processors. We call such list a *local view* as we did for algorithm AN, although the structure is managed differently.

The processors in L_w are partitioned into *layers* consisting of consecutive sublists of L_w: $L_w = \langle \Lambda^0, \Lambda^1, ..., \Lambda^j \rangle$. The number of processors in layer Λ^{i+1}, for $i = 0, 1, ..., j - 1$, is the double of the number of processors in layer Λ^i. Layer Λ^j may contain less processors. So far the local views are exactly as in algorithm AN. The difference is that processors in a local view do not necessarily appear in the order of processor identifiers: restarted processors are appended at the end of the local view in the order of the identifiers of the restarted processors.

Example 5.5. Suppose that we have a system of $p = 31$ processors. Assume that for a phase ℓ all processors are in the local view of a worker w, in order of processor identifier, and that the view is a tree-like view (e.g., at the beginning of the computation, for $\ell = 0$). We now assume that the processors crash as in Example 3.17 and that the local view of processor w for phase $\ell+2$ is as given in Figure 3.2. If in phase $\ell + 2$ processor 3 fails and processors $5, 22, 29, 31$ restart (phase $\ell + 2$ is unattended) and in phase $\ell + 3$ processors $4, 6$ fail and processors $1, 2, 9$ restart (phase $\ell+3$ is unattended) then the view of processor w for phase $\ell + 4$ is the one in Figure 5.1.

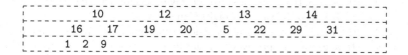

Fig. 5.1. A local view for phase $\ell + 4$.

The local view is used to implement the martingale principle of appointing coordinators as in algorithm AN. The local view is updated at the end of each phase. As we will explain shortly, the update rule for algorithm AR is different.

Phase structure and task allocation. The structure of each phase of the algorithm is the same as for algorithm AN. The differences are as follows.

1. If a processor restarts, it informs all other processors of this fact.
2. Any processors that restarted during a phase are not considered available, since they might not have up to date information about the computation.
3. Following the receipt of messages from any restarted processors, they are reintegrated in the local views of all processors receiving these messages, and become available for computation in the subsequent phase.

Details of Algorithm AR

We now present algorithm AR in greater detail, with the focus on handling restarted processors. After the restart, processor q broadcasts $\mathtt{restart}(q)$ messages in each step until it receives a response. Processors receiving such messages, ignore them if these messages are not received in the receive substage of stage 2 of a phase. Thus we can imagine that a restarted processor q broadcasts a $\mathtt{restart}(q)$ in the send substage of stage 1 of a phase ℓ (however we will count all the $\mathtt{restart}$ messages in the message complexity). This message is then received by all the live and restarted processors of that phase, and, as we will see shortly, processor q is re-integrated in the view for phase $\ell+1$. Processor q needs to be informed about the status of the ongoing computation. Hence processors that have this information send the $\mathtt{info}(U_\ell, L_\ell)$ messages to processor q with the set U_ℓ of unaccounted tasks and the local view L_ℓ. In Figure 5.2 we provide the detailed description for each phase. The parts that are new or that are different in algorithm AR as compared to algorithm AN are *italicized* in the figure.

Phase ℓ of algorithm AR:

STAGE 1.
> RECEIVE: The receive substage is not used.
> COMPUTE: In the compute substage any processor w performs a specific task z according to the load balancing rule.
> SEND: In the send substage w sends a $\texttt{report}(z)$ to any coordinator, that is, to any processor in the first layer of $L_{\ell,w}$. *Any restarted processor q broadcasts the $\texttt{restart}(q)$ message informing all live processors of its restart.*

STAGE 2.
> RECEIVE: In the receive substage the coordinators gather $\texttt{report}$ messages *and all processors gather $\texttt{restart}$ messages. Let R be the set of processors that sent a $\texttt{restart}$ message.* For any coordinator c, let $z_c^1, ..., z_c^{k_c}$ be the set of TIDs received in $\texttt{report}$ messages.
> COMPUTE: In the compute substage c sets $D_c \leftarrow D_c \cup \bigcup_{i=1}^{k_c}\{z_c^i\}$ and P_c to the set of processors from which c received $\texttt{report}$ messages.
> SEND: In the send substage, coordinator c multicasts the message $\texttt{summary}(D_c, P_c)$ to the processors in P_c *and R. Any processor in P_c sends the message $\texttt{info}(U_\ell, L_\ell)$ to processors in R.*

STAGE 3.
> RECEIVE: *In the receive substage processors in R receive $\texttt{info}(U_\ell, L_\ell)$ messages and processors in P_c and R receive $\texttt{summary}(D_c, P_c)$ messages.*
> COMPUTE: *In the compute substage, a restarted processor q sets $L_{\ell,q} \leftarrow L_\ell$ and $U_{\ell,q} \leftarrow U_\ell$.* Let $(D_w^1, P_w^1), ..., (D_w^{k_w}, P_w^{k_w})$ be the sets received in $\texttt{summary}$ messages by processor w. Processor w sets $D_w \leftarrow D_w^i$ and $P_w \leftarrow P_w^i$ for an arbitrary $i \in 1, ..., k_w$ and updates its local view $L_{\ell,w}$ *as described below.*
> RECEIVE: The send substage is not used.

Fig. 5.2. Phase ℓ of algorithm AR (text in *italics* highlights differences between algorithm AR and algorithm AN).

Local view update rule. In phase 0 the local view $L_{0,w}$ of any processor w contains all the processors in $\mathcal{P}$ ordered by their PIDs, and the first layer is a singleton set. Let $L_{\ell,w} = \langle \Lambda^0, \Lambda^1, ..., \Lambda^j \rangle$ be the local view of processor w for phase ℓ. We distinguish two possible cases.

Case 1: Phase ℓ is unattended. Let R^ℓ be the set of restarted processors which send $\texttt{restart}$ messages. Let R' be the set of processors of R^ℓ that are not already in the local view $L_{\ell,w}$. Let $\langle R' \rangle$ be the processors in R' ordered according to their PIDs. The local view for the next phase is $L_{\ell+1,w} = \langle \Lambda^1, ..., \Lambda^j \rangle \oplus \langle R' \rangle$. The operator $\oplus$ places processors of R', in the order $\langle R' \rangle$, into the last layer Λ^j till this layer contains exactly the double of the processors of layer Λ^{j-1} and possibly adds a new layer Λ^{j+1} to accommodate the remaining processors of $\langle R' \rangle$. That is, newly restarted processors which are not yet in the view, are appended at the end of the old view. Notice that restarted processors, which receive info messages, know the old view L_ℓ.

Case 2: Phase ℓ is attended. Let R^ℓ be the set of restarted processors. Since the phase is attended summary messages are received by all the live processors (including the restarted ones). Any processor w updates P_w as described in stage 3. Processor w knows the set R^ℓ. The local view $L_{\ell+1,w}$ for the next phase is structured according to the martingale principle and contains all the processors in $P_w \cup R^\ell$ ordered according to their PIDs.

If there are no restarts, algorithm AR behaves exactly as algorithm AN. Figure 5.3 provides a graphical description of both algorithms. The main differences deal with the messages involving restarted processors and corresponding updates.

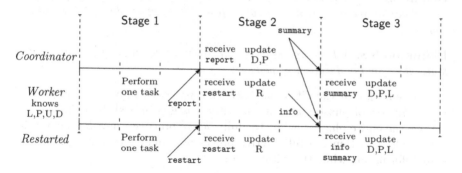

Fig. 5.3. A phase of algorithm AR.

Remark 5.6. Algorithm AR tolerates crash/restart patterns that are 26-restricted. Recall that a 26-restricted failure pattern is one such that for any 26 consecutive steps of the algorithm there is at least one processor alive in all the 26 steps. The constant 26 depends on the algorithm. In algorithm AR some substages are not used (see Figure 5.2). The algorithm can be modified by "squeezing" the full phase into two stages, instead of the three (the three stages were used in the presentation for the sake of clarity). With this modification, 17-restricted failure patterns can be tolerated.

5.3.2 Correctness of Algorithm AR

Here we show that algorithm AR solves the *Do-All* problem under adversary $\mathcal{A}_{CR}^{(26)}$. Given an execution of the algorithm we say that the execution is *good* if it is an execution allowed by $\mathcal{A}_{CR}^{(26)}$. Hence we have to prove that the algorithm solves the problem for any good execution.

A restarted processor has no information about the ongoing computation, and thus cannot actively participate in the computation, until it gets a chance to communicate with other processors. Moreover, if a processors completes two consecutive phases it is able to acquire information about the computation in the first of the two phases and to transfer it to other processors in the second of the two phases. We will show that having, at any point during any execution, a processor that is operational for 26 consecutive steps is sufficient for our algorithm. This allows for the largest number of steps, 8, that may be "wasted" because this is just short of the 9 steps that constitute a phase, plus two complete phases, i.e., 18 steps, as described above. This intuition is made formal in the proofs in this section.

Formally we use the following definitions.

Definition 5.7. *A live processor is said to be "fully active" at a particular time t during phase ℓ, if it stays alive from the start of phase $\ell - 1$ through time t.*

Definition 5.8. *A live processor is said to be a "witness" for phase ℓ if it stays alive for the duration of phases $\ell - 1$ and ℓ.*

We remark that the difference between a processor fully active in phase ℓ and a witness of phase ℓ is that the witness is guaranteed, by definition, to survive the entire phase ℓ, while the fully active processor may fail before the end of phase ℓ. Hence a fully active processor cannot guarantee transfer of state information while the witness can.

Lemma 5.9. *In a good execution, there is a witness for any phase.*

Proof. A good execution has a 26-restricted adversarial pattern. Thus for any step i, there is at least one processor that stays alive for the next 26 steps. Notice that 8 of these step may be spent waiting for the beginning of the next phase (if the processor has just restarted in step i). However the remaining 18 steps are enough to guarantee that the processor stays alive for the next two phases, since each phase consists of 9 steps. □

The witness of phase ℓ is always a processor fully active in phase ℓ. Next we show that at the beginning of each phase every fully active processor has consistent knowledge of the ongoing computation.

Lemma 5.10. *In a good execution of algorithm AR, for any two processors w, v fully active at the beginning of phase ℓ, we have that $L_{\ell,w} = L_{\ell,v}$ and that $U_{\ell,w} = U_{\ell,v}$.*

Proof. By induction on the number of phases. For the base case we need to prove that the lemma is true for the first phase. Initially we have that $L_{0,w} = L_{0,v} = \langle \mathcal{P} \rangle$ and $U_w = U_v = \mathcal{T}$. Hence the base case is true.

Assume that the lemma is true for phase ℓ. We need to prove that it is true for phase $\ell + 1$. Let w and v be two processors fully active at the beginning of phase $\ell + 1$.

First we claim that at the beginning of stage 3 of phase ℓ, we have $L_{\ell,w} = L_{\ell,v}$ and $U_{\ell,w} = U_{\ell,v}$. Indeed, if w and v are fully active also at the beginning of phase ℓ, then the claim follows by the inductive hypothesis. If processor w (resp. v) has just restarted and is not yet fully active in phase ℓ, then it sends a `restart` message in stage 1 of phase ℓ. By Lemma 5.9, there is a witness for phase ℓ. Hence processor w (resp. v) receives a `info` message from the witness and thus at the beginning of stage 3 of phase ℓ it has $U_{\ell,w} = U_\ell$ (resp. $U_{\ell,v} = U_\ell$) and $L_{\ell,w} = L_\ell$ (resp. $L_{\ell,v} = L_\ell$).

We now distinguish two cases: phase ℓ is attended and phase ℓ is unattended.

Case 1: Phase ℓ is not attended. Then no `summary` messages are received by w and v and in stage 3 of phase ℓ they do not modify their sets $U_{\ell,w}$ and $U_{\ell,v}$. The local view of both processors is modified in the same way (case 1 of the local view update). Hence we have that $U_{\ell+1,w} = U_{\ell+1,v}$ and $L_{\ell+1,w} = L_{\ell+1,v}$.

Case 2: Phase ℓ is attended. Then there is at least one coordinator completing the phase. Let $c_1, ..., c_k$ be the coordinators for phase ℓ. Since we have reliable multicast, the `report` message of each worker reaches all coordinators that are alive. Thus the `summary` messages sent by coordinators are all equal. Let `summary`(D, P) one such a message. Since we have reliable multicast, both processors w and v receive `summary`(D, P) messages from the coordinators. Hence in stage 3 of phase ℓ processors w and v set $D_{\ell+1,w} = D_{\ell+1,v} = D$ and thus we have $U_{\ell+1,w} = U_{\ell+1,v}$. Processors w and v also set $P_{\ell+1,w} = P_{\ell+1,v} = P$ and use the same rule (case 2 of the local view update rule) to update the local view. Hence we have $L_{\ell+1,w} = L_{\ell+1,v}$. $\qquad\square$

Because of the previous lemma we can define the view $L_\ell = L_{\ell,w}$, the set of available processors $P_\ell = P_{\ell,w}$, the set of done tasks $D_\ell = D_{\ell,w}$ and the set of unaccounted tasks $U_\ell = U_{\ell,w}$, all of them referred to the beginning of phase ℓ, where w is any fully active processor. Notice that restarted (non-fully-active) processors may have inconsistent knowledge of these quantities.

Remember that we denote by p_ℓ the cardinality of the set of live processors for phase ℓ, i.e., $p_\ell = |P_\ell|$, and by u_ℓ the cardinality of the set of unaccounted tasks for phase ℓ, i.e., $u_\ell = |U_\ell|$.

In the following lemmas we prove safety (no live processor or undone task is forgotten) and progress (tasks execution) properties, which imply the correctness of the algorithm.

Lemma 5.11. *In any execution of algorithm* AR, *a processor fully active at the beginning of phase ℓ belongs to P_ℓ.*

Proof. If processor w is fully active at the beginning of phase $\ell - 1$, then by the inductive hypothesis it belongs to $P_{\ell-1}$. Processor w is taken out of the set P_ℓ only if a coordinator does not receive a **report** message from w in phase $\ell - 1$. Since processor w survives phase $\ell - 1$ then it sends the **report** message in phase $\ell - 1$. Hence it belongs to P_ℓ.

If processor w is not fully active at the beginning of phase $\ell - 1$, then it restarted in phase $\ell - 1$. Thus at the end of phase $\ell - 1$ processor w is re-integrated in the local views of phase ℓ. Hence it belongs to P_ℓ. □

Lemma 5.12. *In any execution of algorithm AR, if a task z does not belong to U_ℓ then it has been executed in phases $1, 2, ..., \ell - 1$.*

Proof. The proof is the same as the proof of Lemma 3.20. □

Lemma 5.13. *In a good execution of algorithm AR, for any phase ℓ we have that $u_{\ell+1} \leq u_\ell$.*

Proof. Consider phase ℓ. If there are no restarts, then, by the code, no task is added to the set of undone tasks. If there are restarts, a restarted processor w has $U_{\ell,w} = T$. By Lemma 5.9, there is a processor v which is a witness for phase ℓ. Then processor w receives the $\text{info}(U_\ell, L_\ell)$ message from processor v and hence sets $U_{\ell,w} = U_\ell$. Hence also when processors restart no task is added to the set of undone tasks. □

Lemma 5.14. *In any good execution of algorithm AR, for any attended phase ℓ we have that $u_{\ell+1} < u_\ell$.*

Proof. Since phase ℓ is attended, there is at least one coordinator c alive in phase ℓ. A coordinator must be a fully active processor (a restarted processor needs to complete a phase in order to known the current view and become coordinator). By Lemma 5.11 processor c belongs to P_ℓ and thus it executes one task. Hence at least one task is executed and consequently at least one task is taken out of U_ℓ. By Lemma 5.13, no task is added to U_ℓ during phase ℓ. □

As for algorithm AN, given a particular execution, we denote by $\alpha_1, \alpha_2, ..., \alpha_\tau$ the attended phases and by π_i the unattended period in between phases α_i and α_{i+1}.

Lemma 5.15. *In a good execution of algorithm AR any unattended period consists of at most $\min\{\log p, \log f\}$ phases.*

Proof. Consider the unattended period π_i. As argued in Lemma 3.23 the views at the beginning of π_i is a tree-like view.

By Lemma 5.11 and by the local view update rule for unattended phases, any processor fully active at the beginning of a phase ℓ of π_i belongs to P_ℓ and thus to L_ℓ. By the local view update rule for unattended phases, we have that eventually there is a phase ℓ' such that all fully active processors are supposed to be coordinators of phase ℓ' (that is, the first layer of $L_{\ell'}$ contains all the processors fully active at the beginning of phase ℓ'). By Lemma 5.9, phase ℓ' has a witness. The witness is a fully active processor and by definition it survives the entire phase. Hence, phase ℓ' is attended.

The upper bounds on the number of phases follow from the tree-like structure of the views. With the same argument used in Lemma 3.23 we have that the number of phases of π_i is at most $\log f$. The $\log p$ bound follows from the fact that by doubling the number of expected coordinators for each unattended phase, after at most $\log p$ phases all processors are expected to be coordinators and thus at least one of them (the witness) survives the phase.   □

Theorem 5.16. *In a good execution of algorithm* AR *the algorithm terminates and all the units of work are performed.*

Proof. By Lemma 5.11 fully active processors are always part of the computation, so the computation never ends if there are fully active processors and U_ℓ is not empty. By Lemma 5.9 any phase has a witness which is a fully active processor. The local knowledge about the outstanding tasks is sound, by Lemma 5.12. For every $1 + \log p$ phases there is at least one attended phase, by Lemma 5.15. Hence, by Lemmas 5.13 and 5.14, the number of unaccounted tasks decreases by at least one in every $1 + \log p$ phases. Thus after at most $O(n \log p)$ phases all the tasks have been performed. During the next attended phase this information is disseminated and the algorithm terminates.   □

5.3.3 Complexity Analysis of Algorithm AR

We next analyze the performance of algorithm AR in terms of total-work complexity S used message complexity M. To assess S we partition it into S_a spent during the attended phases and S_u spent during the unattended phases. So $S = S_a + S_u$. In the following lemmas we assess the available processor steps of algorithm AR.

Recall that good executions are those executions whose adversarial pattern is allowed by $\mathcal{A}_{CR}^{(26)}$. We also recall that $\alpha_1, \alpha_2, ..., \alpha_\tau$ denote the attended phases, π_i denote the unattended period in between phases α_i and α_{i+1} and that p_ℓ and u_ℓ denote, respectively, the size of the set P_ℓ of fully active processors for phase ℓ and the size of the set U_ℓ of undone tasks for phase ℓ.

Lemma 5.17. *In a good execution of algorithm* AR *we have* $S_a = O(n + p \log p + f)$.

Proof. By Theorem 5.16 the algorithm terminates.

We first account for all those steps spent by a processor after a restarts and before the processor either fails again or becomes fully active, that is, it is included in the set P_ℓ for a phase ℓ, and thus is counted for in p_ℓ. The number of such steps spent for each restart is bounded by a constant. Hence the available processor steps spent is $O(r)$, which is $O(f)$.

Next we account for all the remaining part of S_a by distinguishing two possible cases:

Case 1: All attended phases α_k such that $p_{\alpha_k} \leq u_{\alpha_k}$. The load balancing rule assures that at most one processor is assigned to a task. Hence the available processor steps used in this case can be charged to the number of tasks executed, which is at most $n + f$.

Case 2: All attended phases such that $p_{\alpha_k} > u_{\alpha_k}$. We arrange the tasks that were executed and accounted for during such phases in the order by the phase in which they are performed (for tasks executed in the same phase the order does not matter). Let $\langle b_1, b_2, \ldots, b_m \rangle$ be such a list. Notice that $m \leq p$ because $u_{\alpha_k} < p_{\alpha_k} \leq p$, and once the inequality $u_{\alpha_k} \leq p$ starts to hold, it remains true in phases α_i for $i \geq k$. We then partition these tasks into disjoint adjacent segments Z_i:

$$Z_i = \left\{ b_k : \frac{p}{i+1} \leq m - k + 1 < \frac{p}{i} \right\}.$$

By the load balancing rule, at most

$$\frac{p}{m-k+1} \leq p\frac{i+1}{p} = i+1$$

processors are assigned to each task in Z_i, because when a processor is assigned for the last time to task b_k, there are at least $m - k + 1$ unaccounted tasks. The size of Z_i can be estimated as follows:

$$|Z_i| \leq \frac{p}{i} - \frac{p}{i+1} \leq p\left(\frac{1}{i} - \frac{1}{i+1}\right) = \frac{p}{i(i+1)}.$$

Hence the total-work used is less than

$$\sum_{1 \leq i \leq m} \frac{p}{i(i+1)} \cdot (i+1) \leq p \sum_{1 \leq i \leq p} \frac{1}{i} = O(p \log p) .$$

Combining all the cases we obtain $S_a = O(n + p \log p + f)$. $\square$

Lemma 5.18. *In a good execution of algorithm* AR *we have* $S_u = O(S_a + f) \cdot \min\{\log p, \log f\})$.

Proof. Consider the unattended period π_i. At the beginning of this period there are p_i available processors. By Lemma 5.15, for each of these processors we need to account for $\min\{\log p, \log f\}$ steps spent in period i. Summing up over all attended phases, we have that the part of S_u for these processors is

$$\min\{\log p, \log f\} \cdot \sum_{i=1}^{\tau} p_{\alpha_i} = S_a \cdot \min\{\log p, \log f\}.$$

Each restart can contribute additionally at most $\min\{\log p, \log f\}$ processor steps because if the processor stays alive past phase α_{i+1}, its contribution is already accounted for. Since the number of restarts r is $r \leq f$, the bound follows. $\square$

Theorem 5.19. *In a good execution of algorithm* AR *its total-work is* $S = O((n + p \log p + f) \cdot \min\{\log p, \log f\})$.

Proof. The total S of algorithm AR is given by $S = S_a + S_u$. The theorem follows from Lemmas 5.18 and 5.17.   □

Remark 5.20. We recall that a lower bound on work in the setting with processor restarts is $\Omega(t + p \log p)$. This bound holds even for algorithms that performs tasks by perfectly balancing loads of surviving processors in each computation step. The work of algorithm AR includes a contribution that comes within a factor of $\min\{\log p, \log f\}$ relative to that lower bound. As we have similarly remarked for algorithm AN, this suggests that improving the work result is difficult and that better solutions may have to involve a trade-off between the work and message complexities.

We now assess the message complexity. The analysis is similar to the one done for algorithm AN. The difference is that we need to account also for messages sent by restarted processors. However the approach used to analyze the message complexity of algorithm AN works also for algorithm AR.

We distinguish between the attended phases preceded by a nonempty unattended period and the attended phases not preceded by unattended periods. We let M_u be the number of messages sent in $\pi_{i-1}\alpha_i$, for all those i's such that π_{i-1} is nonempty and we let M_a be the number of messages sent in $\pi_{i-1}\alpha_i$, for all those i's such that π_{i-1} is empty (clearly in these cases we have $\pi_{i-1}\alpha_i = \alpha_i$). Next we estimate M_a and M_u and thus the message complexity M of algorithm AR.

Lemma 5.21. *In a good execution of algorithm* AR *we have* $M_a = O(n + p \log p / \log \log p + f)$.

Proof. We first account for messages sent by restarted processors and responses to those messages. For each restart the number of **restart** messages sent is bounded by a constant and one **info** and one **summary** message are sent to a restarted processor before it becomes fully active. Hence the total number of messages sent due to restarts is $O(r) = O(f)$.

The remaining messages can be estimated as in Lemma 3.30. In a phase ℓ where there is a unique coordinator the number of messages sent is $2p_\ell$. By the definition of M_a, messages counted in M_a are messages sent in a phase α_i such that π_{i-1} is empty. This means that the phase previous to α_i is α_{i-1} which, by definition, is attended. Hence by the local view update rule of attended phases we have that α_i has a unique coordinator. Thus phase α_i gives a contribution of at most $2p_{\alpha_i}$ messages to M_a. Hence $M_a \leq \sum_{i=1}^{\tau} 2p_{\alpha_i} = 2S_a$. The lemma follows from Lemma 5.17.   □

Lemma 5.22. *In any good execution of algorithm* AR *we have* $M_u = O(fp)$.

Proof. We first account for messages sent by restarted processors and responses to those messages. The argument is the same as in Lemma 5.21. The total number of messages sent because of restarts is $O(f)$.

Next we estimate the remaining messages as done in Lemma 3.31. First we notice that in any phase the number of messages sent is $O(cp)$ where c is the number of coordinators for that phase. Hence to estimate M_u we simple count all the supposed coordinators in the phases included in $\pi_{i-1}\alpha_i$, where π_{i-1} is nonempty.

Let i be such that π_{i-1} is not empty. Because of the structure of the local view, we have that the total number of supposed coordinators in all the phases of $\pi_{i-1}\alpha_i$ is $2f_{i-1} + 1 = O(f_{i-1})$ where f_{i-1} is the number of failures during π_{i-1}. Hence the total number of supposed coordinators, in all of the phases contributing to M_u, is $\sum_{i=1}^{\tau} O(f_{i-1}) = O(f)$.

Thus M_u is $O(fp)$. $\qquad\square$

Theorem 5.23. *In a good execution of algorithm* AR *the number of messages sent is* $M = O(n + p\log p + fp)$.

Proof. The total number of messages sent is $M = M_a + M_u$. The theorem follows from Lemmas 5.21 and 5.22. $\qquad\square$

5.4 Open Problems

The algorithm presented in this chapter depends on the availability of reliable multicast. In algorithm AR it appears not difficult to show that worker-to-coordinator multicasts need not be reliable. A more difficult problem is to design algorithms that use the aggressive coordinator paradigm and unreliable coordinator-to-worker communication.

For the crash/restart models we assume that a processor loses its state upon a crash and that its state is reset to some known initial state upon a restart. Algorithm AR cannot take direct advantage of such a possibility, and it would be interesting to explore the benefits of having stable storage. This may also help reduce the reliance on broadcasts as the sole means for information propagation.

Developing stronger lower bounds is another challenging area of research. In order to reduce the existing gap between the upper and lower bounds, one needs to exploit the fact that communication is necessary to share the knowledge among the processors. Additionally trade-offs between work and communication need to be studied. For example, it is trivial to reduce communication to 0 while increasing work to $\Theta(n \cdot p)$ by requiring each processor to perform all tasks. Exploring meaningful trade-off relations between work and communication will lead to specialized lower bounds and to algorithms that can be tuned to specific distributed computing environments depending on the relative costs of computation and communication. Another area of interest is exploring lower bounds that show how the complexity of the problem depends on the number of crashes and the number of restarts.

Finally, it is also interesting to consider adversaries where κ-restriction is imposed not on at least one processor as is done here, but on at least q processors, where q is an adversarial model parameter. Such definition yields families of adversaries $\mathcal{A}_{CR}^{(\kappa,q)}$, and more efficient algorithms could be sought for these models. This is because the adversaries are more benign, i.e., $\mathcal{A}_{CR}^{(\kappa,1)} \supseteq \mathcal{A}_{CR}^{(\kappa,q)}$ for $q > 1$.

A different algorithmic approach may be necessary to solve the problem for κ-restricted executions with a smaller κ, for example, $\kappa < 17$. However, recall the problem is not solvable for 1-restricted executions (unless processors are assisted by an oracle) and there is a qualitative difference between 1-restricted executions and κ-restricted executions, with $\kappa \geq 2$. It appears that in order to achieve solutions for κ-restricted executions for small κ it is necessary to use more messages. For example for 2-restricted executions there must be transfer of some state information in each step, otherwise any progress information is lost.

5.5 Chapter Notes

The lower bound and its matching upper bound result on total-work for $Do\text{-}All_{\mathcal{A}_{CR}}^{\mathcal{O}}(n, p, f)$ presented in Section 5.2 was first shown by Kanellakis and Shvartsman [67] while studying the $Do\text{-}All$ problem in shared-memory using unit-time memory snapshots (processors can read all memory in unit-time). As already discussed in Section 3.5, the memory snapshot assumption in shared-memory is equivalent to the assumption of perfect knowledge (processors are assisted by an oracle for load-balancing and termination information). In fact, the proofs of Theorems 5.2 and 5.3 are slight modifications of the corresponding proofs presented in [67].

The presentation of Sections 5.1 and 5.3 on the $Do\text{-}All$ problem under processor crashes and restarts in message-passing systems is based on the work by Chlebus, De Prisco, and Shvartsman [15]. The $Do\text{-}All$ problem has also been studied under processor crashes and restarts in shared-memory systems by Kanellakis and Shvartsman [67].

6

Synchronous Do-All with Byzantine Failures

S O far we have studied the *Do-All* problem under relatively benign failure
types, where faulty processors may stop working, but do not perform
any actions harmful to the computation. We now move to study the *Do-All*
problem under an adversary, called $\mathcal{A}_B$, that can cause Byzantine processor
failures. A faulty processor may perform arbitrary actions, including those
that interfere with the ongoing computation. The distributed environment is
still assumed to be synchronous and the underlying network is fully connected.
More specifically, for a system with p processors, f of which may be faulty,
and the *Do-All* problem with n tasks we present upper and lower bounds on
the complexity of $Do\text{-}All_{\mathcal{A}_B}(n, p, f)$ for several cases: (a) the case where the
maximum number of faulty processors f is known *a priori*, (b) the case where
f is not known, (c) the case where a task execution can be verified (without
re-executing the task), and (d) the case where task executions cannot be
verified. The efficiency of algorithms is evaluated in terms of total-work and
message complexities. We also consider time of computation, measured in
terms of parallel global steps taken by the processors, and referred to simply
as the number of steps. Interestingly, we show that in some cases obtaining
work $\Theta(n \cdot p)$ is the best one can do, that is, each of the p processors must
perform all of the n tasks, and that in certain cases communication cannot
help improve work efficiency.

Chapter structure.

We define adversary $\mathcal{A}_B$ in Section 6.1. In Section 6.2 we present upper and
lower bound results when the task executions cannot be verified, first for
the case when the maximum number of faulty processors f is known (Section 6.2.1) and then for the case when f is unknown (Section 6.2.2). In Section 6.3 we present upper and lower bound results when the task executions
can be verified, first when f is known (Section 6.3.1) and then when f is
unknown (Section 6.3.2). We discuss open problems in Section 6.4.

6.1 Adversarial Model

We denote by $\mathcal{A}_B$ an omniscient (on-line) adversary that can cause Byzantine processor failures, as defined in Section 2.2.1. Consider an algorithm A that performs a computation in the presence of adversary $\mathcal{A}_B$. Let ξ be an execution in $\mathcal{E}(A, \mathcal{A}_B)$. Then, the adversarial pattern $\xi|_{\mathcal{A}_B}$ is a set of triples (*event*, PID, t), where *event* is an arbitrary action (including *crash* and *restart*) that the adversary forces processor PID to perform at time t in the execution, where t is given according to some external global clock not available to the processors.

For each processor PID, we are normally interested in only the *first time* when the processor behaves differently from what is prescribed by algorithm A for processor PID. We say that processor PID *survives* step i of the execution ξ if $\xi|_{\mathcal{A}_B}$ does not contain a triple (*event*, PID, t) such that $t \leq i$. We say that processor PID *fails* in $\xi|_{\mathcal{A}_B}$, if there exists a triple (*event*, PID, t) $\in \xi|_{\mathcal{A}_B}$, for some t. For an adversarial pattern $\xi|_{\mathcal{A}_B}$ we define $f_b(\xi|_{\mathcal{A}_B}) = \|\xi|_{\mathcal{A}_B}\|$ to be the number of processors that fail in $\xi|_{\mathcal{A}_B}$. As in $\mathcal{A}_C$, we consider only executions ξ where $f_b(\xi|_{\mathcal{A}_B}) < p$ to ensure computational progress. For this adversary we consider the case where $f_b(\xi|_{\mathcal{A}_B})$ is known to the algorithms, and the case where it is unknown.

Observe that when no restrictions on the number of failures are imposed on the adversaries, then $\mathcal{A}_C \subset \mathcal{A}_{CR} \subset \mathcal{A}_B$.

6.2 Task Execution without Verification

We first consider the setting where a processor cannot verify whether or not a task was performed. Thus a faulty processor can "lie" about doing a task without any other processor being able to detect it.

6.2.1 Known Maximum Number of Failures

We assume here that the upper bound f on the number of processors that can fail is known *a priori*; of course the set of processors that may actually fail in any give execution is not known. We first present lower bounds for this setting.

Theorem 6.1. *Any fault-free execution of an algorithm that solves Do-All$_{\mathcal{A}_B}(n, p, f)$ with f known, takes at least $\lceil \frac{n(f+1)}{p} \rceil$ steps.*

Proof. By way of contradiction, assume that there is an algorithm A that solves the *Do-All* problem for all adversarial patterns of size at most f, and that it has some failure-free execution R that solves the problem in $s < \lceil (n(f+1)/p) \rceil$ steps. Then, in R there is a task z that has been performed by less than $f + 1$ processors, since $\lfloor \frac{sp}{n} \rfloor \leq \lfloor \frac{(\lceil \frac{n(f+1)}{p} \rceil - 1)p}{n} \rfloor < f + 1$.

Now construct an execution R' of A that behaves exactly like R except that in the first s steps each processor that is supposed to execute task z is in fact faulty and does not execute z. Since z is executed by less than $f+1$ processors, z is not executed. Since verification is not available, no correct processor in R' can distinguish R from R', hence R' stops after s steps and the problem is not solved (since at least one task was not performed), a contradiction. □

Corollary 6.2. *Any fault-free execution of an algorithm that solves Do-All$_{\mathcal{A}_B}(n, p, f)$ with f known, has total-work at least $S = \lceil \frac{n(f+1)}{p} \rceil p$.*

We now present algorithm *Cover* that solves *Do-All* in the case where f is known and task execution cannot be verified. The algorithm is simple: each task is performed by $f + 1$ processors. Since there can be at most f faulty processors, this guarantees that each task is performed at least once. This implies the correctness of the algorithm. The pseudocode of the algorithm is given in Figure 6.1. We now show that algorithm *Cover* is optimal.

---

for each processor q, $1 \leq q \leq p$ **do:**
1   **for** $k_\ell = 1$ **to** $\lceil \frac{n(f+1)}{p} \rceil$ **do**
2   execute task $((\lceil \frac{nq}{p} \rceil + k_\ell) \mod n) + 1$

Fig. 6.1. Algorithm *Cover*. The code is for processor q.

Theorem 6.3. *Algorithm Cover solves Do-All$_{\mathcal{A}_B}(n, p, f)$ with f known, in optimal number of steps $\lceil \frac{n(f+1)}{p} \rceil$ and total-work $S = \lceil \frac{n(f+1)}{p} \rceil p$, without any communication.*

Proof. The proof follows from the fact that each task is executed by at least $f + 1$ different processors. Since at most f processors are faulty, at least one correct processor executes the task.

For simplicity we will remove the modular algebra (see Figure 6.1) for both processor and task indices. We do this by assuming that any task number z, $z < 1$, is in fact the task number $z + n$, any task number $z > n$ is in fact the task number $z - n$, and any processor q, with $q < 1$, is in fact processor $q + p$. Let us consider the tasks between $\lceil \frac{nq}{p} \rceil + 2$ and $\lceil \frac{n(q+1)}{p} \rceil + 1$. We show that these tasks are executed by processors $q - f$ to q. For that, it is enough to show that the last task executed by processor $q - f$ is at least task number $\lceil \frac{n(q+1)}{p} \rceil + 1$. This can be simply observed, since $\lceil \frac{n(q-f)}{p} \rceil + \lceil \frac{n(f+1)}{p} \rceil + 1 \geq \lceil \frac{n(q+1)}{p} \rceil + 1$, from the fact that $\lceil x \rceil + \lceil y \rceil \geq \lceil x + y \rceil$. □

It is worth observing that algorithm *Cover* is work-optimal and time-optimal even though no communication took place. This shows that in this setting communication does not help obtaining better performance.

6.2.2 Unknown Maximum Number of Failures

Now we consider the case where the upper bound f is not known, i.e., all that is known is that $f < p$. In this setting we observe that no algorithm can do better than having each processor perform each task, as shown in the following theorem.

Theorem 6.4. *Any fault-free execution of an algorithm that solves Do-All$_{\mathcal{A}_B}(n, p, p - 1)$ takes at least n steps and has total-work at least $S = n \cdot p$.*

This is an immediate corollary of the above discussion.

In summary, it is not very interesting to study fault-tolerant computation in this model:

Corollary 6.5. *When f is unknown and the task execution cannot be verified, the trivial algorithm in which each processor executes all the tasks is optimal.*

6.3 Task Execution with Verification

In this section we consider the setting where a task execution can be *verified* without re-executing the task. The verification mechanism reinforces the ability of correct processors to detect faulty processors: if a faulty processor "lies" about having done a task, a correct processor can detect this by separately verifying the execution of the task.

We assume that up to v tasks, $1 \leq v \leq n$, can be verified by a processor in one step. Thus performing a task or verifying v tasks corresponds to a unit of work. Furthermore, we do not count as part of the message complexity of an algorithm the messages used to verify tasks, as this is dependent on the specific verification method used (which here we leave as an abstraction) and need not be a function of the number of verifications. Because the setting is synchronous, we assume that if the same task is verified by several processors in the same step, then either all processors find the task done or all of them find the task undone.

Recall from Section 2.2.3 that given an execution ξ of an algorithm A that performs a computation in the presence of adversary $\mathcal{A}_B$ we let $f_b = f_b(\xi|_{\mathcal{A}_B}) = \|\xi|_{\mathcal{A}_B}\|$ to be the (exact) number of processors that fail in adversarial pattern $\xi|_{\mathcal{A}_B}$.

For brevity of presentation, in this section we define and use Λ_{p,f_b} as follows:

$$\Lambda_{p,f_b} = \begin{cases} \log(\frac{p}{f_b}) & \text{when } f_b \leq p/\log p, \\ \\ \log\log n & \text{when } p/\log p < f_b < p. \end{cases}$$

6.3.1 Known Maximum Number of Failures

As before, we first consider the case where the upper bound f on the number of faulty processors is known. We first show lower bounds on steps and total-work required by any $Do\text{-}All$ algorithm in this case. Then we present an algorithm, called $Minority$, designed to efficiently solve $Do\text{-}All_{A_B}(n, p, f)$ when $f \geq p/2$. Next we present algorithm $Majority$ that is designed to efficiently solve $Do\text{-}All_{A_B}(n, p, f)$ when $f < p/2$. Finally, we combine algorithms $Minority$ and $Majority$, yielding an algorithm, called $Complete$, that efficiently solves $Do\text{-}All_{A_B}(n, p, f)$ for the whole range of f. The complexity of algorithm $Complete$ depends on f and comes close to matching the corresponding lower bound.

Lower Bounds

We now present lower bounds on time steps and total-work for any execution of an algorithm that solves the $Do\text{-}All$ problem with verification and known f. The first result is a bound on total-work that follows directly from the analogous result shown in Section 3.2.2 for $Do\text{-}All_{A_C}^{O}(n, p, f)$.

Lemma 6.6. *Any execution of an algorithm that solves $Do\text{-}All_{A_B}(n, p, f)$ with f known, in the presence of $f_b \leq f$ Byzantine failures, requires total-work $S = \Omega(n + p \log p / \Lambda_{p, f_b})$.*

Proof. Theorem 3.10 in Section 3.2.2 gives a lower bound on the amount of total-work any algorithm that solves the $Do\text{-}All$ problem requires. Recall that the mentioned theorem assumes Adversary $\mathcal{A}_C$, and the existence of an oracle that gives information about termination and that balances the undone tasks among the correct processors. Implicitly, the oracle can verify the execution of up to n tasks in constant time. The theorem shows that, just in executing tasks, any execution with f failures of an algorithm that solves $Do\text{-}All$ in this model requires work $\Omega(n + p \log n / \Lambda_{p, f_c})$. Since crashes are a special case of Byzantine failures, that is, $\mathcal{A}_C \subset \mathcal{A}_F$, the lower bound applies here as well. $\square$

We now present a lower bound on the steps of any algorithm that solves the $Do\text{-}All$ problem.

Lemma 6.7. *Any fault-free execution of an algorithm that solves $Do\text{-}All_{A_B}(n, p, f)$ with f known and with task verification, takes at least $\lceil \frac{n(f+v)}{pv} \rceil$ steps.*

Proof. By way of contradiction, assume that there is an algorithm A that solves the $Do\text{-}All$ problem with verification for all adversarial patterns of length at most f and it has some failure-free execution R that solves the problem in $s < \lceil \frac{n(f+v)}{pv} \rceil$ steps (since s is an integer, we can drop the ceiling: $s < \frac{n(f+v)}{pv}$). The work in this execution is $s \cdot p$. Note that in these steps each task has been executed at least once. Counting just one task execution, n

units of work have been spent on executing the tasks. The remaining work is $sp - n$, and each work unit can be used to either perform a task or to verify v of them. Then there is a task z that, in addition to having been executed once, has been "looked at" (executed or verified) at most $f - 1$ more times, since

$$\lfloor \frac{(sp-n)v}{n} \rfloor < \lfloor \frac{(\frac{n(f+v)}{pv}p - n)v}{n} \rfloor = \lfloor (\frac{f+v}{v} - 1)v \rfloor = f \text{ (by the pigeonhole principle)}.$$

Thus task z has been "looked at" at most f times.

Now construct an execution R' of A that behaves exactly like R except that in the first s steps each processor that is supposed to execute task z is in fact faulty and does not execute it, and every processor that is supposed to verify z is also faulty and behaves as if z was executed. Then, no correct processor in R' can distinguish R from R', hence R' stops after s steps and the problem is not solved (since at least one task was not performed), a contradiction. □

The above lemma leads to the following result.

Theorem 6.8. *Any fault-free execution of an algorithm that solves Do-All$_{A_B}(n, p, f)$ with f known and with task verification, requires total-work at least $S = \lceil \frac{n(f+v)}{pv} \rceil \cdot p$.*

Proof. Using Lemma 6.7 and the fact that none of the p processors fail, we compute the work of any algorithm as $\lceil \frac{n(f+v)}{pv} \rceil \cdot p$. □

From the above we obtain the following lower bound result.

Theorem 6.9. *Any algorithm that solves Do-All$_{A_B}(n, p, f)$ with f known, in the presence of $f_b \leq f$ Byzantine failures, and with task verification, takes total-work $S = \Omega(n + nf/v + p\log p/\Lambda_{p,f_b})$.*

Proof. It follows directly from Lemma 6.6 and Theorem 6.8. □

Algorithm *Minority*

Now we present algorithm *Minority* that is designed to solve *Do-All* in the case when at most half of the processors are guaranteed not to fail, i.e., $f \geq p/2$. Algorithm *Minority* is detailed in Figure 6.2. The code is given for a generic processor $q \in [p]$.

As can be seen in Figure 6.2, the main body of the algorithm is formed by a while loop. Within the loop the variables P, T, and ψ are updated so they always hold the current set of the processors assumed to be correct, the tasks whose completion status is unknown, and the number of processors that can still fail, respectively. The iterations of the while loop are executed synchronously by every correct processor. An important correctness condition of the algorithm is that every correct processor has the same value in these variables at the beginning of each loop iteration (that is why we do not index the variables with the processor's id). The exit conditions of the loop are that there is no remaining work or no remaining processor is faulty. If the latter

Minority(q, P, T, ψ):

1   **while** $T \neq \emptyset$ and $\psi > 0$ **do**
2   execute one task allocated to q as a function of q, P, and T
3       $\Phi \leftarrow \emptyset$
4       $C \leftarrow$ tasks allocated to the processors in P, as a list of $\lceil \frac{\min\{|P|,|T|\}}{v} \rceil$
            sets of at most v tasks each
5   **for** $l = 1$ to $\lceil \frac{\min\{|P|,|T|\}}{v} \rceil$ **do**
6   verify the tasks in the lth set $C[l]$
7           $\Phi \leftarrow \Phi \cup \{\kappa : \text{task } z \in C[l] \text{ was allocated to processor } \kappa \text{ and}$
                was not done$\}$
8   **end for**
9       $P \leftarrow P \setminus \Phi$
10      $T \leftarrow T \setminus \{z : z \text{ was allocated to some } \kappa \in P\}$
11      $\psi \leftarrow \psi - |\Phi|$
12 **end while**
13 execute up to $\lceil |T|/|P| \rceil$ tasks allocated to q as a function of q, P, and T

Fig. 6.2. Algorithm for the case $f \geq p/2$. The code is for processor q. The call to the procedure is made with $P = [p]$, $T = [n]$, and $\psi = f$.

condition holds, then the remaining tasks are evenly distributed among the remaining processors in P, so that every tasks is assigned to at least one processor, and the problem is solved.

Consider an execution of algorithm *Minority*. Let k be the number of iterations of the while loop in this execution. The iterations are numbered starting with 1. We denote by P_i, T_i, and ψ_i the values of the sets P and T, and the variable ψ, respectively, at the *end* of iteration i. We also use P_0, T_0, and ψ_0 to denote the initial values of P, T, and ψ, respectively. To abbreviate, we use $p_i = |P_i|$ and $n_i = |T_i|$.

For an iteration i of the loop, each processor first chooses one of the tasks in T_{i-1} deterministically with an allocating function of q, P_{i-1}, and T_{i-1}. The allocating function is known to every processor and must ensure that, if $n_{i-1} \geq p_{i-1}$, different processors in P_{i-1} choose different tasks in T_{i-1}. It must also ensure that if $n_{i-1} < p_{i-1}$, each task is assigned to at least $\lfloor p_{i-1}/n_{i-1} \rfloor$ and at most $\lceil p_{i-1}/n_{i-1} \rceil$ processors. One possible allocating function is one that (once the processors in P_{i-1} are indexed from 1 to p_{i-1} and the tasks in T_{i-1} are indexed from 1 to n_{i-1}) assigns to the qth processor in P_{i-1} the $(((q - 1) \mod n_{i-1}) + 1)$st task in T_{i-1}. After executing this task, the processor verifies the execution of all the tasks allocated to processors in P_{i-1} to identify faulty processors. The identities of the newly discovered faulty processors are stored in the set Φ. With this information it updates the sets T_{i-1} and P_{i-1} and the value ψ_{i-1} and obtains T_i, P_i and ψ_i, respectively. The list of sets C is the same for each processor. Then, according to the description of the algorithm all processors verify the tasks allocated to a subset of correct processors simultaneously, either finding each of them done or undone. This guarantees that the sets Φ are the same in all correct processors.

The correctness of algorithm *Minority* can be shown by induction on the number of iterations of the while loop. The induction claims that at the beginning of iteration $i > 0$ all correct processors have the same value of the variables P_{i-1}, T_{i-1}, and ψ_{i-1}, and that $|T_{i-1}| \leq n - i + 1$. Observe that initially all processors have the same P_0, T_0 and ψ_0, and that $|T_0| = n$, which covers the base case. The induction then has to show that if the correct processors begin an iteration i with the same P_{i-1}, T_{i-1} and ψ_{i-1}, then at the end of this iteration all correct processors have the same P_i, T_i, and ψ_i, and at least one new task has been done in the iteration. The first part follows from the fact that all correct processes end up with the same set Φ of failed processes. The second follows from the fact that at least one processor is correct. Then, termination is guaranteed (with all tasks being completed) by the fact that at least one processor is correct ($f < p$), by the fact that after at most n iterations all correct processors will exit the while loop, by the exit conditions of the while loop, and by "line 13" of the code of the algorithm.

We now assess the efficiency of algorithm *Minority*. We denote by Φ_i the value of set Φ at the *end* of iteration i of the loop, and we use $\phi_i = |\Phi_i|$. Note that $\phi_1 \leq \phi_2 \leq \ldots \leq \phi_i \leq \ldots \leq f_b$, f_b being the number of processor failures in a given execution.

The analysis makes use of the upper bound results obtained for *Do-All*$^{\mathcal{O}}_{\mathcal{A}_C}(n, p, f)$ in Section 3.2.3 and the oracle-based algorithm, call it *Oracle*, as given in Figure 3.1. Recall that in this algorithm, oracle $\mathcal{O}$ is queried in each iteration to determine whether there are still undone tasks. The oracle can detect the processors that crashed during an iteration and whether a task has been performed or not by the end of the iteration. If there is at least one undone task by the end of the iteration, then the oracle is queried to allocate undone tasks to the uncrashed processors. The allocation satisfies that the undone tasks are evenly distributed among the uncrashed processors. In fact, we assume here that the function that allocates in each iteration an undone task t to each processor q in line 2 is the same used in algorithm *Oracle* ($t = $ *Oracle-task*(q)). Hence, the difference between algorithm *Oracle* and algorithm *Minority* is that in algorithm *Minority* the task execution verification is performed by the processors to detect faulty processors and undone tasks, as opposed to algorithm *Oracle* where the task execution verification is performed by oracle $\mathcal{O}$. Recall that in Section 3.2.3 was shown (assuming that the queries to the oracle can be done in $O(1)$ time) that in an execution with no more than f_c crashes algorithm *Oracle* requires at most total-work $O(n + p \log p / \Lambda_{p, f_c})$. We will use this result to show Lemma 6.10 for algorithm *Minority*.

Lemma 6.10. *Given an execution of algorithm Minority with f_b failures and where the while loop consists of k iterations, then $\sum_{i=1}^{k} p_i = O(n + p \log p / \Lambda_{p,f_b})$.*

Proof. Consider an execution of the algorithm *Minority* with f_b failures, and let k be the number of iterations of the while loop. We want to bound the sum $\sum_{i=1}^{k} p_i$. For that, let us consider the execution of algorithm *Oracle* in which after the task allocation and before the task execution in each iteration $i \in \{1, ..., k\}$ the processors in Φ_i, and only those, crash. Then, since the same allocation function is used in the executions of *Minority* and *Oracle*, it follows by induction on i that in the execution of algorithm *Oracle*, at the beginning of iteration i the set of correct processors is P_{i-1} and the set of undone tasks is T_{i-1}, and at the end of the iteration the set of correct processors is P_i and the set of undone tasks is T_i. Observe that for algorithm *Oracle*, when the oracle queries can be done in constant time, we have that the work of iteration i, denoted s_i, is a constant multiple of the number of correct processors p_i. Hence, if we denote by S_k the work of the k first iterations of *Oracle*, we have that

$$S_k = \sum_{i=1}^{k} s_i \geq \sum_{i=1}^{k} p_i. \tag{6.1}$$

Now, since the number of failures in the execution of *Minority* is f_b, if we assume that no processor crashes after iteration k in the execution of *Oracle* we have that the number of failures in this execution is $\sum_{i=1}^{k} \phi_i \leq f_b$. Hence, from the upper bound result of Section 3.2.3, mentioned above, we have that

$$S_k = O(n + p \log p / \Lambda_{p,f_b}). \tag{6.2}$$

The thesis of the lemma follows from equations (6.1) and (6.2). $\square$

We now state and prove the work complexity of algorithm *Minority*.

Lemma 6.11. *Any execution of algorithm Minority has total-work $S = O(n + np/v + p \log p / \Lambda_{p,f_b})$.*

Proof. We begin by computing the work incurred in the while loop. We break the analysis into two parts. In the first part we consider only the iterations i of the while loop where initially the number of remaining tasks is at least as large as the number of remaining processors, i.e., $n_{i-1} \geq p_{i-1}$, and we compute the work incurred in these iterations. In the second part we consider only the iterations i where $n_{i-1} < p_{i-1}$ and we compute the work incurred in such iterations.

(1) *Iterations i with $n_{i-1} \geq p_{i-1}$.* In these iterations no task is done twice by correct processors. Hence, at most n tasks are done in these iterations. For

each task done, no more than $\lceil p/v \rceil < p/v + 1$ verification steps are taken. Hence, the total work incurred in these iterations is $S_1 = O(n + np/v)$.

(2) *Iterations i with $n_{i-1} < p_{i-1}$.* Let us assume there are r such iterations out of a total of k iterations ($r \leq k$), with indices $\ell^{(1)}$ to $\ell^{(r)}$, and $1 \leq \ell^{(1)} < \ell^{(2)} < ... < \ell^{(r)} \leq k$. In iteration $\ell^{(i)}$, there are initially $p_{\ell^{(i)}-1}$ processors and $n_{\ell^{(i)}-1}$ tasks, with $n_{\ell^{(i)}-1} < p_{\ell^{(i)}-1}$. In this iteration each (correct) processor performs a task and verifies $\min\{p_{\ell^{(i)}-1}, n_{\ell^{(i)}-1}\} = n_{\ell^{(i)}-1}$ tasks. Hence, the total work incurred in all r iterations is

$$S_2 = \sum_{i=1}^{r} p_{\ell^{(i)}} \left(1 + \left\lceil \frac{n_{\ell^{(i)}-1}}{v} \right\rceil \right) < 2 \sum_{i=1}^{r} p_{\ell^{(i)}} + \frac{1}{v} \sum_{i=1}^{r} p_{\ell^{(i)}} n_{\ell^{(i)}-1}.$$

The first sum is bounded by using Lemma 6.10, since

$$\sum_{i=1}^{r} p_{\ell^{(i)}} \leq \sum_{i=1}^{k} p_i = O\left(n + p \log p / \Lambda_{p,f_b}\right).$$

To bound the second sum, we bound first the value of $n_{\ell^{(i)}}$ using the fact that, in iteration $\ell^{(i)}$, each task is assigned to at most $\lceil p_{\ell^{(i)}-1}/n_{\ell^{(i)}-1} \rceil$ processors,

$$n_{\ell^{(i)}} \leq n_{\ell^{(i)}-1} - \frac{p_{\ell^{(i)}}}{\lceil p_{\ell^{(i)}-1}/n_{\ell^{(i)}-1} \rceil} < n_{\ell^{(i)}-1} - \frac{p_{\ell^{(i)}} n_{\ell^{(i)}-1}}{n_{\ell^{(i)}-1} + p_{\ell^{(i)}-1}}.$$

Then, since $n_{\ell^{(i)}-1} < p_{\ell^{(i)}-1}$, we have

$$p_{\ell^{(i)}} n_{\ell^{(i)}-1} < 2\, p_{\ell^{(i)}-1}\left(n_{\ell^{(i)}-1} - n_{\ell^{(i)}}\right) \tag{6.3}$$

Then, the second sum can be bounded as follows:

$$\sum_{i=1}^{r} p_{\ell^{(i)}} n_{\ell^{(i)}-1} < \sum_{i=1}^{r} 2\, p_{\ell^{(i)}-1}\left(n_{\ell^{(i)}-1} - n_{\ell^{(i)}}\right)$$

$$\leq 2\left(p_{\ell^{(1)}-1} n_{\ell^{(1)}-1} + \sum_{i=2}^{r} p_{\ell^{(i)}-1} n_{\ell^{(i)}-1} - \sum_{i=1}^{r-1} p_{\ell^{(i)}-1} n_{\ell^{(i)}}\right)$$

$$\leq 2\left(p_{\ell^{(1)}-1} n_{\ell^{(1)}-1} + \sum_{i=1}^{r-1} n_{\ell^{(i)}}\left(p_{\ell^{(i+1)}-1} - p_{\ell^{(i)}-1}\right)\right)$$

$$\leq 2\, p_{\ell^{(1)}-1} n_{\ell^{(1)}-1} \leq 2\, np$$

The first inequality follows from Eq. (6.3), the third inequality follows from the fact that $n_{\ell^{(i)}-1} \leq n_{\ell^{(i-1)}}$, and the fourth inequality follows from the facts that $\ell^{(i+1)} - 1 > \ell^{(i)} - 1$ and that $p_i \leq p_j$ when $i > j$.

Then, we have that the work incurred in these iterations is $S_2 = O(n + np/v + p \log p / \Lambda_{p,f_b})$.

We now compute the work incurred after the exit conditions are satisfied, say at the end of iteration k. If $T_k = \emptyset$ then each processor takes at most one step before halting for the total of $O(p)$ work. Otherwise, at most $p\lceil n/p \rceil < n + p \le 2n$ work is done. Hence this work is $S_3 = O(n)$. Therefore, the total-work is $S = S_1 + S_2 + S_3 = O\left(n + np/v + p\log p/\Lambda_{p,f_b}\right).$ □

Note that the work complexity of the algorithm is asymptotically optimal as long as $f = \Omega(n)$. It is worth observing that algorithm *Minority* is asymptotically optimal even though it does not use communication. This shows that for relatively large number of failures communication cannot improve work complexity (asymptotically).

Algorithm *Majority*

We now present algorithm *Majority* that is designed to efficiently solve *Do-All* in the case where the majority of the processors does not fail, i.e., $f < p/2$. At a high level algorithm *Majority* proceeds as follows. Each non-faulty processor is given a set of tasks to be done and a set of processors whose tasks it has to verify. The processor executes its tasks and verifies the tasks of its set of processors, detecting faulty processors. Then a check-pointing algorithm is executed in which all non-faulty processors agree on a set of processors identified as faulty in this stage, and update their information of completed tasks and non-faulty processors accordingly. Algorithm *Majority* is detailed in Figure 6.3. The code is given for a processor $q \in [p]$.

```
Majority(q, P, T, ψ):
1    while |T| > n/p and ψ > 0 do
2        Do_Work_and_Verify(q, P, T, ψ, Φ)
3        Checkpoint(q, P, ψ, Φ)
4        P ← P \ Φ
5        T ← T \ {z : z was allocated to some κ ∈ P}
6        ψ ← ψ − |Φ|
7    end while
8    if ψ = 0 then
9        execute ⌈|T|/|P|⌉ tasks allocated to q as a function of q, P, and T
10   else
11       execute all the tasks in T
12   end if
```

Fig. 6.3. Algorithm for the case $f < p/2$. The code is for processor q. The call parameters are $P = [p]$, $T = [n]$, and $\psi = f$.

As in algorithm *Minority*, the parameters of algorithm *Majority* are the identifier q of the invoking processor, the set of processors P that have not been identified as faulty, the set of tasks T that may still need to be completed, and the maximum number ψ of processors in set P that can be faulty. We adopt the parameter notations we used for an iteration of the while loop of algorithm *Minority* to the parameters of algorithm *Majority*. Specifically, for an iteration i, we let P_i, T_i and ψ_i denote the values of P, T, and ψ, respectively, at the *end* of iteration i. Then, $p_i = |P_i|$ and $n_i = |T_i|$. Finally, $p_0 = p$ and $n_0 = n$.

The iterations of the while loop of *Majority* in all the correct processors work synchronously, i.e., the ith iteration starts at exactly the same step in each correct processor. An important correctness condition of the algorithm, which can be checked by induction, is that the values of P_i, T_i, and ψ_i must be the same for each iteration i in different *correct* processors.

Before starting a new iteration i, a processor first checks whether all the processors in P_{i-1} are correct or whether the total number of remaining tasks is no more than n/p. If either condition holds, it exits the loop. Then, if all the processors in P_{i-1} are correct, it computes a balanced distribution of the remaining set of tasks so that, overall, all the tasks are done by the processors in P_{i-1}. Otherwise the total number of remaining tasks is no more than n/p, and in that case the processor does all the remaining tasks itself. Overall, in either case, this implies $O(n)$ work.

If none of the above conditions hold, a new iteration i starts. The processor first calls the subroutine *Do_Work_and_Verify*. In this subroutine each processor in P_{i-1} gets allocated some subset of the tasks in T_{i-1} that it must execute, and a subset of the processors in P_{i-1} that it must *supervise*, that is, whose tasks it will *verify*. More formally,

Definition 6.12. *For an iteration i of an execution of algorithm Majority, we say that a processor $q \in P_{i-1}$ supervises a processor $w \in P_{i-1}$, if q is assigned to verify all the tasks from T_{i-1} that w was assigned to perform in iteration i.*

If a processor detects in this subroutine that some supervised processor in that subset is not doing the tasks it was assigned, it includes it in a set of faulty processors, returned as set Φ. We denote by $\Phi_{i,q}$ the processors that processor q suspects to be faulty at the *end* of subroutine *Do_Work_and_Verify* of iteration i. Then the processor calls the subroutine *Checkpoint*, which uses a check-pointing algorithm to combine the sets of suspected processors from all the processors in P_i into a common consistent set Φ_i; this denotes the consistent set of faulty processors at the *end* of iteration i. Finally, knowing which processors have been identified as faulty in this iteration, it updates the values of P_{i-1}, T_{i-1}, and ψ_{i-1} and obtains P_i, T_i, and ψ_i, respectively. Note that since $\psi_0 = f < p/2$ initially, at any point it is satisfied that $\psi_i < |P_i|/2$.

We now detail more the subroutines *Do_Work_and_Verify* and *Checkpoint*. We begin the first one. The code of subroutine *Do_Work_and_Verify* is shown in Figure 6.4.

$Do\_Work\_and\_Verify(q, P, T, \psi, \Phi)$:
1   $W \leftarrow Allocate\_Tasks(q, P, T)$
2   $S \leftarrow Allocate\_Processors(q, P, T, \psi)$
3   $\Phi \leftarrow \emptyset$
4   **for** $z = 1$ to $|W|$ **do**
5   perform the zth task in W
6   **for** $\kappa = 1$ to $\lceil \frac{2\psi}{v} \rceil + 2$ **do**
7   verify the zth task of each processor in set $S[\kappa]$
8           $\Phi \leftarrow \Phi \cup \{r : l$ is the zth task allocated to $r \in S[\kappa]$ and was not done$\}$
9   **end for**
10 **end for**

Fig. 6.4. Subroutine $Do\_Work\_and\_Verify$. Code for processor q

In the subroutine, W is an ordered list of tasks. We denote by W_i the value of W after the *end* of routine $Allocate\_Tasks$ of iteration i. Hence, W_i is an ordered list of tasks, all of them in T_{i-1}. This is needed to ensure that it is known the order in which a given processor is supposed to perform the tasks in its list W_i. That also allows us to ensure that all processors supervising a processor r verify the zth task allocated to r at the same time (and hence all find it either done or undone). Note also that to ensure that all correct processors finish the call to $Do\_Work\_and\_Verify$ at the same time, they all must be allocated the same number of tasks to perform.

Similarly, S is a sequence of sets $S[1], ..., S[\lceil \frac{2\psi}{v} \rceil + 2]$, each with at most v processors. We denote by S_i the value of S after the *end* of the routine $Allocate\_Processors$ of iteration i. These sets must also satisfy (in order for the same task to be verified at the same time by all the processors that do so) that the same processor r is in the same set $S_i[k]$ in all the processors that supervise r. Then, all the tasks of r will be verified at the same time in the kth iteration of the inner "for" loop.

Let us now look at the allocation of tasks. For iteration i, we impose that $\lceil n_{i-1}/p_{i-1} \rceil$ different tasks from T_{i-1} are allocated to each processor in P_{i-1} by subroutine $Allocate\_Tasks$, and that the number of processors allocated to execute two different tasks in T_{i-1} differs in at most one. Other than these, there are no other restrictions. For instance, if we enumerate the tasks in T_{i-1} from 1 to n_{i-1} and the processors in P_{i-1} from 1 to p_{i-1}, the qth processor could be allocated the tasks with numbers $((kp_{i-1} + q - 1) \mod n_{i-1}) + 1$, for $k = 0, ..., \lceil n_{i-1}/p_{i-1} \rceil - 1$.

We look now at the allocation of processors done in subroutine $Allocate\_Processors$, for iteration i. We require that at least $2\psi_{i-1} + 1$ processors supervise any other processor (to be able to use Lemma 6.13, stated later). A processor implicitly supervises itself. Then, any deterministic function that assigns at least $2\psi_{i-1}$ other processors to each processor in P_{i-1} so that each processor is supervised by at least other $2\psi_{i-1}$ processors is valid.

We also need to choose the sets S_{i-1} appropriately, as described above. All these could be done as follows. First, define a cyclic order in P_{i-1} and allocate to each processor the $2\psi_{i-1}$ processors that follow it in that order. Then, group the processors in sets of size v using the cyclic order and starting from some distinguished processor (e.g., the one with smallest PID). Number these sets from 1 to $\lceil p_{i-1}/v \rceil$. Each processor then gets assigned the sets that contain processors it has to supervise. To enforce that the same set is verified simultaneously, set number k is verified in the $(k \bmod (\lceil \frac{2\psi_{i-1}}{v} \rceil + 2)) + 1$st iteration of the inner loop. Since $2\psi_{i-1}$ adjacent processors can span at most $\lceil \frac{2\psi_{i-1}}{v} \rceil + 2$ sets (out of which at least $\lceil \frac{2\psi_{i-1}}{v} \rceil + 1$ have v processors each), there is a way to schedule the verification of all the sets.

$Checkpoint(q, P, \psi, \Phi)$:
1    $C \leftarrow$ the first $2\psi + 1$ processors in P with smallest PID
2   send set Φ to every processor in C
3   if $q \in C$ then
4   attempt to receive set Φ_w from each processor $w \in P$
5        $\Phi \leftarrow \{b : \text{processor } b \text{ is in at least } \psi + 1 \text{ received sets } F_w\}$
6   send Φ to every processor in P
7   else
8   idle for the rest of the step
9   attempt to receive set Φ_c from each processor $c \in C$
10       $\Phi \leftarrow \{b : \text{processor } b \text{ is in at least } \psi + 1 \text{ received sets } \Phi_c\}$
11   end if

Fig. 6.5. Subroutine $Checkpoint$. Code for processor q.

We now consider subroutine $Checkpoint$. Its code is detailed in Figure 6.5. We denote by C_i the value of C at the *end* of the assignment at line 1 of the code, of iteration i. The subroutine uses two communication rounds. At iteration i, first each processor q sends its set $\Phi_{i,q}$ (computed in the subroutine $Do\_Work\_and\_Verify$) to the processors in set C_i. Set C_i contains the first $2\psi_{i-1} + 1$ processors in P_{i-1} with the smallest PID. An elementary, but important, invariant of the algorithm is that set C_i is the same in all correct processors.

The processors in C_i attempt to receive all sets $\Phi_{i,q}$ from the processors in P_{i-1}. Note that a faulty processor b may not send its corresponding set $\Phi^{i,b}$ or send an erroneous set $\Phi_{i,b}$. That is allowed and no note is taken of it by the correct processors. Also, messages received from processors not in P_{i-1} are disregarded by the correct processors. Only those processors that are in at least $\psi_{i-1} + 1$ received sets from processors in P_{i-1} are considered faulty by the processors in set C_i. Then, the processors c in C_i send their updated sets $\Phi_{i,c}$ to the processors in P_{i-1}. Each processor q in P_{i-1} updates its set $\Phi_{i,q}$ by considering as faulty only the processors that are in at least $\psi_{i-1} + 1$

received sets from processors in C_i and obtains Φ_i. Since P_{i-1} contains at least $2\psi_{i-1} + 1$ processors, we have the following claim.

Lemma 6.13. *For an iteration i of an execution of algorithm Majority, if each processor in P_{i-1} is supervised by at least $2\psi_{i-1} + 1$ different processors in P_{i-1}, then after subroutine Checkpoint has been executed, the set Φ_i is the same for every correct processor in P_{i-1}, it only contains faulty processors, and all the tasks allocated to processors in $P_i \setminus \Phi_i$ have been performed.*

Proof. Assuming the correct processors do the supervision properly, if some correct processor q detects a faulty processor w, and includes w in $\Phi_{i,q}$ in the subroutine *Do_Work_and_Verify*, then all correct processors that supervise w also do so. Then, each correct processor in C_i receives at least $\psi_{i-1} + 1$ sets $\Phi_{i,q}$ containing w, since in any set of $2\psi_{i-1} + 1$ processors (including the set of processors that supervised w) at least $\psi_{i-1} + 1$ processors are correct. This also implies that the processors in P_{i-1} will receive at least $\psi_{i-1} + 1$ sets $\Phi_{i,c}$ containing w (even if the faulty processors b in C_i send erroneous sets $\Phi_{i,b}$). Hence processor w will be in the final set Φ_i of each correct processor. Note that if processor w is not faulty and the faulty processors b send erroneous sets $\Phi_{i,b}$ that include w, w will not be included in a set Φ_i of a correct processor since there will not be more than ψ_{i-1} sets $\Phi_{i,b}$ containing w. Since this is true for each processor $w \in P_{i-1}$, after the subroutine *Checkpoint* has been executed the set Φ_i is the same for every correct processor in P_{i-1}, and it only contains faulty processors. This implies that the processors in $P_{i-1} \setminus \Phi_i$ performed the tasks allocated to them correctly (otherwise they would not be in $P_{i-1} \setminus \Phi_i$ but in Φ_i). This completes the proof of the lemma. □

Lemma 6.15 below shows that algorithm *Majority* solves the *Do-All* problem efficiently when $f < p/2$. Here $f_b \leq f$ is the exact number of faulty processors in the execution of interest of the algorithm. This value can be much smaller, for a particular execution, than the upper bound f.

In the proof of Lemma 6.15 we use the following fact.

///**I am not convinced this applies here. Tell me more**///

Fact 6.14 *If in every stage of a synchronous algorithm α the work to be performed is evenly divided among the processors, then the total number of stages executed in algorithm α is bounded by $O(\log p)$.*

Lemma 6.15. *Algorithm Majority, can be used to solve Do-All$_{AB}(n, p, f)$ with known f, $f_b \leq f$ actual Byzantine failures, and v task verifications per processor per step, with total-work $S = O(n + nf/v + p(1 + f/p) \cdot \min\{f_b + 1, \log p\})$ and message complexity $M = O(p(f + 1) \cdot \min\{f_b + 1, \log p\})$.*

Proof. It can be shown by induction that after each iteration i of the while loop of the algorithm, each correct processor has the same values of T_i, P_i, and $\psi_i \leq f$ and that the tasks not in T_i have been executed. Specifically, based on Lemma 6.13, if the correct processors begin an iteration i with common values of P_{i-1}, T_{i-1} and ψ_{i-1}, it follows that the (remaining) correct processors conclude this iteration with common values of P_i, T_i and ψ_i. Of course, initially all processors have the same P_0, T_0 and ψ_0. If there is at least one correct processor, then each iteration has a set T_i of smaller size. This implies that the algorithm terminates with all tasks performed and at least one correct processor being aware of this.

As algorithm *Majority* fully divides the work in each iteration, $f < p/2$, and only the tasks of failed processors are performed again, it follows from Fact 6.14 that at most $O(\log p)$ iterations are required by algorithm *Majority*.

We are going to study separately those iterations i of the while loop in which $n_{i-1} \geq p_{i-1}$ from those in which $n_{i-1} < p_{i-1}$. Since we assume $p \leq n$, initially $n_0 \geq p_0$. Furthermore, it is easy to show that once (if ever) $n_{i-1} < p_{i-1}$, this holds until the end of the execution as follows. Since less than half the processors in P_{i-1} can fail, if $n_{i-1} < p_{i-1}/2$, clearly at the end of the iteration i $n_i < p_i$. Otherwise, if $p_{i-1} > n_{i-1} \geq p_{i-1}/2$, then any task is assigned to at most two processors, and at the end of the iteration n_i has been reduced to less than half. Then, we can consider both kind of iterations separately. Let us first consider iterations i of the while loop where $n_{i-1} \geq p_{i-1}$. Note that there is no such iteration in which more than $\lceil n/p \rceil$ tasks are allocated to any processor. This is so because initially $\lceil n/p \rceil$ tasks are allocated, and the number of failures required to have more than $\lceil n/p \rceil$ tasks in any other iteration is more than $p/2$. Hence, a faulty processor can force at most $\lceil n/p \rceil$ tasks to be redone. Thus, we have that at most $n + f_b\lceil n/p \rceil < 2n + f_b = O(n)$ work spent executing tasks in these iterations. Similarly, in the iterations i where $n_{i-1} < p_{i-1}$, one task is allocated to each processor. We have from above that the number of iterations is $O(\log p)$, and it can be trivially observed that there can be at most $f_b + 1$ iterations. Hence, at most $O(p \cdot \min\{f_b + 1, \log p\})$ work is spent executing tasks in this case. Hence, in both kinds of iterations the work incurred in executing tasks is $O(n + p \cdot \min\{f_b + 1, \log p\})$. Since for each task executed there is one call to the checkpoint subroutine (each such call takes constant time) and at most $\lceil \frac{2f}{v} \rceil + 2$ verifications, the work bound follows. Note that the work incurred after the exit conditions of the while loop are satisfied is $O(n)$ (see discussion on the exit conditions in the description of the algorithm).

For the message bound, we use a similar argument. There are $O(\min\{f_b + 1, \log p\})$ iterations, with one call to the checkpoint subroutine in each, and at most $2p(2f + 1)$ messages required in each checkpoint call. The message complexity bound follows. Note that no communication takes place after the exit conditions of the while loop are satisfied. $\square$

It is worth observing that in this case, communication helps improve work complexity.

Algorithm *Complete*

By combining the two cases considered by algorithms *Minority* and *Majority* for different ranges of f, we obtain an algorithm that efficiently solves the *Do-All* problem for the entire range of f. We refer to this algorithm as algorithm *Complete*. The correctness and the efficiency of algorithm *Complete* follows directly from the correctness and efficiency of algorithms *Minority* and *Majority*.

Theorem 6.16. *Algorithm Complete solves Do-All$_{A_B}(n, p, f)$ with f known, $f_b \leq f$ actual Byzantine failures, and v verifications per processor per step, with work $S = O(n + np/v + p \log p / \Lambda_{p,f_b})$ and no communication when $f = \Omega(p)$, and with work $S = O(n + nf/v + p(1 + f/v) \cdot \min\{f_b + 1, \log p\})$ and message complexity $M = O(p(f + 1) \cdot \min\{f_b + 1, \log p\})$ otherwise.*

6.3.2 Unknown Maximum Number of Failures

In this section we assume that all we know about the number of faulty processors is that $f < p$. Using Lemma 6.7 and Theorem 6.8 of Section 6.3.1. we obtain the following lower bound.

Lemma 6.17. *Any fault-free execution of an algorithm that solves Do-All$_{A_B}(n, p, f)$ with f unknown and with task verification, requires $\Omega(n/p + n/v)$ steps and has total-work $S = \Omega(n + np/v)$.*

Proof. Since all that is known about the number of failures is that $f < p$, any algorithm that solves the problem under these assumptions has to solve it for $f = p - 1$. Then, the result follows from Lemma 6.7 and Theorem 6.8. □

Note that the lower bound of Lemma 6.6 does not depend on the knowledge of f_b or f and is hence applicable to this case as well. Then, we have the following theorem.

Theorem 6.18. *Any algorithm that solves Do-All$_{A_B}(n, p, f)$ with f unknown, in the presence of $f_b \leq f$ Byzantine failures, and with task verification, has total-work $S = \Omega(n + np/v + p \log p / \Lambda_{p,f_b})$.*

Since f is unknown, a given algorithm must solve *Do-All* efficiently even for the case $f = p - 1$. Hence, if we use algorithm *Minority* assuming that $p = n - 1$, then Lemma 6.11 gives us an asymptotically matching upper bound on work for the setting that f is unknown. Taken together with the above lower bound result (Theorem 6.18), we conclude the following.

Corollary 6.19. *The total-work complexity of algorithm Minority for solving Do-All$_{A_B}(n, p, f)$ with f unknown, $f_b \leq f$ actual Byzantine failures, and with task verification, is $S = \Theta(n + np/v + p \log p / \Lambda_{p,f_b})$.*

6.4 Open Problems

In most cases we showed asymptotically matching upper and lower bound results. For the case where $f = o(p)$ and known, and task execution is verifiable, the upper bound, produced by the analysis of algorithm *Majority* is not tight. Obtaining tight bounds for this case is an interesting open question.

A promising research direction is to study the *Do-All* problem with Byzantine failures in the presence of asynchrony.

6.5 Chapter Notes

The presentation in this Chapter is based on a paper by Fernandez, Georgiou, Russell and Shvartsman [35]. This is the first and only paper to date to consider the *Do-All* problem under Byzantine processor failures both for message-passing and shared-memory settings.

Fact 6.14 used in the proof of Lemma 6.15 is an adaptation of Theorem 4 of [25]. Although the theorem is given for the crash failure model, the proof makes use of the fact that the work previously assigned to a correct processor is not re-performed (tasks of only crashed processors are executed again). This is also the case for the model considered in this chapter, as malicious nodes cannot undo already performed tasks and hence only the tasks not performed by malicious nodes need to be executed. More details can be obtained in [35].

The model of Byzantine processor failures was introduced by Lamport, Pease, and Shostak [78] in the context of the consensus problem (a set of processors must agree on a common value).

Fernandez, Georgiou, Lopez and Santos [34] considered an asynchronous distributed system formed by a master processor and a collection of p worker processors that can execute tasks on behalf of the master and that may act maliciously (i.e., workers are Byzantine) by deliberately returning fallacious results. The master decides on the correctness of the results by assigning the same task to several workers. The master is charge one work-unit for each tasked assigned to a worker. The goal is to have the master accept the correct value of the task with high probability and with the smallest possible amount of work. They explore two ways of bounding the number of faulty processors: (a) they consider a fixed bound $f < p/2$ on the maximum number of workers that may fail, and (b) a probability $q < 1/2$ of any processor to be faulty. They assume that f or q are known to the master processor. Furthermore, processors can be slow, and messages can get lost or arrive late; these assumptions are modeled by considering a probability d (which may depend on p) of the master receiving the reply from a given worker on time (d is known to the master processor).

Fernandez et al. demonstrated that it is possible to obtain high probability of correct acceptance with low work. In particular, by considering both mechanisms of bounding the number of malicious workers, they show lower bounds on the minimum amount of (expected) work required, so that any algorithm accepts the correct value with probability of success $1 - \varepsilon$, where $\varepsilon \ll 1$ (e.g., $1/p$). They also develop and analyze two algorithms, each using a different decision strategy, and show that both algorithms obtain the same probability of success $1 - \varepsilon$, and in doing so, they require similar upper bounds on the (expected) work. Furthermore, under certain conditions, these upper bounds are shown to be asymptotically optimal with respect to the lower bounds.

Konwar, Rajasekaran and Shvartsman [72] have studied an extension of the problem in which there are p workers and p tasks to be performed. The computational model considered is somewhat stronger than the one considered in [34], as they assume a synchronous system in which the result of a task assigned to a non-faulty worker is always received by the master on time. This enables them to obtain efficient algorithms even if the failure parameters f and p are unknown (in fact they efficiently estimate these parameters). More specifically, they consider a failure model where f-fraction, $0 < f < 1/2$, of the workers provide faulty results with probability $0 < q < 1/2$, given that the master has no a priori knowledge of the values of f and q. For this model they provide an algorithm that can estimate f and q with (ϵ, δ)-approximation, for any $0 < \delta < 1$ and $\epsilon > 0$. They also provide a randomized algorithm for detecting the faulty processors. A lower bound on the total-work complexity of performing p tasks correctly with high probability is shown. Finally, a randomized algorithm to perform p tasks with high probability is given with closely matching upper bound on total-work.

Asynchrony and Delay-Sensitive Bounds

COMMON impediments to effective coordination in distributed settings, as we have seen, include failures and asynchrony that manifest themselves, e.g., in disparate processor speeds and varying message latency. Fortunately, the *Do-All* problem can always be solved as long as at least one processor continues to make progress. In particular, assuming that initially there n tasks that need to be performed, and the tasks are known to all p processors, the problem can be solved by a communication-oblivious algorithm where each processor performs all tasks. Such a solution has total-work $S = O(n \cdot p)$, and either it requires no communication, or it cannot rely on communication because of very long delays. On the other hand, $\Omega(n)$ is the obvious lower bound on work; additionally we show in this chapter that a lower bound of $S = \Omega(n + p \log p)$ holds for any asynchronous algorithm for *Do-All*, no matter how small is the message delay. Therefore it is reasonable to have the goal that, given a non-trivial and non-negligible delay d, effective use of messaging should result in the decrease in work from the trivial upper bound of $S = O(n \cdot p)$ so that work becomes sub-quadratic in n and p.

Obtaining algorithmic efficiency in asynchronous models of computation is difficult. For an algorithm to be interesting, it must be better than the oblivious algorithm, in particular, it must have sub-quadratic work complexity. However, if messages can be delayed for a "long time", then the processors cannot coordinate their activities, leading to an immediate lower bound on work of $\Omega(n \cdot p)$. In particular, it is sufficient for messages to be delayed by $\Theta(n)$ time for this lower bound to hold. Algorithmic techniques for synchronous processors assume constant-time message delay. In general it is not clear how such algorithms can be adapted to deal with asynchrony. Thus it is interesting to develop algorithms that are correct for any pattern of asynchrony and failures (with at least one surviving processor), and whose work depends on the message latency upper bound, such that work increases gracefully as the latency grows. The quality of the algorithms can be assessed by comparing their work to the corresponding *delay-sensitive* lower bounds.

In this chapter our goal is to obtain complexity bounds for work-efficient message-passing algorithms for the *Do-All* problem. We require that the algorithms tolerate any pattern of processor crashes with at least one surviving processor. More significantly, we are interested in algorithms whose work degrades gracefully as a function of the worst case message delay d. Here the requirement is that work must be subquadratic in n and p as long as $d = o(n)$. Thus for our algorithms we aim to develop *delay-sensitive* analysis of work and message complexity. Noting again that work must be $\Omega(p \cdot n)$ for $d \geq n$, we give a comprehensive analysis for $d < n$, achieving substantially better work complexity.

Chapter structure.

We define the model of adversity and expand on complexity measures in Section 7.1. In Section 7.2 we develop a delay-sensitive lower bounds for *Do-All*. In Section 7.3 we deal with permutations and their combinatorial properties used in the algorithm analysis. In Section 7.4 we present and analyze a work-efficient asynchronous deterministic *Do-All* algorithm. In Section 7.5 we present and analyze two randomized and one deterministic algorithm that satisfy our efficiency criteria. We discuss open problems in Section 7.6.

7.1 Adversarial Model and Complexity

Processors communicate over a fully connected network by sending point-to-point messages via reliable asynchronous channels. When a processor sends a message to a group of processors, we call it a multicast message, however in the analysis we treat a multicast message as multiple point-to-point messages. Messages are subject to delays, but are not corrupted or lost.

We assume an omniscient (on-line) adversary that introduces delays. We call this adversary $\mathcal{A}_D$. The adversary can introduce arbitrary delays between local processor steps and cause processor crashes (crashes can be viewed as infinite delays). The only restriction is that at least one processor is non-faulty. Adversary $\mathcal{A}_D$ also causes arbitrary message delays.

We specialize adversary $\mathcal{A}_D$ by imposing a constraint on message delays. We assume the existence of a global real-timed clock that is unknown to the processors. For convenience we measure time in terms of units that represent the smallest possible time between consecutive clock-ticks of any processor. We define the delay-constrained adversary as follows. We assume that there exists an integer parameter d, that is not assumed to be a constant and that is *unknown* to the processors, such that messages are delayed by at most d time units. We call this adversary $\mathcal{A}_D^{(d)}$. It is easy to see that $\mathcal{A}_D^{(d)} \subseteq \mathcal{A}_D^{(d+1)}$ for any $d \geq 0$, because increasing the maximum delays introduces new adversarial behaviors. We also note that $\mathcal{A}_D = \bigcup_{d \in \mathbb{N}} \mathcal{A}_D^{(d)}$.

In this chapter we are interested in algorithms that are correct against adversary $\mathcal{A}_D$, i.e., for any message delays. For the purpose of analysis of such algorithms, we are interested in complexity analysis under adversary $\mathcal{A}_D^{(d)}$, for some specific positive d that is unknown to the algorithm. Note that by the choice of the time units, a processor can take at most d local steps during any global time period of duration d.

For an algorithm A, let $\mathcal{E} = \mathcal{E}(A, \mathcal{A}_D^{(d)})$ be the set of all executions of the algorithm in our model of computation subject to adversary $\mathcal{A}_D^{(d)}$. For the purposes of this chapter, we define the *weight* of an adversarial pattern to be the *maximum delay incurred by any message*. Thus, for any execution $\xi \in \mathcal{E}$, the maximum weight of the adversarial pattern $\xi|_{\mathcal{A}_D^{(d)}}$ is d, that is $||\xi|_{\mathcal{A}_D^{(d)}}|| \leq d$.

We assess the efficiency of algorithms in terms of total-work (Definition 2.4) and message complexity (Definition 2.6) under adversary $\mathcal{A}_D^{(d)}$. We use the notation $S(n, p, d)$ to denote work, and $M(n, p, d)$ to denote message complexity. Expected work and message complexity are denoted by $ES(n, p, d)$ and $EM(n, p, d)$ respectively.

When work or messages complexities do not depend d we omit d and use, for example, $S(n, p)$ and $M(n, p)$ for work and message complexity (and $ES(n, p)$ and $EM(n, p)$ for expected work and message complexity).

Next we formulate a proposition leading us to not consider algorithms where a processor may halt voluntarily before learning that all tasks have been performed.

Proposition 7.1. *Let Alg be a Do-All algorithm such that there is some execution ξ of Alg in which there is a processor that (voluntarily) halts before it learns that all tasks have been performed. Then there is an execution ξ' of Alg with unbounded work in which some task is never performed.*

Proof. For the proof we assume a stronger model of computation where in one local step any processor can learn the complete state of another processor, including, in particular, the complete computation history of the other processor. Assume that, in some execution ξ, the *Do-All* problem is solved, but some processor i halts in ξ without learning the a certain task z was performed. First we observe that for any other processor j that i learns about in ξ, j does not perform task z by the time i learns j's state. (Otherwise i would know that z was performed.) We construct another execution ξ' from ξ as follows. Any processor j (except for i) proceeds as in ξ until it attempts to perform task z. Then j is delayed forever. We show that processor i can proceed exactly as in ξ. We claim that i is not able to distinguish between ξ and ξ'. Consider the histories of all processors that i learned about in ξ' (directly or indirectly). None of the histories contain information about task z being performed. Thus the history of any processor j was recorded in advance of j's delay in ξ'. Then by the definition of ξ' these histories are identical to those in ξ. This means that in ξ' processor i halts as in ξ. Since the problem remains unsolved, processor i continues to be charged for each local clock tick (recall that work is charged until the problem is solved).   □

As the result of Proposition 7.1, we will only consider algorithms where a processor may voluntarily halt only after it knows that all tasks are complete, i.e., for each task the processor has local knowledge that either it performed the task or that some other processor did.

Note that for large message delays the work of any *Do-All* algorithm is necessarily $\Omega(n \cdot p)$. The following proposition formalizes this lower bound and motivates our delay-sensitive approach.

Proposition 7.2. *Any algorithm that solves the Do-All problem in the presence of adversary* $\mathcal{A}_D^{(c \cdot n)}$, *for a constant* $c > 0$, *has work* $S(n,p) = \Omega(n \cdot p)$.

Proof. We choose the adversary that delays each message by $c \cdot n$ time units, and does not delay any processor. If a processor halts voluntarily before learning that all tasks are complete, then by Proposition 7.1 work may be unbounded. Assume then that no processor halts voluntarily until it learns that all tasks are done. A processor may learn this either by performing all the tasks by itself and contributing n to the work of the system, or by receiving information from other processors by waiting for messages for $c \cdot n$ time steps. In either case the contribution is $\Omega(n)$ to the work of the algorithm. Since there are p processors, the work is $\Omega(n \cdot p)$.   □

Lastly we note that since in this chapter we are trading communication for work, we design algorithms with the focus on work.

7.2 Delay-Sensitive Lower Bounds on Work

In this section we develop delay-sensitive lower bounds for asynchronous algorithms for the *Do-All* problem. for deterministic and randomized algorithms. We show that any deterministic (randomized) algorithm with p asynchronous processors and n tasks has worst-case total-work (respectively expected total-work) of $\Omega(n + p\,d \log_{d+1} n)$ under adversary $\mathcal{A}_D^{(d)}$, where d is the upper bound on message delay (unknown to the processors). This shows that work grows with d and becomes $\Omega(p\,n)$ as d approaches n.

We start by showing that the lower bound on work of $\Omega(n + p \log p)$ from Theorem 5.2 for the model with crashes and restarts also applies to the asynchronous model of computation, regardless of the delay. Note that the explicit construction in the proof below shows that the same bound holds in the asynchronous setting where no processor crashes.

Theorem 7.3. *Any asynchronous p-processor algorithm solving the Do-All problem on inputs of size n has total-work $S(n,p) = n + \Omega(p \log p)$.*

Proof. We present a strategy for the adversary that results in the worst case behavior. Let A be the best possible algorithm that solves the *Do-All* problem. The adversary imposes delays on the processor steps (regardless of what the message delay is) as described below:

Stage 1: Let $u > 1$ be the number of remaining tasks. Initially $u = n$. The adversary induces no delays as long as the number of remaining tasks, u, is more than p. The work needed to perform $n - p$ tasks when there are no delays is at least $n - p$.

Stage 2: As soon as a processor is about to perform some task $n - p + 1$ making $u \leq p$, the adversary uses the following strategy. For the upcoming iteration, the adversary examines the algorithm to determine how the processors are assigned to the remaining tasks. The adversary then lists the remaining tasks with respect to the number of processors assigned to them. The adversary delays the processors assigned to the first half remaining tasks ($\lfloor \frac{u}{2} \rfloor$) with the least number of processors assigned to them. By an averaging argument, there are no more than $\lceil \frac{p}{2} \rceil$ processors assigned to these $\lfloor \frac{u}{2} \rfloor$ tasks. Hence at least $\lfloor \frac{p}{2} \rfloor$ processors will complete this iteration having performed no more than half of the remaining tasks.

The adversary continues this strategy which results in performing at most half of the remaining tasks at each iteration. Since initially $u = p$ in this stage, the adversary can continue this strategy for at least $\log p$ iterations. Considering these two stages the work performed by the algorithm is:

$$S(n, p) \geq \underbrace{n - p}_{\text{Stage 1}} + \underbrace{\lfloor p/2 \rfloor \log p}_{\text{Stage 2}} = n + \Omega(p \log p). \qquad \square$$

The above lower bound holds for arbitrarily small delays. We next develop a lower bound for the settings where the delay is non-negligible, specifically we assume $d \geq 1$.

7.2.1 Deterministic Delay-Sensitive Lower Bound

First we prove a lower bound on work that shows how the efficiency of work-performing deterministic algorithms depends on the number of processors p, the number of tasks n, and the message delay d.

Theorem 7.4. *Any deterministic algorithm solving Do-All with n tasks using p asynchronous message-passing processors against adversary $\mathcal{A}_D^{(d)}$ performs work $S(n, p, d) = \Omega(n + p \min\{d, n\} \log_{d+1}(d + n))$.*

Proof. That the required work is at least n is obvious — each task must be performed. We present the analysis for $n > 5$ and n that is divisible by 6 (this is sufficient to prove the lower bound). We present the following adversarial strategy. The adversary partitions computation into stages, each containing $\min\{d, n/6\}$ steps. We assume that the adversary delivers all messages sent to a processor in stage s at the end of stage s (recall that the receiver can process any such message later, according to its own local clock) — this is allowed since the length of stage s is at most d. For stage s we will define the set of processors P_s such that the adversary delays all processors not in P_s. More precisely, each processor in P_s is not delayed during stage s, but any processor not in P_s is delayed so it does not complete any step during stage s.

Consider stage s. Let $u_s > 0$ be the number of tasks that remain unperformed at the beginning of stage s, and let U_s be the set of such tasks. We now show how to define the set P_s. Suppose first that each processor is not delayed during stage s (with respect to the time unit). Let $J_s(i)$, for every processor i, $i \in \mathcal{P}$ (recall that $\mathcal{P}$ is the set of all processors), denote the set of tasks from U_s (we do not consider tasks not in U_s in the analysis of stage s since they performed before) which are performed by processor i during stage s (recall that inside stage s processor i does not receive any message from other processors, by the assumption on consider kind of the adversary). Note that $|J_s(i)|$ is at most $\min\{d, n/6\}$, which is the length of a stage.

Claim. There are at least $\frac{u_s}{3\min\{d, n/6\}}$ tasks z such that each of them is contained in at most $2p\min\{d, n/6\}/u_s$ sets in the family $\{J_s(i) \mid i \in \mathcal{P}\}$.

We prove the claim by the pigeonhole principle. If the claim is not true, then there would be more than $u_s - \frac{u_s}{3\min\{d, t/6\}}$ tasks such that each of them would be contained in more than $2p\min\{d, n/6\}/u_s$ sets in the family $\{J_s(i) \mid i \in \mathcal{P}\}$. This yields a contradiction because the following inequality holds

$$
\begin{aligned}
p \min\{d, n/6\} &= \sum_{i \in \mathcal{P}} |J_s(i)| \\
&\geq \left(u_s - \frac{u_s}{3\min\{d, n/6\}}\right) \cdot \frac{2p\min\{d, n/6\}}{u_s} \\
&= \left(2 - \frac{2}{3\min\{d, n/6\}}\right) \cdot p\min\{d, n/6\} \\
&> p \min\{d, n/6\} \,,
\end{aligned}
$$

since $d \geq 1$ and $n > 4$. This proves the claim.

We denote the set of $\frac{u_s}{3\min\{d, n/6\}}$ tasks from the above claim by J_s. We define P_s to be the set $\{i : J_s \cap J_s(i) = \emptyset\}$. By the definition of tasks $z \in J_s$ we obtain that

$$
|P_s| \geq p - \frac{u_s}{3\min\{d, n/6\}} \cdot \frac{2p\min\{d, n/6\}}{u_s} \geq p/3 \,.
$$

Since all processors, other that those in P_s, are delayed during the whole stage s, work performed during stage s is at least $\frac{p}{3} \cdot \min\{d, n/6\}$, and all tasks from J_s remains unperformed. Hence the number u_{s+1} of undone tasks after stage s is still at least $\frac{u_s}{3\min\{d, n/6\}}$.

If $d < n/6$ then work during stage s is at least $p\,d/6$, and there remain at least $\frac{u_s}{3d}$ unperformed tasks. Hence this process may be continued, starting with n tasks, for at least $\log_{3d} n = \Omega(\log_{d+1}(d+n))$ stages, until all tasks are performed. The total work is then $\Omega(p\,d\log_{d+1}(d+n))$.

If $d \geq n/6$ then during the first stage work performed is at least $p\,n/18 = \Omega(p\,n\log_{d+1}(d+n)) = \Omega(p\,n)$, and at the end of stage 1 at least $\frac{n}{3n/6} = 2$ tasks remain unperformed. Notice that this asymptotic value does not depend on whether the minimum is selected among d and n, or among d and $n/6$. More precisely, the works is

$$\Omega(p\min\{d,n\}\log_{d+1}(d+n)) = \Omega(p\min\{d,n/6\}\log_{d+1}(d+n)),$$

which completes the proof. $\square$

7.2.2 Delay-sensitive Lower Bound for Randomized Algorithms

In this section we prove a delay-sensitive lower bound for randomized work-performing algorithms. We first state a technical lemma (without a proof) that we put to use in the lower bound proof.

Lemma 7.5. *For* $1 \leq d \leq \sqrt{u}$ *the following holds* $\dfrac{1}{4} \leq \dfrac{\binom{u-d}{u/(d+1)}}{\binom{u}{u/(d+1)}} \leq \dfrac{1}{e}$.

The idea behind the lower bound proof for randomized algorithms we present below is similar to the one for deterministic algorithms in the previous section, except that sets $J_s(i)$ are random, hence we have to modify the construction of set P_s also. We partition the execution of the algorithms into stages, similarly to the lower bound for deterministic algorithms. Recall that $\mathcal{P}$ is the set of p processors. Let U_s denote the remaining tasks at the beginning of stage s. Suppose first that all processors are not delayed during stage s, and the adversary delivers all messages sent to processor i during stage s at the end of stage s. The set $J_s(i)$, for processor $i \in \mathcal{P}$, denotes a certain set of tasks from U_s that i is going to perform during stage s. The size of $J_s(i)$ is at most d, because we consider at most d steps in advance (the adversary may delay all messages by d time steps, and so the choice of $J_s(i)$ does not change during next d steps, provided $|J_s(i)| \leq d$). The key point is that the set $J_s(i)$ is random, since we consider randomized algorithms, and so we deal with the probabilities that $J_s(i) = Y$ for the set of tasks $Y \subseteq U_s$ of size at most d. We denote these probabilities by $p_i(Y)$. For some given set of processors P, let $J_s(P)$ denote set $\bigcup_{i \in P} J_s(i)$.

The goal of the adversary is to prevent the processors from completing some sufficiently large set J_s of tasks during stage s. Here we are interested in the events where there is a set of processors P_s that is "large enough" (linear size) so that the processors do not perform any tasks from J_s.

In the next lemma we prove that, for some set J_s, such set of processors P_s exists with high probability. This is the main difference compared to the deterministic lower bound — instead of finding a suitably large set J_s *and a* linear-size set P_s, we prove that the set J_s exists, and we prove that the set P_s of processors not performing this set of tasks during stage s *exists with high probability*. However in the final proof, the existence with high probability is sufficient — we can define the set on-line using the rule that if some processor wants to perform a task from the chosen set J_s, then we delay it, and do not put it in P_s. In the next lemma we assume that s is known, so we skip lower index s from the notation for clarity of presentation.

Lemma 7.6. *There exists set $J \subseteq U$ of size $\frac{u}{d+1}$ such that*

$$\Pr[\exists_{P \subseteq \mathcal{P}} : |P| = p/64 \ \wedge \ J(P) \cap J = \emptyset] \geq 1 - e^{-p/512} .$$

Proof. First observe that

$$\sum_{\left(J:\ J \subseteq U,\ |J| = \frac{u}{d+1}\right)} \ \sum_{(v \in \mathcal{P})} \ \sum_{(Y:\ Y \subseteq U,\ Y \cap J = \emptyset,\ |Y| \leq d)} p_v(Y) \ =$$

$$= \sum_{(v \in \mathcal{P})} \ \sum_{(Y:\ Y \subseteq U,\ |Y| \leq d)} p_v(Y) \cdot \binom{u - |Y|}{u/(d+1)}$$

$$\geq \ p \cdot \binom{u - d}{u/(d+1)} .$$

It follows that there exists set $J \subseteq U$ of size $\frac{u}{d+1}$ such that

$$\sum_{(v \in \mathcal{P})} \ \sum_{(Y:\ Y \subseteq U,\ Y \cap J = \emptyset,\ |Y| \leq d)} p_v(Y) \geq \frac{p \cdot \binom{u-d}{u/(d+1)}}{\binom{u}{u/(d+1)}} \geq \frac{p}{4} , \tag{7.1}$$

where the last inequality follows from Lemma 7.5. Fix such a set J. For every node $v \in \mathcal{P}$, let

$$Q_v = \sum_{(Y:\ Y \subseteq U,\ Y \cap J = \emptyset,\ |Y| \leq d)} p_v(Y) .$$

Notice that $Q_v \leq 1$. Using the pigeonhole principle to Inequality 7.1, there is a set $V' \subseteq \mathcal{P}$ of size $p/8$ such that for every $v \in V'$

$$Q_v \geq \frac{1}{8} .$$

(Otherwise more than $7p/8$ nodes $v \in \mathcal{P}$ would have $Q_v < 1/8$, and fewer than $p/8$ nodes $v \in \mathcal{P}$ would have $Q_v \leq 1$. Consequently $\sum_{v \in \mathcal{P}} S_v < 7p/64 + p/8 < p/4$, which would contradict (7.1)). For every $v \in V'$, let X_v be the random variable equal 1 with probability Q_v, and 0 with probability $1 - Q_v$. These random variables constitute sequence of independent 0-1 trials. Let $\mu = \mathbb{E}[\sum_{v \in V'} X_v] = \sum_{v \in V'} Q_v$. Applying Chernoff bound we obtain

$$\Pr\left[\sum_{v \in V'} X_v < \mu/2\right] < e^{-\mu/8} ,$$

and consequently, since $\mu \geq \frac{p}{8} \cdot \frac{1}{8} = \frac{p}{64}$, we have

$$\Pr\left[\sum_{v\in V'} X_v < p/64\right] \leq \Pr\left[\sum_{v\in V'} X_v < \mu/2\right]$$
$$< e^{-\mu/8} \leq e^{-p/512}.$$

Finally observe that

$$\Pr\left[\exists_{P\subseteq \mathcal{P}} : |P| = p/64 \ \wedge\ J(P)\cap J = \emptyset\right]$$

$$\geq 1 - \Pr\left[\sum_{v\in V'} X_v < p/64\right],$$

which completes the proof of the lemma.   □

We apply Lemma 7.6 in proving the following lower bound result.

Theorem 7.7. *Any randomized algorithm solving Do-All with n tasks using p asynchronous message-passing processors against adversary $\mathcal{A}_D^{(d)}$ performs expected work $ES(n, p, d) = \Omega(n + p\min\{d, n\}\log_{d+1}(d + n))$.*

Proof. That the lower bound of $\Omega(t)$ holds with probability 1 is obvious. We consider three cases, depending on how large is d comparing to n: in the first case d is very small comparing to n (in this case the thesis follows from the simple calculations), in the second case we assume that d is larger than in the first, but still no more than $\sqrt{n}$ (this is the main case), and in the third case d is large than $\sqrt{n}$ (here the proof is similar to the second case, but is restricted to one stage). We now give the details.

Case 1: Inequalities $1 \leq d \leq \sqrt{n}$ and $1 - e^{-p/512} \cdot \log_{d+1} n < 1/2$ hold.

This case is a simple derivation. It follows that $\log_{d+1} n > e^{p/512}/2$, and next $\sqrt[3]{n} > p + d + \log_{d+1} n$ for sufficiently large p and n. More precisely:

$\sqrt[3]{n} > 3p$ for sufficiently large p, since $n > \log_{d+1} n > e^{p/512}$;

$\sqrt[3]{n} > 3d$ for sufficiently large p, since $d^{e^{p/512}/2} < n$;

$\sqrt[3]{n} > 3\log_{d+1} n$ for sufficiently large n, since $d \geq 1$ and by the properties of the logarithm function.

Consequently, $n = (\sqrt[3]{n})^3 > pd\log_{d+1} n$ for sufficiently large p and n, and the lower bound

$$\Omega(n) = \Omega(p\,d\log_{d+1} n) = \Omega(p\,d\log_{d+1}(d + n))$$

holds, with the probability 1, in this case.

Case 2: Inequalities $1 \leq d \leq \sqrt{n}$ and $1 - e^{-p/512} \cdot \log_{d+1} n \geq 1/2$ hold.

Consider any *Do-All* algorithm. Similarly as in the proof of Theorem 7.4, the adversary partitions computation into stages, each containing d steps.

Let us fix an execution of the algorithm through the end of stage $s - 1$. Consider stage s. We assume that the adversary delivers to a processor all messages sent in stage s at the end of stage s, provided the processor is not delayed at the end of stage s (any such message is processed by the receivers at a later time). Let $U_s \subseteq T$ denote set of tasks that remain unperformed by the end of stage $s-1$. Here, by the adversarial strategy (no message is received and processed during stage s), given that the execution is fixed at the end of stage $s - 1$, one can fix a distribution of processor i performing the set of tasks Y during stage s — this distribution is given by the probabilities $p_i(Y)$. The adversary derives the set $J_s \subseteq U_s$, using Lemma 7.6 according to the set of all processors, the set of the unperformed tasks U_s, and the distributions $p_i(Y)$ fixed at the beginning of stage s according to the action of processors i in stage s. (In applying Lemma 7.6 we use the same notation, except that the quantities are subscripted according to the stage number s.)

The adversary additionally delays any processor i, not belonging to some set P_s, that attempts to perform a task from J_s before the end of stage s. The set P_s is defined on-line (this is one of the difference between the adversarial constructions in the proofs of the lower bounds for deterministic and randomized Do-All algorithms): at the beginning of stage s set P_s contains all processors; every processor i that is going to perform some task $z \in J_s$ at time τ in stage s, is delayed till the end of stage s and removed from set P_s. We illustrate the adversarial strategy for five processors and $d = 5$ in Figure 7.1.

We now give additional details of the adversarial strategy. Suppose $u_s = |U_s| > 0$ tasks remain unperformed at the beginning of stage s. As described above, we apply Lemma 7.6 to the set U_s and probabilities $p_i(Y)$ to find, at the very beginning of stage s, the set $J_s \subseteq U_s$ such that the probability that there exists a subset of processors P_s of cardinality $p/64$ such that none of them would perform any tasks from J_s during stage s is at least $1 - e^{-p/512}$. Next, during stage s the adversary delays (to the end of stage s) all processors that (according to the random choices during stage s) are going to perform some task from J_s. By Lemma 7.6, the set P_s of not-delayed processors contains at least $p - 63p/64 \geq p/64$ processors, and the set of the remaining tasks $U_{s+1} \supseteq J_s$ contains at least $\frac{u_s}{d+1}$ tasks, all with probability at least $1 - e^{-p/512}$. If this happens, we call stage s *successful*.

It follows that the probability, that every stage $s < \log_{d+1} n$ is successful is at least $1 - e^{-p/512} \cdot \log_{d+1} n$. Hence, using the assumption for this case, with the probability at least $1 - e^{-p/512} \cdot \log_{d+1} n \geq 1/2$, at the beginning of stage s there will be at least $n \cdot \left(\frac{1}{d+1}\right)^{\log_{d+1} n - 1} > 1$ unperformed tasks and work will be at least $(\log_{d+1} n - 1) \cdot dp/64$, since the work in one successful stage is at least $p/64$ (the number of non-delayed processors) times d (the duration of one stage). It follows that the expected work of this algorithm in the presence of our adversary is $\Omega(pd \log_{d+1} n) = \Omega(pd \log_{d+1}(d + n))$, because $1 \leq d \leq \sqrt{n}$. This completes the proof of Case 2.

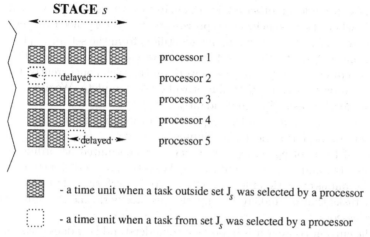

STAGE s

processor 1

delayed

processor 2

processor 3

processor 4

delayed

processor 5

▨ - a time unit when a task outside set J_s was selected by a processor

▢ - a time unit when a task from set J_s was selected by a processor

Strategy of the adversary during stage s, where $p = d = 5$. Using the set J_s, which exists by Lemma 7.6, the adversary delays a processor from the moment where it wants to perform a task from J_s. Lemma 7.6 guarantees that at least a fraction of processors will not be delayed during stage s, with high probability.

Fig. 7.1. Illustration of the adversarial strategy leading to the delay-sensitive lower bound on total-work for randomized algorithms.

Case 3: Inequality $d > \sqrt{t}$ holds.

Here we follow similar reasoning as in the Case 2, except that we consider a single stage.

Consider first $\min\{d, n/6\}$ steps. Let T be the set of all tasks, and $p_i(Y)$ denote the probability that processor $i \in \mathcal{P}$ performs tasks in $Y \subseteq T$ of cardinality $\min\{d, n/6\}$ during the considered steps. Applying Lemma 7.6 we obtain, that at least $p/64$ processors are non-delayed during the considered steps, and after these steps at least $\frac{\min\{d, n/6\}}{d+1} \geq 1$ tasks remain unperformed, all with the probability at least $1 - e^{-p/512}$. Since $1 \leq \log_{d+1}(d+n) < 2$, work is $\Omega(p \min\{d, n/6\}) = \Omega(p \min\{d, n\} \log_{d+1}(d+n))$. This completes the proof of the third case and of the theorem. □

7.3 Contention of Permutations

In this section we present and generalize the notion of *contention* of permutations, and state several properties of contention (without proofs). Contention properties turn out to be important in the analysis of algorithms we present later in this chapter.

We use braces $\langle \ldots \rangle$ to denote an ordered list. For a list L and an element a, we use the expression $a \in L$ to denote the element's membership in the list, and the expression $L - K$ to stand for L with all elements in K removed.

We next provide a motivation for the material in this section. Consider the situation where two asynchronous processors, $\mathfrak{p}_1$ and $\mathfrak{p}_2$, need to perform n independent tasks with known unique identifiers from the set $[n] = \{1, \ldots, n\}$. Assume that before starting a task, a processor can check whether the task is complete; however if both processors work on the task concurrently, then the task is done twice because both find it to be not complete. We are interested in the number of tasks done redundantly.

Let $\pi_1 = \langle a_1, \ldots, a_n \rangle$ be the sequence of tasks giving the order in which $\mathfrak{p}_1$ intends to perform the tasks. Similarly, let $\pi_2 = \langle a_{s_1}, \ldots, a_{s_n} \rangle$ be the sequence of tasks of $\mathfrak{p}_2$. We can view π_2 as π_1 permuted according to $\sigma = \langle s_1, \ldots, s_t \rangle$ (π_1 and π_2 are permutations). With this, it is possible to construct an asynchronous execution for $\mathfrak{p}_1$ and $\mathfrak{p}_2$, where $\mathfrak{p}_1$ performs all t tasks by itself, and any tasks that $\mathfrak{p}_2$ finds to be unperformed are performed redundantly by both processors.

In the current context it is important to understand how does the structure of π_2 affect the number of redundant tasks. Clearly $\mathfrak{p}_2$ may have to perform task a_{s_1} redundantly. What about a_{s_2}? If $s_1 > s_2$ then by the time $\mathfrak{p}_2$ gets to task a_{s_2}, it is already done by $\mathfrak{p}_1$ according to π_1. Thus, in order for a_{s_2} to be done redundantly, it must be the case that $s_2 > s_1$. It is easy to see, in general, that for task a_{s_j} to be done redundantly, it must be the case that $s_j > \max\{s_1, \ldots, s_{j-1}\}$. Such s_j is called the *left-to-right maximum* of σ. The total number of tasks done redundantly by $\mathfrak{p}_2$ is thus the number of left-to-right maxima of σ. Not surprisingly, this number is minimized when $\sigma = \langle n, \ldots, 1 \rangle$, i.e, when π_2 is the reverse order of π_1, and it is maximized when $\sigma = \langle 1, \ldots, n \rangle$, i.e., when $\pi_1 = \pi_2$. In this section we will define the notion *contention* of permutations that captures the relevant left-to-right maxima properties of permutations that are to be used as processor schedules.

Now we proceed with formal presentation. Consider a list of some idempotent computational *jobs* with identifiers from the set $[n] = \{1, \ldots, n\}$. (We make the distinction between *tasks* and *jobs* for convenience to simplify algorithm analysis; a job may be composed of one or more tasks.) We refer to a list of job identifiers as a *schedule*. When a schedule for n jobs is a permutation of job identifiers π in $\mathcal{S}_n$, we call it a *n-schedule*. Here $\mathcal{S}_n$ is the symmetric group, the group of all permutations on the set $[n]$; we use the symbol $\circ$ to denote the composition operator, and $\mathbf{e}_n$ to denote the identity permutation. For a n-schedule $\pi = \langle \pi(1), \ldots, \pi(n) \rangle$ a *left-to-right maximum* is an element $\pi(j)$ of π that is larger than all of its predecessors, i.e., $\pi(j) > \max_{i<j}\{\pi(j-i)\}$.

Given a n-schedule π, we define $\mathrm{LRM}(\pi)$, to be the number of left-to-right maxima in the n-schedule π. For a list of permutations $\Psi = \langle \pi_0, \ldots, \pi_{n-1} \rangle$ from $\mathcal{S}_n$ and a permutation δ in $\mathcal{S}_n$, the *contention* of Ψ with respect to δ is defined as $\mathrm{Cont}(\Psi, \delta) = \sum_{u=0}^{n-1} \mathrm{LRM}(\delta^{-1} \circ \pi_u)$. The *contention of the list of schedules* Ψ is defined as $\mathrm{Cont}(\Psi) = \max_{\delta \in \mathcal{S}_n}\{\mathrm{Cont}(\Psi, \delta)\}$. Note that for any Ψ, we have $n \leq \mathrm{Cont}(\Psi) \leq n^2$. It turns out that it is possible to construct a family of permutations with following low contention (H_n is the nth harmonic number, $H_n = \sum_{j=1}^{n} \frac{1}{j}$).

Lemma 7.8. *For any* $n > 0$ *there exists a list of permutations* $\Psi = \langle \pi_0, \ldots, \pi_{n-1} \rangle$ *with* $\text{Cont}(\Psi) \leq 3nH_n = \Theta(n \log n)$.

For a constant n, a list Ψ with $\text{Cont}(\Psi) \leq 3nH_n$ can be found by exhaustive search. This costs only a constant number of operations on integers (however, this cost might be of order $(n!)^n$).

7.3.1 Contention and Oblivious Tasks Scheduling

Assume now that n distinct asynchronous processors perform the n jobs such that processor i performs the jobs in the order given by π_i in Ψ. We call this oblivious algorithm OBLIDO and give the code in Figure 7.2. (Here each "processor" may be modeling a group of processors, where each processor follows the same sequence of activities.)

```
00 const Ψ = {π_r | 1 ≤ r ≤ n ∧ π_r ∈ S_n}    % Fixed set of n permutations of [n]
01 for each processor PID = 1..n begin
02    for r = 1 to n do
03         perform Job(π_pid(r))
04    od
05 end.
```

Fig. 7.2. Algorithm OBLIDO.

Since OBLIDO does not involve any coordination among the processors the total of n^2 jobs are performed (counting multiplicities). However, it can be shown that if we count only the job executions such that each job has not been previously performed by any processor, then the total number of such job executions is bounded by $\text{Cont}(\Psi)$, again counting multiplicities. We call such job executions *primary*; we also call all other job executions *secondary*. Note that the number of primary executions cannot be smaller than n, since each job is performed at least once for the first time. In general this number is going to be between n and n^2, because several processors may be executing the same job concurrently for the first time.

Note that while an algorithm solving the *Do-All* problem may attempt to reduce the number of secondary job executions by sharing information about complete jobs among the processors, it is not possible to eliminate (redundant) primary job executions in the asynchronous model we consider. The following lemma formalizes the relationship between the primary job executions and the contention of permutations used as schedules.

Lemma 7.9. *In algorithm* OBLIDO *with* n *processors,* n *tasks, and using the list* Ψ *of* n *permutations, the number of primary job executions is at most* $\text{Cont}(\Psi)$.

7.3.2 Generalized Contention

Now we generalize the notion of contention and define *d-contention*. For a schedule $\pi = \langle \pi(1), \ldots, \pi(n) \rangle$, an element $\pi(j)$ of π is a *d-left-to-right maximum* (or *d-lrm* for short) if the number the elements in π preceding and greater than $\pi(j)$ is less than d, i.e., $|\{i : i < j \wedge \pi(i) > \pi(j)\}| < d$.

Given a n-schedule π, we define (d)-LRM(π) as the number of d-lrm's in the schedule π. For a list $\Psi = \langle \pi_0, \ldots, \pi_{p-1} \rangle$ of permutations from $\mathcal{S}_n$ and a permutation δ in $\mathcal{S}_n$, the d-contention of Ψ with respect to δ is defined as

$$(d)\text{-Cont}(\Psi, \delta) = \sum_{u=0}^{p-1} (d)\text{-LRM}(\delta^{-1} \circ \pi_u) .$$

The *d-contention of the list of schedules* Ψ is defined as

$$(d)\text{-Cont}(\Psi) = \max_{\delta \in \mathcal{S}_n} \{(d)\text{-Cont}(\Psi, \delta)\} .$$

We first show a lemma about the d-contention of a set of permutations with respect to $\mathbf{e}_n$, the identity permutation.

Lemma 7.10. *Let Ψ be a list of p random permutations from $\mathcal{S}_n$. For every fixed positive integer d, the probability that (d)-Cont$(\Psi, \mathbf{e}_n) > n \ln n + 8pd \ln(e + n/d)$ is at most $e^{-\left(n \ln n + 7pd \ln(e + \frac{n}{3d})\right) \ln(7/e)}$.*

Proof. For $d \geq n/5$ the thesis is obvious. In the remainder of the proof we assume $d < n/5$.

First we describe a well known method for generating a random schedule by induction on the number of elements $n' \leq n$ to be permuted. For $n' = 1$ the schedule consists of a single element chosen uniformly at random. Suppose we can generate a random schedule of $n' - 1$ different elements. Now we show how to schedule n' elements uniformly and independently at random. First we choose uniformly and independently at random one element among n' and put it as the last element in the schedule. By induction we generate random schedule from remaining $n' - 1$ elements and put them as the first $n' - 1$ elements. Simple induction proof shows that every obtained schedule of n' elements has equal probability (since the above method is a concatenation of two independent and random events).

A random list of schedules Ψ can be selected by using the above method p times, independently.

For a schedule $\pi \in \Psi$, let $X(\pi, i)$, for $i = 1, \ldots, n$, be a random value such that $X(\pi, i) = 1$ if $\pi(i)$ is a d-lrm, and $X(\pi, i) = 0$ otherwise.

Claim. *For any $\pi \in \Psi$, $X(\pi, i) = 1$ with probability $\min\{d/i, 1\}$, independently from other values $X(\pi, j)$, for $j > i$. Restated precisely, we claim that $\Pr[X(\pi, i) = 1 \mid \bigwedge_{j>i} X(\pi, j) = a_j] = \min\{d/i, 1\}$, for any 0-1 sequence $a_{i+1}, \ldots, a_n$.*

This is so because $\pi(i)$ might be a d-lrm if during the $(n - i - 1)$th step of generating π, we select uniformly and independently at random one among the d greatest remaining elements (there are i remaining elements in this step). This proves the claim.

Note that

1. for every $\pi \in \Psi$ and every $i = 1, \ldots, d$, $\pi(i)$ is d-lrm, and
2. $\mathbb{E}\left[\sum_{\pi \in \Psi} \sum_{i=d+1}^{n} X(\pi, i)\right] = p\, d \cdot \sum_{i=d+1}^{n} \frac{1}{i} = p\, d\, (H_n - H_d)$.

Applying the well known Chernoff bound of the following form: for 0-1 independent random variables Y_j and any constant $b > 0$,

$$\Pr\left[\sum_j Y_j > \mathbb{E}\left[\sum_j Y_j\right](1+b)\right] < \left(\frac{e^b}{(1+b)^{1+b}}\right)^{\mathbb{E}[\sum_j Y_j]} < e^{-\mathbb{E}[\sum_j Y_j](1+b)\ln\frac{1+b}{e}},$$

and using the fact that $2 + \dfrac{n\ln n}{pd(H_n - H_d)} > 0$, we obtain

$$\Pr\left[\sum_{\pi \in \Psi} \sum_{i=d+1}^{n} X(\pi, i) > n\ln n + 3pd(H_n - H_d)\right]$$

$$= \Pr\left[\sum_{\pi \in \Psi} \sum_{i=d+1}^{n} X(\pi, i) > pd(H_n - H_d)\left(1 + \left(2 + \frac{n\ln n}{pd(H_n - H_d)}\right)\right)\right]$$

$$\leq e^{-(n\ln n + 3pd(H_n - H_d))\ln\frac{n\ln n + 3pd(H_n - H_d)}{e \cdot pd(H_n - H_d)}}$$

$$\leq e^{-[n\ln n + 3pd(H_n - H_d)]\ln(3/e)}.$$

Since $\ln i \leq H_i \leq \ln i + 1$ and $n > 5d$, we obtain that

$$\Pr\left[\sum_{\pi \in \Psi} \sum_{i=1}^{n} X(\pi, i) > n\ln n + 5pd\ln\left(e + \frac{n}{d}\right)\right]$$

$$\leq \Pr\left[\sum_{\pi \in \Psi} \sum_{i=d+1}^{n} X(\pi, i) > n\ln n + 3pd(H_n - H_d) + pd\right]$$

$$\leq e^{-[n\ln n + 3pd(H_n - H_d)]\ln(3/e)}.$$

$\square$

Now we generalize the result of Lemma 7.10.

Theorem 7.11. *For a random list of schedules Ψ containing p permutations from $\mathcal{S}_n$, the event:*

"for every positive integer d, (d)-Cont$(\Psi) > n\ln n + 8pd\ln(e + n/d)$",

holds with probability at most $e^{-n\ln n \cdot \ln(7/e^2) - p}$.

Proof. For $d \geq n/5$ the result is straightforward, moreover the event holds with probability 0. In the following we assume that $d < n/5$.

Note that since Ψ is a random list of schedules, then so is $\sigma^{-1} \circ \Psi$, where $\sigma \in S_n$ is an arbitrary permutation. Consequently, by Lemma 7.10, $(d)\text{-Cont}(\Psi, \sigma) > n \ln n + 8pd \ln(e + n/d)$ holds with probability at most $e^{-[n \ln n + 7pd \ln(e + \frac{n}{3d})] \ln \frac{7}{e}}$.

Hence the probability that a random list of schedules Ψ has d-contention greater than $n \ln n + 8pd \ln(e + n/d)$ is at most

$$n! \cdot e^{-[n \ln n + 7pd \ln(e + \frac{n}{3d})] \ln \frac{7}{e}} \leq e^{n \ln n - [n \ln n + 7pd \ln(e + \frac{n}{3d})] \ln \frac{7}{e}}$$
$$\leq e^{-n \ln n \cdot \ln \frac{7}{e^2} - 7pd \ln(e + \frac{n}{d})} .$$

Then the probability that, for every d, $(d)\text{-Cont}(\Psi) > n \ln n + 8pd \ln(e + n/d)$, is at most

$$\sum_{d=1}^{\infty} \Pr \left[(d)\text{-Cont}(\Psi) > n \ln n + 8pd \ln(e + n/d) \right]$$

$$\leq \sum_{d=1}^{n/5-1} e^{-n \ln n \cdot \ln(7/e^2) - 7pd \ln(e + n/d)} + \sum_{d=n/5}^{\infty} 0$$

$$\leq e^{-n \ln n \cdot \ln(7/e^2)} \cdot \sum_{d=1}^{n/5-1} (e^{-7p})^d$$

$$\leq e^{-n \ln n \cdot \ln(7/e^2)} \cdot \frac{e^{-7p}}{1 - e^{-7p}}$$

$$\leq e^{-n \ln n \cdot \ln(7/e^2) - p} .$$

$\square$

Using the probabilistic method we obtain the following.

Corollary 7.12. *There is a list of p schedules Ψ from S_n such that $(d)\text{-Cont}(\Psi) \leq n \log n + 8pd \ln(e + n/d)$, for every positive integer d.*

We put to use our generalized notion of contention in the delay-sensitive analysis of work-performing algorithms in Section 7.5.

7.4 Deterministic Algorithms Family DA

We now present a deterministic solution for the *Do-All* problem with p processors and n tasks. We develop a family of deterministic algorithms DA, such that for any constant $\varepsilon > 0$ there is an algorithm with total-work $S = O(np^{\varepsilon} + p \, d\lceil n/d \rceil^{\varepsilon})$ and message complexity $M = O(p \cdot S)$.

More precisely, algorithms from the family DA are parameterized by a positive integer q and a list Ψ of q permutations on the set $[q] = \{1, \ldots, q\}$, where $2 \leq q < p \leq n$. We show that for any constant $\varepsilon > 0$ there is a constant q and a corresponding set of permutation Ψ, such that the resulting algorithm has total-work $S = O(np^\varepsilon + p \ d\lceil n/d \rceil^\varepsilon)$ and message complexity $M = O(p \cdot S)$. The work of these algorithms is within a small polynomial factor of the corresponding lower bound (see Section 7.2.1).

7.4.1 Construction and Correctness of Algorithm DA(q)

Let q be some constant such that $2 \leq q \leq p$. We assume that the number of tasks t is an integer power of q, specifically let $t = q^h$ for some $h \in \mathbb{N}$. When the number of tasks is not a power of q we can use a standard padding technique by adding just enough "dummy" tasks so that the new number of tasks becomes a power of q; the final results show that this padding does not affect the asymptotic complexity of the algorithm. We also assume that $\log_q p$ is a positive integer. If it is not, we pad the processors with at most qp "infinitely delayed" processors so this assumption is satisfied; in this case the upper bound is increased by a (constant) factor of at most q.

The algorithm uses any list of q permutations $\Psi = \langle \pi_0, \ldots \pi_{q-1} \rangle$ from $\mathcal{S}_q$ such that Ψ has the minimum contention among all such lists. We define a family of algorithms, where each algorithm is parameterized by q, and a list Ψ with the above contention property. We call this algorithm DA(q). In this section we first present the algorithm for $p \geq n$, then state the parameterization for $p < n$.

Algorithm DA(q), utilizes a q-ary boolean *progress tree* with n leaves, where the tasks are associated with the leaves. Initially all nodes of the tree are 0 (false) indicating that no tasks have been performed. Instead of maintaining a global data structure representing a q-ary tree, in our algorithms each processor has a replica of the tree.

Whenever a processor learns that all tasks in a subtree rooted at a certain node have been performed, it sets the node to 1 (true) and shares the good news with all other processors. This is done by multicasting the processor's progress tree; the local replicas at each processor are updated when multicast messages are received.

Each processor, acting independently, searches for work in the smallest immediate subtree that has remaining unperformed tasks. It then performs any tasks it finds, and moves out of that subtree when all work within it is completed. When exploring the subtrees rooted at an interior node at height m, a processor visits the subtrees in the order given by one of the permutations in Ψ. Specifically, the processor uses the permutation π_s such that s is the value of the m-th digit in the q-ary expansion of the processor's identifier (pid). We now present this in more detail.

```
00 const q                                              % Arity of the progress tree
01 const Ψ = ⟨π_r | 0 ≤ r < q ∧ π_r ∈ S_q⟩    % Fixed list of q permutations of [q]
02 const l = (qt-1)/(q-1)                          % The size of the progress tree
03 const h = log_q n                               % The height of the progress tree
04 type ProgressTree: array [0 .. l - 1] of boolean        % Progress tree
05 for each processor pid = 1 to p begin
06    ProgressTree Tree_pid                   % The progress tree at processor pid

10    thread                          % Traverse progress tree in search of work
11            integer ν init = 0          % Current node, begin at the root
12            integer η init = 0          % Current depth in the tree
13            DoWork(ν, η)
14    end

20    thread                                % Receive broadcast messages
21            set of ProgressTree B              % Incoming messages
22            while Tree_pid[0] ≠ 1 do        % While not all tasks certified
23                receive B                  % Deliver the set of received messages
24                Tree_pid := Tree_pid ∨ (⋁_{b∈B} b)         % Learn progress
25            od
26    end
27 end.
```

```
40 procedure DoWork(ν, η)                 % Recursive progress tree traversal
41                                % ν : current node index ; η : node depth
42 const array x[0 .. h - 1] = pid_{(base q)}   % h least significant q-ary digits of pid
43    if Tree_pid[ν] = 0 then                % Node not done – still work left
44        if η = h then                      % Node ν is a leaf
45            perform Task(n - l + ν + 1)          % Do the task
46        else                              % Node ν is not a leaf
47            or r = 1 to q do            % Visit subtrees in the order of π_{x[η]}
48                DoWork(qν + π_{x[η]}(r), η + 1)
49            od
50        fi
51        Tree_pid[ν] := 1               % Record completion of the subtree
52        broadcast Tree_pid                  % Share the good news
53    fi
54 end.
```

Fig. 7.3. The deterministic algorithm DA $(p \geq n)$.

Data Structures: Given the n tasks, the progress tree is a q-ary ordered tree of height h, where $n = q^h$. The number of nodes in the progress tree is $l = \sum_{i=0}^{h-1} q^i = (q^{h+1}-1)/(q-1) = (qn-1)/(q-1)$. Each node of the tree is a boolean, indicating whether the subtree rooted at the node is done (value 1) or not (value 0).

The progress tree is stored in a boolean array $Tree[0 .. l-1]$, where $Tree[0]$ is the root, and the q children of the interior node $Tree[\nu]$ being the nodes $Tree[q\nu + 1], Tree[q\nu + 2], \ldots, Tree[q\nu + q]$. The space occupied by the tree is $O(n)$. The n tasks are associated with the leaves of the progress tree, such that the leaf $Tree[\nu]$ corresponds to the task $Task(\nu + n + 1 - l)$.

We represent the pid of each of the p processors in terms of its q-ary expansion. We care only about the h least significant q-ary digits of each pid (thus when $p > n$ several processors may be indistinguishable in the algorithm). The q-ary expansions of each pid is stored in the array $x[0..h-1]$.

Control Flow: The code is given in Figure 7.3. Each of the p processors executes two concurrent threads. One thread (lines 10-14) traverses the local progress tree in search work, performs the tasks, and broadcasts the updated progress tree. The second thread (lines 20-26) receives messages from other processors and updates the local progress tree. (Each processor is asynchronous, but we assume that its two threads run at approximately the same speed. This is assumed for simplicity only, as it is trivial to explicitly schedule the threads on a single processor.) Note that the updates of the local progress tree $Tree$ are always monotone: initially each node contain 0, then once a node changes its value to 1 it remains 1 forever. Thus no issues of consistency arise.

The progress tree is traversed using the recursive procedure DOWORK (lines 40-54). The order of traversals within the progress tree is determined by the list of permutations $\Psi = \langle \pi_0, \pi_1, \ldots, \pi_{q-1} \rangle$. Each processor uses, at the node of depth η, the ηth q-ary digit $x[\eta]$ of its pid to select the permutation $\pi_{x[\eta]}$ from Ψ (recall that we use only the h least significant q-ary digits of each pid when representing the pid in line 42). The processor traverses the q subtrees in the order determined by $\pi_{x[\eta]}$ (lines 47-49); the processors starts the traversal of a subtree only if the corresponding bit in the progress tree is not set (line 43).

In other words, each processor pid traverses its progress tree in a post-order fashion using the q-ary digits of its pid and the permutations in Ψ to establish the order of the subtree traversals, except that when the messages from other processors are received, the progress tree of processor pid can be pruned based on the progress of other processors.

Parameterization for Large Number of Tasks: When the number of input tasks n' exceeds the number of processors p, we divide the tasks into *jobs*, where each job consists of at most $\lceil n'/p \rceil$ tasks. The algorithm in Figure 7.3 is then used with the resulting p jobs ($p = n$), where $Task(j)$ now refers to the job number j ($1 \leq j \leq n$). Note that in this case the cost of work corresponding to doing a single job is $\lceil n'/p \rceil$.

Correctness: We claim that algorithm DA(q) correctly solves the *Do-All* problem. This follows from the observation that a processor leaves a subtree by returning from a recursive call to DOWORK if and only if the subtree contains no unfinished work and its root is marked accordingly. We formalize this as follows.

Lemma 7.13. *In any execution of algorithm* $\mathrm{DA}(q)$, *whenever a processor returns from a call to* $\mathrm{DOWORK}(\nu, \eta)$, *all tasks associated with the leaves that are the descendants of node* ν *have been performed.*

Proof. First, by code inspection (Figure 7.3, lines 45, 51, and 52), we note that processor *pid* reaching a leaf n at depth $\eta = h$ broadcasts its $Tree_{pid}$ with the value $Tree_{pid}[\nu]$ set to 1 if and only if it performs the task corresponding to the leaf.

We now proceed by induction on η.

Base case, $\eta = h$:
In this case, processor *pid* makes the call to $\mathrm{DOWORK}(\nu, \eta)$. If $Tree_{pid}[\nu] = 0$, as we have already observed, the processor performs the task at the leaf (line 45), broadcasts its $Tree_{pid}$ with the leaf value set to 1 (lines 51-52), and returns from the call. If $Tree_{pid}[\nu] \neq 0$ then the processor must have received a message from some other processor indicating that the task at the leaf is done. This can be so if the sender itself performed the task (as observed above), or the sender learned from some other processor the fact that the task is done.

Inductive step, $0 \leq \eta < h$:
In this case, processor *pid* making the call to $\mathrm{DOWORK}(\nu, \eta)$ executes q calls to $\mathrm{DOWORK}(\nu', \eta + 1)$, one for each child ν' of node ν (lines 47-49). By inductive hypothesis, each return from $\mathrm{DOWORK}(\nu', \eta + 1)$ indicates that all tasks associated with the leaves that are the descendants of node ν' have been performed. The processor then broadcasts its $Tree_{pid}$ with the the value $Tree_{pid}[\nu]$ set to 1 (lines 51-52), indicating that all tasks associated with the leaves that are the descendants of node ν have been performed, and returns from the call. □

Theorem 7.14. *Any execution of algorithm* $\mathrm{DA}(q)$ *terminates in finite time having performed all tasks.*

Proof. The progress tree used by the algorithm has finite number of nodes. By code inspection, each processor executing the algorithm makes at most one recursive call per each node of the tree. Thus the algorithm terminates in finite time. By Lemma 7.13, whenever a processor returns from the call to $\mathrm{DOWORK}(\nu \, (= 0), \, \eta \, (= 0))$, all tasks associated with the leaves that are the descendants of the node $\nu = 0$ are done, and the value of node is set to 1. Since this node is the root of the tree, all tasks are done. □

7.4.2 Complexity Analysis of Algorithm $\mathrm{DA}(q)$

We start by showing a lemma that relates the work of the algorithm, against adversary $\mathcal{A}_D^{(d)}$ to its recursive structure.

We consider the case $p \geq n$. Let $S(n, p, d)$ denote total-work of algorithm $\mathrm{DA}(q)$ through the first global step in which some processor completes the last remaining task and broadcasts the message containing the progress tree where $T[0] = 1$. We note that $S(1, p, d) = O(p)$. This is because the progress tree has only one leaf. Each processor makes a single call to DOWORK, performs the sole task and broadcasts the completed progress tree.

Lemma 7.15. *For p-processor, n-task algorithm* $\mathrm{DA}(q)$ *with* $p \geq n$ *and* n *and* p *divisible by* q:

$$S(n, p, d) = O(\mathrm{Cont}(\Psi) \cdot S(p/q, n/q, d) + p \cdot q \cdot \min\{d, n/q\}) \ .$$

Proof. Since the root of the progress tree has q children, each processor makes the initial call to DOWORK$(0,0)$ (line 13) and then (in the worst case) it makes q calls to DOWORK (line 47-49) corresponding to the children of the root. We consider the performance of all tasks in the specific subtree rooted at a child of the progress tree as a job, thus such a job consists of all invocations of DOWORK on that subtree. We now account separately for the primary and secondary job executions (recall the definitions in Section 7.3).

Observe that the code in lines 47-49 of DA is essentially algorithm OBLIDO (lines 02-04 in Figure 7.2) and we intend to use Lemma 7.9. The only difference is that instead of q processors we have q groups of p/q processors where in each group the *pids* differ in their q-ary digit corresponding to the depth 0 of the progress tree. From the recursive structure of algorithm DA it follows that the work of each such group in performing a single job is $S(p/q, n/q, d)$, since each group has p/q processors and the job includes n/q tasks. Using Lemma 7.9 the primary task executions contribute $O(\mathrm{Cont}(\Psi) \cdot S(p/q, n/q, d))$ work.

If messages were delivered without delay, there would be no need to account for secondary job executions because the processors would instantly learn about all primary job completions. Since messages can be delayed by up to d time units, each processor may spend up to d time steps, but no more than $O(n/q)$ steps performing a secondary job (this is because it takes a single processor $O(n/q)$ steps to perform a post-order traversal of a progress tree with n/q leaves). There are q jobs to consider, so for p processors this amounts to $O(p \cdot q \cdot \min\{d, n/q\})$ work.

For each processor there is also a constant overhead due to the fixed-size code executed per each call to DOWORK. The total-work contribution is $O(p \cdot q)$. Finally, given the assumption about thread scheduling, the work of message processing thread does not exceed asymptotically the work of the DOWORK thread. Putting all these work contributions together yields the desired result.   □

We now prove the following theorem about total-work.

Theorem 7.16. *Consider algorithm* $\mathrm{DA}(q)$ *with* p *processors and* n *tasks where* $p \geq n$. *Let* d *be the maximum message delay. For any constant* $\varepsilon > 0$ *there is a constant* q *such that the algorithm has total-work* $S(n, p, d) = O(p \min\{n, d\} \lceil n/d \rceil^\varepsilon)$.

Proof. Fix a constant $\varepsilon > 0$; without loss of generality we can assume that $\varepsilon \leq 1$. Let a be the sufficiently large positive constant "hidden" in the big-oh upper bound for $S(n, p, d)$ in Lemma 7.15. We consider a constant $q > 0$ such that $\log_q(4a \log q) \leq \varepsilon$. Such q exists since $\lim_{q \to \infty} \log_q(4a \log q) = 0$ (however, q is a constant of order $2^{\frac{\log(1/\varepsilon)}{\varepsilon}}$).

First suppose that $\log_q n$ and $\log_q p$ are positive integers. We prove by induction on p and n that

$$S(n, p, d) \leq q \cdot n^{\log_q(4a \log q)} \cdot p \cdot d^{1-\log_q(4a \log q)},$$

For the *base case* of $n = 1$ the statement is correct since $S(1, p, d) = O(p)$. For $n > 1$ we choose the list of permutations Ψ with $\mathrm{Cont}(\Psi) \leq 3q \log q$ per Lemma 7.8. Due to our choice of parameters, $\log_q n$ is an integer and $n \leq p$. Let β stand for $\log_q(4a \log q)$. Using Lemma 7.15 and inductive hypothesis we obtain

$$S(n, p, d) \leq a \cdot \left(3q \log q \cdot q \cdot \left(\frac{n}{q}\right)^\beta \cdot \frac{p}{q} \cdot d^{1-\beta} + p \cdot q \cdot \min\{d, n/q\}\right)$$

$$\leq a \cdot \left(\left(q \cdot n^\beta \cdot p \cdot d^{1-\beta}\right) \cdot 3 \log q \cdot q^{-\beta} + p \cdot q \cdot \min\{d, n/q\}\right).$$

We now consider two cases:

Case 1: $d \leq n/q$. It follows that

$$p \cdot q \cdot \min\{d, n/q\} = p\, q\, d \leq p\, q\, d^{1-\beta} \cdot \left(\frac{n}{q}\right)^\beta.$$

Case 2: $d > n/q$. It follows that

$$p \cdot q \cdot \min\{d, n/q\} = p\, n \leq p\, q\, d^{1-\beta} \cdot \left(\frac{n}{q}\right)^\beta.$$

Putting everything together we obtain the desired inequality

$$S(n, p, d) \leq a\left(\left(q \cdot n^\beta \cdot p \cdot d^{1-\beta} \cdot q^{-\beta}\right) 4 \log q\right) \leq q \cdot n^\beta \cdot p \cdot d^{1-\beta}.$$

To complete the proof, consider any $n \leq p$. We add $n' - n$ new "dummy" tasks, where $n' - n < q\, n - 1$, and $p' - p$ new "virtual" processors, where $p' - p < q\, p - 1$, such that $\log_q n'$ and $\log_q p'$ are positive integers. We assume that all "virtual" crash at the start of the computation (else they can be thought of as delayed to infinity). It follows that

$$S(n, p, d) \leq S(n', p', d) \leq q \cdot (n')^\beta p' \cdot d^{1-\beta} \leq q^{2+\beta} n^\beta p \cdot d^{1-\beta}.$$

Since $\beta \leq \varepsilon$, we obtain that total-work of algorithm $DA(q)$ is $O(\min\{n^\varepsilon p\, d^{1-\varepsilon}, n\, p\}) = O(p \min\{n, d\}\lceil n/d\rceil^\varepsilon)$, which completes the proof of the theorem. □

Now we consider the case $p < n$. Recall that in this case we divide the n tasks into p jobs of size at most $\lceil n/p\rceil$, and we let the algorithm work with these jobs. It takes a processor $O(n/p)$ work (instead of a constant) to process a single job.

Theorem 7.17. *Consider algorithm* DA(q) *with* p *processors and* n *tasks where* $p < n$. *Let* d *be the maximum message delay. For any constant* $\varepsilon > 0$ *there is a constant* q *such that* DA(q) *has total-work* $S(n, p, d) = O(np^\varepsilon + p\min\{n, d\}\lceil n/d\rceil^\varepsilon)$.

Proof. We use Theorem 7.16 with p jobs (instead of n tasks), were a single job takes $O(n/p)$ units of work. The upper bound on the maximal delay for receiving messages about the completion of some job is $d' = \lceil pd/n \rceil = O(1+pd/n)$ "job units", where a single job unit takes $\Theta(n/p)$ time. We obtain the following bound on work:

$$O\left(p\min\{p, d'\}\lceil p/d'\rceil^\varepsilon \cdot \frac{n}{p}\right) = O\left(\min\left\{p^2, p^\varepsilon p(d')^{1-\varepsilon}\right\} \cdot \frac{n}{p}\right)$$

$$= O\left(\min\left\{n\,p, n\,p^\varepsilon + pn^\varepsilon d^{1-\varepsilon}\right\}\right)$$

$$= O\left(n\,p^\varepsilon + p\min\{n, d\}\left\lceil\frac{n}{d}\right\rceil^\varepsilon\right).$$

$\square$

Finally we consider message complexity.

Theorem 7.18. *Algorithm* DA(q) *with* p *processors and* n *tasks has message complexity* $M(n, p, d) = O(p \cdot S(n, p, d))$.

Proof. In each step, a processor broadcasts at most one message to $p-1$ other processors. $\square$

Note again that our focus is on optimizing work on the assumption that performing a task is substantially more costly that sending a message. It may also be interesting to optimize communication costs first.

7.5 Permutation Algorithms Family PA

In this section we present and analyze a family of algorithms that are simpler than algorithms DA and that directly rely on permutation schedules. Two algorithms are randomized (algorithms PARAN1 and PARAN2), and one is deterministic (algorithm PADET).

7.5.1 Algorithm Specification

The common pattern in the three algorithms is that each processor, while it has not ascertained that all tasks are complete, performs a specific task from its local list and broadcasts this fact to other processors. The known complete tasks are removed from the list. The code is given in Figure 7.4. The common code for the three algorithms is in lines 00-29.

The three algorithms differ in two ways:

1. The initial ordering of the tasks by each processor, implemented by the call to procedure ORDER on line 20.
2. The selection of the next task to perform, implemented by the call to function SELECT on line 24.

We now describe the specialization of the code made by each algorithm (the code for ORDER+SELECT in Figure 7.4).

```
00 use package ORDER+SELECT              % Algorithm-specific procedures
01 type TaskId : [n]
02 type TaskList : list of TaskId
03 type MsgBuff : set of TaskList

10 for each processor pid = 1 to p begin
11     TaskList Tasks_pid init [n]
12     MsgBuf B                          % Incoming messages
13     TaskId tid                        % Task id; next to done

20     ORDER(Tasks_pid)
21     while Tasks_pid ≠ ∅ do
22         receive B                     % Deliver the set of received messages
23         Tasks_pid := Tasks_pid − (⋃_{b∈B} b)   % Remove tasks
24         tid := SELECT(Tasks_pid)      % Select next task
25         perform Task(tid)
26         Tasks_pid := Tasks_pid − {tid}          % Remove done task
27         broadcast Tasks_pid           % Share the news
28     od
29 end.
```

```
40 package ORDER+SELECT                  % Used in algorithm PARAN1
41 list Ψ = ⟨TaskList π_r | 1 ≤ r ≤ p  ∧  π_r = random list of [n]⟩
42 % Ψ is a list of p random permutations
43     procedure ORDER(T) begin  T := π_pid end
44     TaskId function SELECT(T) begin  return(T(1))  end
```

```
50 package ORDER+SELECT                  % Used in algorithm PARAN2
51     procedure ORDER(T) begin  no-op end
52     TaskId function SELECT(T) begin  return(random(T))  end
```

```
60 package ORDER+SELECT                  % Used in algorithm PADET
61 const list Ψ = ⟨TaskList π_r | 1 ≤ r ≤ p ∧ π_r ∈ S_n⟩
62 % Ψ is a fixed list of p permutations
63     procedure ORDER(T) begin  T := π_pid end
64     TaskId function SELECT(T) begin  return(T(1))  end
```

Fig. 7.4. Permutation algorithm and its specializations for PARAN1, PARAN2, and PADET ($p \geq n$).

As with algorithm DA, we initially consider the case of $p \geq n$. The case of $p < n$ is obtained by dividing the n tasks into p jobs, each of size at most $\lceil n/p \rceil$. In this case we deal with jobs instead of tasks in the code of permutation algorithms.

Randomized algorithm PARAN1. The specialized code is in Figure 7.4, lines 40-44. Each processor pid performs tasks according to a local permutation π_{pid}. These permutations are selected uniformly at random at the beginning of computation (line 41), independently by each processor. We refer to the collection of these permutation as Ψ. The drawback of this approach is that the number of random selections is $p \cdot \min\{n, p\}$, each of $O(\log \min\{n, p\})$ random bits (we have $\min\{n, p\}$ above because when $p < n$, we use p jobs, each of size $\lceil n/p \rceil$, instead of n tasks).

Randomized algorithm PARAN2. The specialized code is in Figure 7.4, lines 50-52. Initially the tasks are left unordered. Each processor selects tasks uniformly and independently at random, one at a time (line 52). Clearly the expected work ES is the same for algorithms PARAN1 and PARAN2, however the (expected) number of random bits needed by PARAN2 becomes at most $ES \cdot \log n$ and, as we will see, this is an improvement.

Deterministic algorithm PADET. The specialized code is in Figure 7.4, lines 60-64. We assume the existence of the list of permutations Ψ chosen per Corollary 7.12. Each processor pid permutes its list of tasks according to the local permutation $\pi_{pid} \in \Psi$.

7.5.2 Complexity Analysis

In the analysis we use the quantity t defined as $t = \min\{n, p\}$. When $n < p$, t represents the number of tasks to be performed. When $n \geq p$, t represents the number of jobs (of size at most $\lceil n/p \rceil$) to be performed; in this case, each task in Figure 7.4 represents a single job. In the sequel we continue referring to "tasks" only — from the combinatorial perspective there is no distinction between a task and a job, and the only accounting difference is that a task costs $\Theta(1)$ work, while a job costs $\Theta(\lceil n/p \rceil)$ work.

Recall that we measure global time units according to the time steps defined to be the smallest time between any two clock-ticks of any processor (Section 7.1). Thus during any d global time steps no processor can take more than d local steps.

For the purpose of the next lemma we introduce the notion of adversary $\mathcal{A}_D^{(d,\sigma)}$, where σ is a permutation of n tasks. This is a specialization of adversary $\mathcal{A}_D^{(d)}$ that schedules the asynchronous processors so that each of the n tasks is performed for the first time in the order given by σ. More precisely, if the execution of the task σ_i is completed for the first time by some processor at the global time τ_i (unknown to the processor), and the task σ_j, for any $1 \leq i < j \leq n$, is completed for the first time by some processor at time τ_j, then $\tau_i \leq \tau_j$. Note that any execution of an algorithm solving the *Do-All* problem against adversary $\mathcal{A}_D^{(d)}$ corresponds to the execution against some adversary $\mathcal{A}_D^{(d,\sigma)}$ for the specific σ.

Lemma 7.19. *For algorithms* PADET *and* PARAN1, *the respective total-work and expected total-work is at most* (d)-Cont(Ψ) *against adversary* $\mathcal{A}_D^{(d)}$.

Proof. Suppose processor i starts performing task z at (real) time τ. By the definition of adversary $\mathcal{A}_D^{(d)}$, no other processor successfully performed task z and broadcast its message by time $(\tau - d)$. Consider adversary $\mathcal{A}_D^{(d,\sigma)}$, for any permutation $\sigma \in \mathcal{S}_n$.

For each processor i, let J_i contain all pairs (i,r) such that i performs task $\pi_i(r)$ during the computation. We construct function L from the pairs in the set $\bigcup_i J_i$ to the set of all d-lrm's of the list $\sigma^{-1} \circ \Psi$ and show that L is a bijection. We do the construction independently for each processor i. It is obvious that $(i,1) \in J_i$, and we let $L(i,1) = 1$. Suppose that $(i,r) \in J_i$ and we defined function L for all elements from J_i less than (i,r) in lexicographic order. We define $L(i,r)$ as the first $s \leq r$ such that $(\sigma^{-1} \circ \pi_i)(s)$ is a d-lrm not assigned by L to any element in J_i.

Claim. *For every* $(i,r) \in J_i$, $L(i,r)$ *is well defined.*

For $r = 1$ we have $L(i,1) = 1$. For the (lexicographically) first d elements in J_i this is also easy to show. Suppose L is well defined for all elements in J_i less than (i,r), and (i,r) is at least the $(d+1)$st element in J_i. We show that $L(i,r)$ is also well defined. Suppose, to the contrary, that there is no position $s \leq r$ such that $(\sigma^{-1} \circ \pi_i)(s)$ is a d-lrm and s is not assigned by L before the step of the construction for $(i,r) \in J_i$. Let $(i,s_1) < \ldots < (i,s_d)$ be the elements of J_i less than (i,r) such that $(\sigma^{-1} \circ \pi_i)(L(i,s_1)), \ldots, (\sigma^{-1} \circ \pi_i)(L(i,s_d))$ are greater than $(\sigma^{-1} \circ \pi_i)(r)$. They exist from the fact, that $(\sigma^{-1} \circ \pi_i)(r)$ is not a d-lrm and all "previous" d-lrm's are assigned by L. Let τ_r be the global time when task $\pi_i(r)$ is performed by i. Obviously task $\pi_i(L(i,s_1))$ has been performed at time that is at least $d+1$ local steps (and hence also global time units) before τ_r. It follows from this and the definition of adversary $\mathcal{A}_D^{(d,\sigma)}$, that task $\pi_i(r)$ has been performed by some other processor in a local step, which ended also at least $(d+1)$ time units before τ_r. This contradicts the observation made at the beginning of the proof of lemma. This proves the claim.

That L is a bijection follows directly from the definition of L. It follows that the number of performances of tasks – equal to the total number of local steps until completion of all tasks – is at most (d)-Cont(Ψ, σ), against any adversary $\mathcal{A}_D^{(d,\sigma)}$. Hence total work is at most (d)-Cont(Ψ) against adversary $\mathcal{A}_D^{(d)}$. $\square$

Now we give the result for total-work and message complexities for algorithms PARAN1 and PARAN2.

Theorem 7.20. *Algorithms* PARAN1 *and* PARAN2, *under adversary* $\mathcal{A}_D^{(d)}$, *perform expected total-work*

$$ES(n, p, d) = O(n \log t + p \min\{n, d\} \log(2 + n/d))$$

and have expected message complexity

$$EM(n, p, d) = O(n \ p \log t + p^2 \min\{n, d\} \log(2 + n/d)) \ .$$

Proof. We prove the work bound for algorithm PARAN1 using the random list of schedules Ψ and Theorem 7.11, together with Lemma 7.19. If $p \geq n$ we obtain the formula $O(n \log n + p \min\{n, d\} \log(2 + n/d))$ with high probability, in view of Theorem 7.11, and the obvious upper bound for work is np. If $p < n$ then we argue that $d' = \lceil p\, d/n \rceil$ is the upper bound, in terms of the number of "job units", that it takes to deliver a message to recipients, and consequently we obtain the formula

$$O(p \log p + p \ d' \log(2 + p/d')) \cdot O(n/p) = O(t \log p + p \ d \log(2 + n/d)),$$

which, together with the upper bound $n \ p$, yields the formula

$$O(n \log p + p \min\{n, d\} \log(2 + n/d)).$$

Since the only difference in the above two cases is the factor $\log n$ that becomes $\log p$ in the case where $p < n$, we conclude the final formula for work. All these derivations hold with the probability at least $1 - e^{-t \ln t \cdot \ln(7/e^2) - p}$. Since the work can be in the worst case $n \ p$ with probability at most $e^{-t \ln t \cdot \ln(7/e^2) - p}$, this contributes at most the summand n to the expected work.

Message complexity follows from the fact that in every local step each processor sends $p - 1$ messages. The same result applies to PARAN2 (this is given as an observation in the description of the the algorithm.) □

Next is the result for total-work and messages for algorithm PADET.

Theorem 7.21. *There exists a deterministic list of schedules* Ψ *such that algorithm* PADET, *under adversary* $\mathcal{A}_D^{(d)}$, *performs total-work*

$$S(n, p, d) = O(n \log t + p \min\{n, d\} \log(2 + n/d))$$

and has message complexity

$$M(n, p, d) = O(n \ p \log t + p^2 \min\{n, d\} \log(2 + n/d)) \ .$$

Proof. The result follows from using the set Ψ from Corollary 7.12 together with Lemma 7.19, using the same derivation for work formula as in the proof of Theorem 7.20. Message complexity follows from the fact, that in every local step each processor sends $p - 1$ messages. □

We now specialize Theorem 7.20 for $p \leq n$ and $d \leq n$ and obtain our main result for algorithms PARAN1 and PARAN2.

Corollary 7.22. *Algorithms* PARAN1 *and* PARAN2, *under adversary* $\mathcal{A}_D^{(d)}$, *perform expected total-work*

$$ES(n, p, d) = O(n \log p + p \ d \log(2 + n/d))$$

and have expected message complexity

$$EM(n, p, d) = O(n \ p \log p + p^2 d \log(2 + n/d))$$

for any $d < n$, when $p \leq n$.

Finally we specialize Theorem 7.21 for $p \leq n$ and $d \leq n$ and obtain our main result for algorithm PADET.

Corollary 7.23. *There exists a list of schedules Ψ such that algorithm* PADET *under adversary* $\mathcal{A}_D^{(d)}$ *performs work*

$$S(n, p, d) = O(n \log p + p \ d \log(2 + n/d))$$

and has message complexity

$$M(n, p, d) = O(n \ p \log p + p^2 d \log(2 + n/d)),$$

for any $d \leq n$, when $p \leq n$.

7.6 Open Problems

In this chapter we presented the message-delay-sensitive lower and upper bounds for the *Do-All* problem for asynchronous processors. One of the two deterministic algorithms relies on large permutations of tasks with certain combinatorial properties. Such schedules can be constructed deterministically in polynomial time, however the efficiency of the algorithms using these constructions is slightly detuned (polylogarithmically). This leads to the open problem of how to construct permutations with better quality and more efficiently.

There also exists a gap between the upper and the lower bounds shown in this chapter. It will be very interesting to narrow the gap.

The focus of this chapter is on the work complexity. It is also important to investigate algorithms that simultaneously control work and message complexity.

Lastly, we have used the omniscient adversary definition. The analysis of complexity of randomized algorithms against an oblivious adversary is also an interesting open question.

7.7 Chapter Notes

In the message-passing settings, the *Do-All* problem has been substantially studied for synchronous failure-prone processors under a variety of assumptions, e.g., [15, 16, 20, 30, 25, 38, 44]. However there is a dearth of efficient asynchronous algorithms. The presentation in this paper is based on a paper by Kowalski and Shvartsman [77]; the proof of Lemma 7.5 appears there.

A lower bound $\Omega(n + p \log p)$ on work for algorithms in the presence of processor crashes and restarts was shown by Buss, Kanellakis, Ragde, and Shvartsman [14]. The strategy in that work is adapted to the message-passing setting without failures but with delays by Kowalski, Momenzadeh, and Shvartsman [74], where Theorem 7.3 is proved.

The notion of *contention* of permutations was proposed and studied by Anderson and Woll [5]. Lemmas 7.8 and 7.9 appear in that paper [5]. Algorithms in the family DA are inspired by the shared-memory algorithm of the same authors [5]. The notion of the *left-to-right maximum* is due to Knuth [71] (vol. 3, p. 13). Kowalski, Musial, and Shvartsman [75] explore ways of efficiently constructing permutations with low contention. They show that such permutations can be constructed deterministically in polynomial time, however the efficiency of the algorithms using these constructions is slightly detuned.

For applications of Chernoff bounds see Alon and Spencer [4].

8

Analysis of Omni-Do in Asynchronous Partitionable Networks

I N the settings where network partitions may interfere with the progress of computation, the challenge is to maintain efficiency in performing the tasks and learning the results of the tasks, despite the dynamically changing group connectivity. However, no amount of algorithmic sophistication can compensate for the possibility of groups of processors or even individual processors becoming disconnected during the computation. In general, an adversary that is able to partition the network into g components will cause any task-performing algorithm to have work $\Omega(n \cdot g)$ even if each group of processors performs no more than the optimal number of $\Theta(n)$ tasks. In the extreme case where all processors are isolated from the beginning, the work of any algorithm is $\Omega(n \cdot p)$.

When the network can partition into disconnected components, it is not always sufficient to learn that all tasks are complete (e.g., to solve the *Do-All* problem). It may also be necessary for the processors in each network component to learn the results of the task completion. Thus here we pursue solutions to the *Omni-Do* problem (Definition 2.3): Given a set of n tasks and p message-passing processors, each processor must learn the results of all tasks.

Even given the pessimistic lower bound of $\Omega(n \cdot p)$ on work for partitionable networks, it is desirable to design and analyze efficient algorithmic approaches that can be shown to be better than the oblivious approach where each processor or each group performs all tasks. In particular, it is important to develop complexity bounds that are *failure-sensitive*, namely that capture the dependence of work complexity on the nature of network partitions. In this chapter we present an asynchronous *Omni-Do* algorithm, called AX, and we show that it is optimal in terms of worst case task-oriented work, under network *fragmentations* and *merges*. The algorithm uses a group communication service to provide membership and communication services.

Chapter structure.

We define the model of adversity in Section 8.1. In Section 8.2 we present the group communication service used for providing membership and communication services along with the notation we use to describe algorithm AX. In Section 8.3 we define *view-graphs* that we use in the algorithm's analysis. In Section 8.4 we describe algorithm AX and show its correctness. In Section 8.5 we present the complexity analysis of the algorithm. We discuss open problems in Section 8.6.

8.1 Models of Adversity

In this chapter we consider two adversaries, one causing only fragmentations, called $\mathcal{A}_F$, and one causing fragmentations and merges, called $\mathcal{A}_{FM}$.

We use the term *group* to denote a completely connected component of the network. The processors within a given group can communicate, while processors from two distinct groups can not. At any given point in time the adversary determines what groups comprise the network. The processors are asynchronous and no time bounds are assumed on local processor steps or message delay.

We represent each processor group g as a pair $\langle g.id, g.set \rangle$, where $g.id$ is the unique identifier of group g and $g.set$ is the set of processor identifiers that constitute the membership of the group. For reasons of notational simplicity and where it clear from the context, when using set operations on groups, we mean that the operations are on the membership sets (e.g., $g_1 \cup g_2$ stands for $g_1.set \cup g_2.set$); when using comparisons on groups, we mean that the comparisons are on the group identifiers (e.g., $g_1 < g_2$ stands for $g_1.id < g_2.id$).

Adversary $\mathcal{A}_F$: We denote by $\mathcal{A}_F$ an omniscient (on-line) adversary that can cause only group fragmentations (Section 2.2.2). Once a group fragments, it cannot be merged. We assume that initially all processors belong in a *single* group.

When adversary $\mathcal{A}_F$ forces group g to fragment into k groups $g_1, g_2, \ldots, g_k$, we require that:

(a) $\bigcup_{i \in [k]} g_i = g$ (complete partition), and
(b) for all i and j, s.t. $1 \leq i < j \leq k$, $g_i \cap g_j = \emptyset$ (the groups are disjoint).

We call the parameter k the *fragmentation-number* of such a fragmentation.

Consider an execution ξ of an algorithm A that solves a specific problem under $\mathcal{A}_F$, i.e., $\xi \in \mathcal{E}(A, \mathcal{A}_F)$. Syntactically, we represent an adversarial pattern $\xi|_{\mathcal{A}_F}$ of an execution ξ as the set of triples $(fragmentation, g, \{g_1, g_2, \ldots, g_k\})$.

For an execution ξ, we define the fragmentation-number $f_r = f_r(\xi|_{\mathcal{A}_F}) = \|\xi|_{\mathcal{A}_F}\|$ to be the sum of the fragmentation-numbers of all the fragmentations in $\xi|_{A_F}$. In other words, $f_r(\xi|_{A_F})$ is the total number of new groups created due to the fragmentations in $\xi|_{A_F}$. By convention, when a group is regrouped in such a way that it forms a new group with the same participants, we view this as a fragmentation.

Adversary A_{FM}: We denote by A_{FM} an omniscient (on-line) adversary that can cause fragmentations *and* merges. As for adversary A_F, we assume that initially all processors belong in a single group.

When adversary A_{FM} forces groups $g_1, g_2, \ldots, g_\ell$ to merge and form a group g, we require that $g = \bigcup_{i \in [\ell]} g_i$, and we say that the *merge-number* of this single merge is 1 (note that a merge creates only one new group).

Consider an execution ξ of an algorithm A that solves a specific problem under A_{FM}, i.e., $\xi \in \mathcal{E}(A, A_{FM})$. Syntactically, we represent a merge in the adversarial pattern $\xi|_{A_{FM}}$ as the triple $(merge, \{g_1, g_2, \ldots, g_\ell\}, g)$. Fragmentations are represented as for adversary A_F. Therefore, we represent an adversarial pattern $\xi|_{A_{FM}}$ of an execution ξ as a set of "fragmentation" and "merge" triples.

We define the merge-number $f_m = f_m(\xi|_{A_{FM}})$ to be the number of all merges in $\xi|_{A_{FM}}$. We define $\|\xi|_{A_{FM}}\|$ to be $f_r(\xi|_{A_{FM}}) + f_m(\xi|_{A_{FM}})$. In other words, $\|\xi|_{A_{FM}}\|$ is the total number of new groups created due to the fragmentations and merges in $\xi|_{A_{FM}}$.

Observe that adversary A_{FM} is more powerful than A_F, and that $\mathcal{E}(A, A_F) \subseteq \mathcal{E}(A, A_{FM})$. Since we consider only executions ξ where all processors initially belong in a single group, and from the definition of A_F, it follows that $f_r(\xi|_{A_{FM}}) > f_m(\xi|_{A_{FM}})$.

In this chapter we are interested in assessing complexity bounds in terms of task-oriented work $W(n, p, f)$ (Definition 2.5) and message complexity $M(n, p, f)$ (Definition 2.6), where for adversary A_F we have $f = f_r$ and for adversary A_{FM} we have $f = f_r + f_m$.

We conclude this section with a simple lower bound result.

Theorem 8.1. *For any algorithm solving the Omni-Do problem with n tasks using p processor there exists an adversarial pattern with fragmentation-number f_r such that its task-oriented work is $\Omega(\min\{n \cdot f_r + n, \ n \cdot p\})$*

Proof. We will construct an adversarial strategy for fragmentation-number f_r as required. If $f_r \leq p$, then the adversary partitions the processors into f_r groups at the beginning of the computation, and then lets the f_r groups perform tasks in isolation for the remainder of the computation. This adversarial strategy causes any Omni-Do algorithm to have task-oriented work $\Omega(n \cdot f_r + n)$. (The $\Omega(n)$ part follows trivially from the fact that n tasks must be performed.)

If $f_r > p$ (which means there are merges), then the adversary divides its alloted fragmentation-number f_r as follows. First the adversary "uses up" $f_r - p$ group creations due to fragmentations by repeatedly fragmenting and merging groups without allowing any tasks to be performed until the remaining fragmentation-number is exactly p. Then the adversary creates p singleton groups, where processors work in isolation. In this case any *Omni-Do* algorithm will have task-oriented work $\Omega(n \cdot p)$.

Putting the two cases together yields the lower bound.   □

8.2 A Group Communication Service and Notation

Group communication services are effective building blocks for the construction of fault-tolerant distributed applications. The basis of a group communication service is a *group membership service* (GCS). Each processor, at each time, has a unique *view* of the membership of the group. The view includes a list of the processors that are members of the group. Views can change from time to time, and may become different at different processors.

We assume a group communication service with certain properties. The assumptions are basic, and they are provided by several group communication systems and specifications. We will use the service to maintain group membership information and to communicate information concerning the executed tasks within each group. The GCS provides the following primitives:

- NEWVIEW$(v)_i$: informs processor i of a new view $v = \langle id, set \rangle$, where id is the identifier of the view and set is the set of processor identifiers in the group. When a NEWVIEW$(v)_i$ primitive is invoked, we say that processor i *installs* view v.
- GPMSND$(message)_i$: processor i multicasts a message to the group members.
- GPMRCV$(message)_i$: processor i receives multicasts from other processors.
- GP1SND$(message, destination)_i$: processor i unicasts a message to another member of the current group.
- GP1RCV$(message)_i$: processor i receives unicasts from another processor.

To distinguish between the messages sent in different send events, we assume that each message sent by the application is tagged with a unique message identifier.

We assume the following *safety properties* on any execution ξ of an algorithm that uses GCSs:

1. A processor is always a member of its view. If NEWVIEW$(v)_i$ occurs in ξ then $i \in v.set$.
2. The view identifiers of the views that each processor installs are monotonically increasing. If event NEWVIEW$(v_1)_i$ occurs in ξ before event NEWVIEW$(v_2)_i$, then $v_1.id < v_2.id$. This property implies that: (a) A processor does not install the same view twice, and (b) if two processors install the same two views, they install these views in the same order.

3. For every receive event, there exists a preceding send event of the same message. If $\text{GPMRCV}(m)_i$ ($\text{GP1RCV}(m)_i$) occurs in ξ, then there exists $\text{GPMSND}(m)_j$ ($\text{GP1SND}(m,i)_j$) earlier in execution ξ.

4. Messages are not duplicated. If $\text{GPMRCV}(m_1)_i$ ($\text{GP1RCV}(m_1)_i$) and $\text{GPMRCV}(m_2)_i$ ($\text{GP1RCV}(m_2)_i$) occur in ξ, then $m_1 \neq m_2$.

5. A message is delivered in the same view it was sent in. If processor i receives message m in view v_1 and processor j (it is possible that $i = j$) sends m in view v_2, then $v_1 = v_2$.

6. In the initial state s_0, all processors are in the initial view v_0, such that $v_0.set = \mathcal{P}$.

We assume the following additional *liveness properties* on any execution ξ of an algorithm that uses GCSs:

7. If a processor i sends a message m in the view v, then for each processor j in $v.set$, either j delivers m in v, or i installs another view (or i crashes).

8. If a new view event occurs at any processor i in view v (or i crashes), then a view change will eventually occur at all processors in $v.set - \{i\}$.

Notation

In this chapter we use the Input/Output Automata notation to formally describe our algorithm. Each automaton is a state machine with states and transitions between states, where *actions* are associated with sets of state transitions. Actions are defined using the precondition-effect notation. There are *input*, *output*, and *internal* actions. A particular action is enabled if the preconditions of that action are satisfied. Input actions are always enabled. The statements given as effects are executed as a program started in the existing state and atomically producing the next state as the result of the transition.

An execution ξ of an Input/Output automaton *Aut* is a finite or infinite sequence of alternating states and actions (events) of *Aut* starting with the initial state, i.e., $\xi = s_0, e_1, s_1, e_2, \ldots$, where s_i's are states (s_0 is the initial state) and e_i's are actions (events).

Considering an algorithm A that is specified in Input/Output automata that solves a specific problem under an adversary $\mathcal{A}$, the set of all executions of A can be represented as $\mathcal{E}(A, \mathcal{A})$ using the notation from Section 2.2.3.

Input/Output Automata are composable. Our algorithm in this chapter will be represented as the composition of the automata defining the behavior of each processor with a suitable GCS automaton that satisfies the properties 1 through 7 given above. For an execution of the composed algorithm, each invocation of a primitive of the GCS is represented as a unique action (event) in the execution.

8.3 View-Graphs

We now describe *view-graphs* that represent view changes at processors in executions and that are used to analyze properties of executions. View-graphs are directed graphs (digraphs) that are defined by the states and by the NEWVIEW events of executions of algorithms that use group communication services. Representing view changes as digraphs enables us to use common graph analysis techniques to formally reason about the properties of executions.

Consider the specification of algorithm A that uses a group communication service (GCS). For each processor i, we augment the algorithm specification with the history variable cv_i that keeps track of the current view at i as follows: In the initial state, we set cv_i to be v_0, the distinguished initial view for all processors $i \in \mathcal{P}$. In the effects of the NEWVIEW$(v)_i$ action for processor i, we include the assignment $cv_i := v$. From this point on we assume that algorithms are modified to include such history variables. We now formally define *view-graphs* by specifying how a view-graph is induced by an execution of an algorithm.

Definition 8.2. *Given an execution ξ of algorithm A, the* view-graph $\Gamma_\xi = \langle V, E, L \rangle$ *is defined to be the labeled directed graph as follows:*

1. *Let V_ξ be the set of all views v that occur in NEWVIEW$(v)_i$ events in ξ. The set V of nodes of Γ_ξ is the set $V_\xi \cup \{v_0\}$. We call v_0 the initial node of Γ_ξ.*
2. *The set of edges E of Γ_ξ is a subset of $V \times V$ determined as follows. For each NEWVIEW$(v)_i$ event in ξ that occurs in state s, the edge $(s.cv_i, v)$ is in E.*
3. *The edges in E are labeled by $L : E \to 2^\mathcal{P}$, such that $L(u,v) = \{i : $ NEWVIEW$(v)_i$ occurs in state s in ξ such that $s.cv_i = u\}$.*

Observe that the definition ensures that all edges are labeled.

Example 8.3. Consider the following execution ξ (we omit all events other than NEWVIEW and any states that do not precede NEWVIEW events).

$$\xi = s_0, \text{NEWVIEW}(v_1)_{p_1}, \ldots, s_1, \text{NEWVIEW}(v_2)_{p_2}, \ldots, s_2, \text{NEWVIEW}(v_3)_{p_4}, \ldots,$$
$$s_3, \text{NEWVIEW}(v_4)_{p_1}, \ldots, s_4, \text{NEWVIEW}(v_1)_{p_3}, \ldots, s_5, \text{NEWVIEW}(v_4)_{p_2}, \ldots,$$
$$s_6, \text{NEWVIEW}(v_4)_{p_3}, \ldots$$

Let $v_1.set = \{p_1, p_3\}$, $v_2.set = \{p_2\}$, $v_3.set = \{p_4\}$ and $v_4.set = \{p_1, p_2, p_3\}$. Additionally, $v_0.set = \mathcal{P} = \{p_1, p_2, p_3, p_4\}$.

The view-graph $\Gamma_\xi = \langle V, E, L \rangle$ is given in Figure 8.1. The initial node of Γ_ξ is v_0. The set of nodes of V of Γ_ξ is $V = V_\xi \cup \{v_0\} = \{v_0, v_1, v_2, v_3, v_4\}$. The set of edges E of Γ_ξ is $E = \{(v_0, v_1), (v_0, v_2), (v_0, v_3), (v_1, v_4), (v_2, v_4)\}$, since for each of these (v_k, v_ℓ) the event NEWVIEW$(v_\ell)_i$ occurs in state s_t where $s_t.cv_i = v_k$ for some certain i (by the definition of the history variable). The

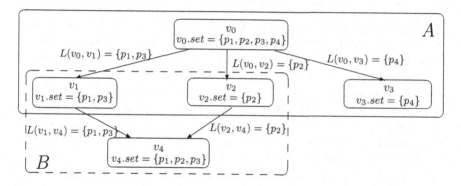

Fig. 8.1. Example of a view-graph

labels of the edges are $L(v_0, v_1) = \{p_1, p_3\}$, $L(v_0, v_2) = \{p_2\}$, $L(v_0, v_3) = \{p_4\}$, $L(v_1, v_4) = \{p_1, p_3\}$ and $L(v_2, v_4) = \{p_2\}$, since for each $p_i \in L(v_k, v_\ell)$ the event NEWVIEW$(v_\ell)_{p_i}$ occurs in state s_t where $s_t.cv_{p_i} = v_k$.

We now show certain properties of view-graphs. Given a graph H and a node v of H, we define $indegree(v, H)$ ($outdegree(v, H)$) to be the indegree (outdegree) of v in H.

Lemma 8.4. *For any execution ξ, $indegree(v_0, \Gamma_\xi) = 0$.*

Proof. In the initial state s_0, $s_0.cv$ is defined to be v_0 for all processors in $\mathcal{P}$ and $v_0.set = \mathcal{P}$. Assume that $indegree(v_0, \Gamma_\xi) > 0$. By the construction of view-graphs, this implies that some processor $i \in \mathcal{P}$ installs v_0 a second time. But this contradicts the property 2(a) of GCS. $\square$

Lemma 8.5. *Let ξ be an execution and $\Gamma_\xi|_i$ be the projection of Γ_ξ on the edges whose label includes i, for some $i \in \mathcal{P}$. $\Gamma_\xi|_i$ is an elementary path and v_0 is the path's source node.*

Proof. Let execution ξ be $s_0, e_1, s_1, e_2, \ldots$. Let $\xi^{(k)}$ be the prefix of ξ up to the kth state. i.e., $\xi^{(k)} = s_0, e_1, s_1, e_2, \ldots, s_k$. Let Γ_ξ^k be the view-graph that is induced by $\xi^{(k)}$. Then define $\Gamma_\xi^k|_i$ to be the projection of Γ_ξ^k on the edges whose label includes i, for some $i \in \mathcal{P}$. For an elementary path π, we define $\pi.sink$ to be its sink node.
We prove by induction on k that $\Gamma_\xi^k|_i$ is an elementary path, that $\Gamma_\xi^k|_i.sink = s_k.cv_i$ and that v_0 is the path's source node.
Basis: $k = 0$. $\Gamma_\xi^0|_i$ has only one vertex, v_0, and no edges ($\xi^{(0)} = s_0$). Thus, $\Gamma_\xi^0|_i.sink = s_0.cv_i = v_0$ and v_0 is the source node of this path.
Inductive Hypothesis: Assume that $\forall n \leq k$, $\Gamma_\xi^n|_i$ is an elementary path, that $\Gamma_\xi^n|_i.sink = s_n.cv_i$ and that v_0 is the path's source node.
Inductive Step: $n = k + 1$. For state s_{k+1} we consider two cases:

Case 1: If event e_{k+1} is not a NEWVIEW event involving processor i, then $\Gamma_\xi^{k+1}|_i = \Gamma_\xi^k|_i$. Thus, by inductive hypothesis, $\Gamma_\xi^{k+1}|_i$ is an elementary path and v_0 is its source node. From state s_k to state s_{k+1}, processor i did not witness any new view. By the definition of the history variable, $s_{k+1}.cv_i = s_k.cv_i$. Thus, $\Gamma_\xi^{k+1}|_i.sink = s_k.cv_i = s_{k+1}.cv_i$.

Case 2: If event e_{k+1} is a NEWVIEW$(v)_i$ event that involves processor i, then by the construction of the view-graph, $(s_k.cv_i, v)$ is a new edge from node $s_k.cv_i$ to node v. By inductive hypothesis, $\Gamma_\xi^k|_i.sink = s_k.cv_i$. Since our GCS does not allow the same view to be installed twice (property 2(a)), $v \neq u$ for all $u \in \Gamma_\xi^k|_i$. Thus, $\Gamma_\xi^{k+1}|_i$ is also an elementary path, with v_0 its source node and $\Gamma_\xi^{k+1}|_i.sink = v$. From state s_k to state s_{k+1}, processor i installs the new view v. By the definition of the history variable, $s_{k+1}.cv_i = v$. Thus, $\Gamma_\xi^{k+1}|_i.sink = s_{k+1}.cv_i$. This completes the proof. □

Theorem 8.6. *Any view-graph Γ_ξ, induced by any execution ξ of algorithm A is a connected graph.*

Proof. The result follows from Definition 8.2(2), from the observation that all edges of the view-graph are labeled and from Lemma 8.5 □

We now demonstrate how we can use view-graphs to represent group fragmentations and merges. We begin with fragmentations.

Definition 8.7. *For a view-graph $\Gamma_\xi = \langle V, E, L \rangle$, a fragmentation subgraph is a connected labeled subgraph $H = \langle V_H, E_H, L_H \rangle$ of Γ_ξ such that:*

1. *H contains a unique node v such that $indegree(v, H) = 0$; v is called the fragmentation node of H.*
2. *$V_H = \{v\} \cup V_H'$, where V_H' is defined to be $\{w : (v, w) \in E\}$.*
3. *$E_H = \{(v, w) : w \in V_H'\}$.*
4. *L_H is the restriction of L on E_H.*
5. *$\bigcup_{w \in V_H'} (w.set) = v.set$.*
6. *$\forall u, w \in V_H'$ such that $u \neq w$, $u.set \cap w.set = \emptyset$.*
7. *$\forall w \in V_H'$, $L_H(v, w) = w.set$.*

We refer to all NEWVIEW events that collectively induce a fragmentation subgraph for a fragmentation node v as a fragmentation.

Example 8.8. The subgraph contained in the solid box A in Figure 8.1 shows the fragmentation subgraph $H = \langle V_H, E_H, L_H \rangle$ of Γ_ξ from Example 8.3. Here $V_H = \{v_0, v_1, v_2, v_3\}$, $E_H = \{(v_0, v_1), (v_0, v_2), (v_0, v_3)\}$ and the labels are the labels of Γ_ξ restricted on E_H. We can confirm that H is a fragmentation subgraph by examining the individual items of Definition 8.7.

We continue with the representation of group merges using view-graphs.

Definition 8.9. *For a view-graph $\Gamma_\xi = \langle V, E, L \rangle$, a merge subgraph is a connected labeled subgraph $H = \langle V_H, E_H, L_H \rangle$ of Γ_ξ such that:*

1. H contains a unique node v such that $outdegree(v, H) = 0$ and $indegree(v, H) > 1$; v is called the merge node of H.
2. $V_H = \{v\} \cup V'_H$, where V'_H is defined to be $\{w : (w, v) \in E\}$.
3. $E_H = \{(w, v) : w \in V'_H\}$.
4. L_H is the restriction of L on E_H.
5. $\bigcup_{w \in V'_H}(w.set) = v.set$.
6. $\forall u, w \in V'_H$ such that $u \neq w$, $u.set \cap w.set = \emptyset$.
7. $\bigcup_{w \in V'_H} L_H(w, v) = v.set$.

We refer to all NEWVIEW events that collectively induce a merge subgraph for a merge node v as a merge.

Note that a regrouping of a group g_1 to a group g_2 with the same membership ($g_1.set = g_2.set$) can be represented either as a fragmentation subgraph (fragmentation) or as a merge subgraph (merge). Following the convention established in the definition of adversary $\mathcal{A}_{FM}$ (Section 8.1), we represent it as a fragmentation subgraph by requiring that $indegree(v, H) > 1$ for any merge node v.

Example 8.10. The subgraph contained in the dashed box B in Figure 8.1 of Example 8.3 shows the merge subgraph $H = \langle V_H, E_H, L_H \rangle$ of Γ_ξ, where $V_H = \{v_1, v_2, v_3, v_4\}$, $E_H = \{(v_1, v_4), (v_2, v_4)\}$ and the labels are the labels of Γ_ξ restricted on E_H. We can verify this by examining all conditions of Definition 8.9.

We now give some additional definitions and show that any view graph is a directed acyclic graph (DAG).

Definition 8.11. *Given a view-graph Γ_ξ we define:*

(a) $frag(\Gamma_\xi)$ *to be the set of all the distinct fragmentation nodes in Γ_ξ,*
(b) $merg(\Gamma_\xi)$ *to be the set of all the distinct merge nodes in Γ_ξ.*

Definition 8.12. *Given a view-graph Γ_ξ:*

(a) *if all of its non-terminal nodes are in $frag(\Gamma_\xi)$, then Γ_ξ is called a fragmentation view-graph.*
(b) *if each of its non-terminal nodes is either in $frag(\Gamma_\xi)$, or it is an immediate ancestor of a node which is in $merg(\Gamma_\xi)$, then Γ_ξ is called an fm view-graph.*

For Γ_ξ in the example in Figure 8.1 we have $v_0 \in frag(\Gamma_\xi)$ by Definition 8.11(a). Also, $v_4 \in merg(\Gamma_\xi)$ per Definition 8.11(b); additionally, the nodes v_1 and v_2 are immediate ancestors of $v_4 \in merg(\Gamma_\xi)$. By Definition 8.12(b), Γ_ξ is an fm view-graph. Observe that Γ_ξ is a DAG. This is true for all view-graphs:

Theorem 8.13. *Any view-graph $\Gamma_\xi = \langle V, E, L \rangle$ is a Directed Acyclic Graph (DAG).*

Proof. Assume that Γ_ξ is not a DAG. Thus, it contains at least one cycle. Let $((v_1, v_2)(v_2, v_3) \ldots (v_k, v_1))$ be an elementary cycle of Γ_ξ. By the construction of view-graphs (Definition 8.2(3)) and by the monotonicity property (property 2) of GCS, $v_i.id < v_{i+1}.id$ for $1 \leq i \leq k$ and $v_k.id < v_1.id$. But, by the transitivity of "<", $v_1.id < v_k.id$, a contradiction. $\square$

Corollary 8.14. *Any fm view graph is a DAG and any fragmentation view-graph is a rooted tree.*

In the complexity analysis of algorithm AX, we exploit the fact that view graphs are DAGs. In particular we use the following fact.

Fact 8.15 *In any (non-empty) DAG, there is at least one vertex, such that all of its descendants have outdegree 0.*

Remark 8.16. Consider an execution ξ of algorithm A under adversary $\mathcal{A}_{FM}$. In Section 8.1 we defined the fragmentation-number $f_r(\xi|_{\mathcal{A}_{FM}})$ and merge-number $f_m(\xi|_{\mathcal{A}_{FM}})$ of the adversarial pattern $\xi|_{\mathcal{A}_{FM}}$ of execution ξ. We can also use view-graphs to define these quantities. Namely, $f_r(\xi|_{\mathcal{A}_{FM}}) = |\{w : \text{NEWVIEW}(w)_i \text{ occurs in } \xi \land (v, w) \in E \land v \in frag(\Gamma_\xi)\}|$, and $f_m(\xi|_{\mathcal{A}_{FM}}) = |\{v : \text{NEWVIEW}(v)_i \text{ occurs in } \xi \land v \in merg(\Gamma_\xi)\}|$, where Γ_ξ is the view-graph of execution ξ.

8.4 Algorithm AX

We present Algorithm AX, that deals with fragmentations and merges and that relies on the GCS as specified in Section 8.2, and prove its correctness. We give its complexity analysis in Section 8.5.

8.4.1 Description of the Algorithm

Algorithm AX uses a coordinator approach within each group view. The high level idea of the algorithm is that each processor performs (remaining) tasks according to a load balancing rule, and a processor completes its computation when it learns the results of all the tasks.

Task Allocation. The set T of the initial tasks is known to all processors. During the execution each processor i maintains a local set D of tasks already done, a local set R of the corresponding results, and the set G of processors in the current group. (The set D may be an underestimate of the set of tasks done globally.) The processors allocate tasks based on the shared knowledge of the processors in G about the tasks done. For a processor i, let $rank(i, G)$ be the rank of i in G when processor identifiers are sorted in ascending order. Let U be the tasks in $T - D$. For a task u in U, let $rank(u, U)$ be the rank of u in U when task identifiers are sorted in ascending order. Our *load balancing rule* for each processor i in G is that:

- if $rank(i, G) \leq |U|$, then processor i performs task u such that $rank(u, U) = rank(i, G)$;
- if $rank(i, G) > |U|$, then processor i does nothing.

Algorithm Structure. The algorithm code is given in Figure 8.2 using the Input/Output automata notation. The algorithm uses the group communication service to structure its computation in terms of *rounds* numbered sequentially within each group view.

Initially all processors are members of the distinguished initial view v_0, such that $v_0.set = \mathcal{P}$. Rounds numbered 1 correspond to the initial round either in the original group or in a new group upon a regrouping as notified via the NEWVIEW event. If a regrouping occurs, the processor receives the new set of members from the group membership service and starts the first round of this view (NEWVIEW action). At the beginning of each round, denoted by a round number Rnd, processor i knows G, the local set D of tasks already done, and the set R of the results. Since all processors know G, they "elect" the group coordinator to be the processor which has the highest processor id (no communication is required since the coordinator is uniquely identified). In each round each processor reports D and R to the coordinator of G (GP1SND action). The coordinator receives and collates these reports (GP1RCV action) and sends the result to the group members (GPMSND action). Upon the receipt of the message from the coordinator, processors update their D and R, and perform work according to the load balancing rule (GPMRCV action).

For generality, we assume that the messages may be delivered by the GCS out of order. The set of messages within the current view is saved in the local variable X. The saved messages are also used to determine when all messages for a given round have been received. Processing continues until each member of G knows all results (the processors enter the *sleep* stage).

The variables cv and MSG are *history variables* that do not affect the algorithm, but play a role in its analysis.

8.4.2 Correctness of the Algorithm

We now show the safety of algorithm AX. We first show that no processor stops working as long as it knows of any undone tasks.

Theorem 8.17. (Safety 1) *For all states of any execution of Algorithm AX it holds that*

$$\forall i \in \mathcal{P} : D_i \neq T \Rightarrow Phase \neq sleep.$$

Proof. The proof follows by examination of the code of the algorithm, and more specifically from the code of the input action GPMRCV($\langle j, Z, Q, round \rangle)_i$. □

Data types and identifiers:

T : tasks
$\mathcal{R}$: results
$Result : T \to \mathcal{R}$
$\mathcal{M}es$: messages
$\mathcal{P}$: processor ids
$\mathcal{G}$: group ids
$views = \mathcal{G} \times 2^{\mathcal{P}}$: views, selectors id and set

$m \in \mathcal{M}es$
$i, j \in \mathcal{P}$
$v \in views$
$Z \in 2^{T}$
$Q \in 2^{\mathcal{R}}$
$round \in \mathbb{N}$
$results \in 2^{\mathcal{R}}$

States:

$T \in 2^{T}$, the set of $n = |T|$ tasks
$D \in 2^{T}$, the set of done tasks, initially $\emptyset$
$R \in 2^{\mathcal{R}}$, the set of known results, initially $\emptyset$
$G \in 2^{\mathcal{P}}$, current members, init. $v_0.set = \mathcal{P}$
$X \in 2^{\mathcal{M}es}$, messages since last NEWVIEW,
    initially $\emptyset$
$Rnd \in \mathbb{N}$, round number, initially 1
$Phase \in$
    $\{send, receive, sleep, mcast, mrecv\}$,
    initially $send$

Derived variables:

$U = T - D$, the set of remaining tasks
$Coordinator(i)$: Boolean,
    if $i = \max_{j \in G}\{j\}$
    then $true$ else $false$
$Next(U, G)$, next task u, such that
    $rank(u, U) = rank(i, G)$

History variables:

$cv_i \in views$ $(i \in \mathcal{P})$,
    initially $\forall i$, $cv_i = v_0$.
$\text{MSG}_i \in 2^{\mathcal{M}es}$ $(i \in \mathcal{P})$,
    initially $\forall i$, $\text{MSG}_i = \emptyset$.

Transitions at i:

input NEWVIEW$(v)_i$
Effect:
    $G \leftarrow v.set$
    $X \leftarrow \emptyset$
    $Rnd \leftarrow 1$
    $Phase \leftarrow send$
    $cv := v$

output GP1SND$(m, j)_i$
Precondition:
    $Coordinator(j)$
    $Phase = send$
    $m = \langle i, D, R, Rnd \rangle$
Effect:
    $\text{MSG} := \text{MSG} \cup \{m\}$
    $Phase \leftarrow receive$

input GP1RCV$(\langle j, Z, Q, round \rangle)_i$
Effect:
    $X \leftarrow X \cup \{\langle j, Z, Q, round \rangle\}$
    $R \leftarrow R \cup Q$
    $D \leftarrow D \cup Z$
    if $G = \{j : \langle j, *, *, Rnd \rangle \in X\}$ then
        $Phase \leftarrow mcast$

output GPMSND$(m)_i$
Precondition:
    $Coordinator(i)$
    $m = \langle i, D, R, Rnd \rangle$
    $Phase = mcast$
Effect:
    $\text{MSG} := \text{MSG} \cup \{m\}$
    $Phase \leftarrow mrecv$

input GPMRCV$(\langle j, Z, Q, round \rangle)_i$
Effect:
    $D \leftarrow D \cup Z$
    $R \leftarrow R \cup Q$
    if $D = T$ then
        $Phase \leftarrow sleep$
    else
        if $rank(i, G) < |U|$ then
            $R \leftarrow R \cup \{Result(Next(U, G))\}$
            $D \leftarrow D \cup \{Next(U, G)\}$
        $Rnd \leftarrow Rnd + 1$
        $Phase \leftarrow send$

Fig. 8.2. Input/Output Automata specification of algorithm AX.

Note that the implication in Theorem 8.17 cannot be replaced by iff ($\Leftrightarrow$). This is because if $D_i = T$, we may still have $Phase \neq sleep$. This is the case where processor i becomes a member of a group in which the processors do not know all the results of all the tasks.

Next we show that if some processor does not know the result of some task, this is because it does not know that this task has been performed (Theorem 8.19 below). We show this using the history variables MSG_i ($i \in \mathcal{P}$).

We define MSG_i to be a history variable that keeps on track all the messages sent by processor $i \in \mathcal{P}$ in all GP1SND and GPMSND events of an execution of algorithm AX. Formally, in the effects of the $\text{GP1SND}(m, j)_i$ and $\text{GPMSND}(m)_i$ actions we include the assignment $\text{MSG}_i := \text{MSG}_i \cup \{m\}$. Initially, $\text{MSG}_i = \emptyset$ for all i. We define UMSG to be $\bigcup_{i \in \mathcal{P}} \text{MSG}_i$.

Lemma 8.18. *If m is a message received by processor $i \in \mathcal{P}$ in a $\text{GP1RCV}(m)_i$ or $\text{GPMRCV}(m)_i$ event of an execution of algorithm AX, then $m \in$ UMSG.*

Proof. Property 3 of the GCS (Section 8.2) requires that for every receive event there exists a preceding send event of the same message (the GCS does not generate messages). Hence, m must have been sent by some processor $j \in \mathcal{P}$ (possible $j = i$) in some earlier event of the execution. Messages can be sent only in $\text{GP1SND}(m, i)_j$ or $\text{GPMSND}(m)_j$ events. By definition, $m \in \text{MSG}_j$. Hence, $m \in$ UMSG.   □

Theorem 8.19. (Safety 2) *For all states of any execution of Algorithm AX:*
  (a) $\forall t \in T, \ \forall i \in \mathcal{P} : result(t) \notin R_i \Rightarrow t \notin D_i$, *and*
  (b) $\forall t \in T, \forall \langle i, D', R', Rnd \rangle \in$ UMSG $: result(t) \notin R' \Rightarrow t \notin D'$.

Proof. Let ξ be an execution of AX and ξ^k be the prefix of ξ up to the kth state, i.e., $\xi^k = s_0, e_1, s_1, e_2, \ldots, s_k$. The proof is done by induction on k.

Base Case: $k = 0$. In s_0, $\forall i \in \mathcal{P}, D_i = \emptyset, R_i = \emptyset$ and UMSG $= \emptyset$.

Inductive Hypothesis: For a state s_ℓ such that $\ell \leq k$, $\forall t \in T$, $\forall i \in \mathcal{P}$: $result(t) \notin R_i \Rightarrow t \notin D_i$, and $\forall t \in T, \forall \langle i, D', R', Rnd \rangle \in$ UMSG $: result(t) \notin R' \Rightarrow t \notin D'$.

Inductive Step: $\ell = k+1$. Consider the following seven types of actions leading to the state s_{k+1}:

1. $e_{k+1} = \text{NEWVIEW}(v')_i$: The effect of this action does not affect the invariant. By the inductive hypothesis, in state s_{k+1}, the invariant holds.
2. $e_{k+1} = \text{GP1SND}(m, j)_i$: Clearly, the effect of this action does not affect part (a) of the invariant but it affects part (b). Since $m = \langle i, D_i, R_i, Rnd \rangle$, by the inductive hypothesis part (a), the assignment $m \in$ UMSG reestablishes part (b) of the invariant. Thus, in state s_{k+1}, the invariant is reestablished.
3. $e_{k+1} = \text{GP1RCV}(\langle j, Z, Q, round \rangle)_i$: Processor i updates R_i and D_i according to Q and Z respectively. The action is atomic, i.e., if R_i is updated, then D_i must be also updated. By Lemma 8.18, $\langle j, Z, Q, round \rangle \in$ UMSG. Thus, by the inductive hypothesis part (b), $\forall t \in T : result(t) \notin Z \Rightarrow$

$t \notin Q$. From the fact that D_i and R_i are updated according to Z and Q respectively and by the inductive hypothesis part (a), in state s_{k+1}, the invariant is reestablished.

4. $e_{k+1} = \text{GPMSND}(m)_i$: Clearly, the effect of this action does not affect part (a) of the invariant but it affects part (b). Since $m = \langle i, D_i, R_i, Rnd \rangle$, by the inductive hypothesis part (a), the assignment $m \in \text{UMSG}$ reestablishes part (b) of the invariant. Thus, in state s_{k+1}, the invariant is reestablished.

5. $e_{k+1} = \text{GPMRCV}(\langle j, Z, Q, round \rangle)_i$: By Lemma 8.18, $\langle j, Z, Q, round \rangle \in \text{UMSG}$. By the inductive hypothesis part (b), $\forall t \in T : result(t) \notin Z \Rightarrow t \notin Q$. Processor i updates R_i and D_i according to Q and Z respectively. Since Z and Q have the required property, by the inductive hypothesis part (a), the assignments to D_i and R_i reestablish the invariant.

   In the case where $D_i \neq T$, processor i performs a task according to the load balancing rule. Let $u \in T$ be this task. Because of the action atomicity, when processor i updates R_i with $result(u)$, it must also update D_i with u. Hence, in state s_{k+1}, the invariant is reestablished.

6. $e_{k+1} = \text{REQUEST}_{q,i}$: The effect of this action does not affect the invariant.

7. $e_{k+1} = \text{REPORT}(results)_{q,i}$: The effect of this action does not affect the invariant.

This completes the proof. □

8.5 Analysis of Algorithm AX

We first assess the efficiency of algorithm AX under adversary $\mathcal{A}_{FM}$ in terms of task-oriented work $W_{\mathcal{A}_{FM}}(n, p, f)$ and message complexity $M_{\mathcal{A}_{FM}}(n, p, f)$, where $f = f_r + f_m$. Then we examine the efficiency of the algorithm under adversary $\mathcal{A}_F$ as a special case.

8.5.1 Work Complexity

We begin the analysis of algorithm AX by first providing definitions and then proving several lemmas that lead to the work complexity of the algorithm.

Definition 8.20. *Let ξ^μ be any execution of algorithm AX in which all the processors learn the results of all tasks and that includes a merge of groups $g_1, \ldots, g_k$ into the group μ, where the processors in μ undergo no further view changes. We define $\bar{\xi}^\mu$ to be the execution we derive by removing the merge from ξ^μ as follows: (1) We remove all states and events that correspond to the merge of groups $g_1, \ldots, g_k$ into the group μ and all states and events for processors within μ. (2) We add the appropriate states and events such that the processors in groups $g_1, \ldots, g_k$ undergo no further view changes and perform any remaining tasks.*

Definition 8.21. *Let ξ^φ be any execution of algorithm AX in which all the processors learn the results of all tasks and that includes a fragmentation of the group φ to the groups $g_1, \ldots, g_k$ where the processors in these groups undergo no further view changes. We define $\bar{\xi}^\varphi$ to be the execution we derive by removing the fragmentation from ξ^φ as follows: (1) We remove all states and events that correspond to the fragmentation of the group φ to the groups $g_1, \ldots, g_k$ and all states and events of the processors within the groups $g_1, \ldots, g_k$. (2) We add the appropriate states and events such that the processors in the group φ undergo no further view changes and perform any remaining tasks.*

Note: In Definitions 8.20 and 8.21, we claim that we can remove states and events from an execution and add some other states and events to it. This is possible because if the processors in a single view installed that view and there are no further view changes, then the algorithm will continue making computation progress. So, if we remove all states and events corresponding to a view change, then the algorithm can always proceed as if this view change never occurred.

Lemma 8.22. *In algorithm AX, for any view v, including the initial view, if the group is not subject to any regroupings, then the work required to complete all tasks in the view is no more than $n - \max_{i \in v.set}\{|D_i|\}$, where D_i is the value of the state variable D of processor i at the start of its local round 1 in view v.*

Proof. In the first round, all the processors send messages to the coordinator containing D_i. The coordinator computes $\cup_{i \in v.set}\{D_i\}$ and broadcasts this result to the group members. Since the group is not subject to any regroupings, the number of tasks t, that the processors need to perform is: $t = n - |\cup_{i \in v.set}\{D_i\}|$. In each round of the computation, by the load balancing rule, the members of the group perform distinct tasks and no task is performed more than once. Therefore, t is the work performed in this group. On the other hand, $\max_{i \in v.set}\{|D_i|\} \leq |\cup_{i \in v.set}\{D_i\}|$, thus, $t \leq n - \max_{i \in v.set}\{|D_i|\}$.   □

In the following lemma, groups $\mu, g_1, \ldots, g_k$ are defined as in Definition 8.20.

Lemma 8.23. *Let ξ^μ be an execution of Algorithm AX as in Definition 8.20. Let W_1 be the work performed by the algorithm in the execution ξ^μ. Let W_2 be the work performed by Algorithm AX in the execution $\bar{\xi}^\mu$. Then $W_1 \leq W_2$.*

Proof. For the execution ξ^μ, let W' be the work performed by the processors in $\mathcal{P} - \cup_{1 \leq i \leq k}(g_i.set) - \mu.set$. Observe that the work performed by the processors in $\mathcal{P} - \cup_{1 \leq i \leq k}(g_i.set)$ in the execution $\bar{\xi}^\mu$ is equal to W'. The work that is performed by processor j in $g_i.set$ prior to the NEWVIEW$(\mu)_j$ event in ξ^μ, is the same in both executions. Call this work $W_{i,j}$. Define $W'' = \sum_{i=1}^{k}\sum_{j \in g_i.set} W_{i,j}$. Define $W_s = W' + W''$. Thus, W_s is the same in both executions, ξ^μ and $\bar{\xi}^\mu$. Define W_μ to be the work performed by all processors in $\mu.set$ in execution ξ^μ. For each processor j in $g_i.set$, let D_j be the value of the state variable D just prior to the NEWVIEW$(\mu)_j$ event in ξ^μ. For each g_i, define: $d_i = |\bigcup_{j\in g_i.set} D_j|$. Thus there are at least $n - d_i$ tasks that remain to be done in each g_i.

In execution $\bar{\xi}^\mu$, the processors in each group g_i proceed and complete these remaining tasks. This requires work at least $n - d_i$. Define this work as W_{g_i}. Thus, $W_{g_i} \geq (n - d_i)$. In execution ξ^μ, groups $g_1, \ldots, g_k$ merge into group μ. The number of tasks that need to be performed by the members of μ is at most $n - d_j$, where $d_j = \max_i\{d_i\}$ for some j. By Lemma 8.22, $W_\mu \leq n - d_j$. Observe that

$$W_1 = W_s + W_\mu \leq W_s + n - d_j \leq W_s + \sum_{i=1}^{k}(n - d_i) \leq W_s + \sum_{i=1}^{k} W_{g_i} = W_2$$

as desired. $\square$

In the following lemma, groups $\varphi, g_1, \ldots, g_k$ are defined as in Definition 8.21.

Lemma 8.24. *Let ξ^φ be an execution of Algorithm AX as in Definition 8.21. Let W_1 be the work performed by the algorithm in the execution ξ^φ. Let W_2 be the worked performed by Algorithm AX in the execution $\bar{\xi}^\varphi$. Then $W_1 \leq W_2 + W_3$, where W_3 is the work performed by all processors in $\bigcup_{1\leq i\leq k}(g_i.set)$ in the execution ξ^φ.*

Proof. Let W' be the work performed by all processors in $\mathcal{P} - \bigcup_{1\leq i\leq k}(g_i.set) - \varphi.set$ in the execution ξ^φ. Observe that the work performed by all processors in $\mathcal{P} - \varphi.set$ in the execution $\bar{\xi}^\varphi$ is equal to W'. The work that is performed by processor j in $\varphi.set$ prior to the NEWVIEW$(g_i)_j$ event in ξ^φ, is the same in both executions. Call this work $W_{\varphi,j}$. Define $W'' = \sum_{j\in\varphi.set} W_{\varphi,j}$. Define $W_s = W' + W''$. Thus, W_s is the same in both executions, ξ^φ and $\bar{\xi}^\varphi$. Define W_φ to be the work performed by all processors in $\varphi.set$ in execution $\bar{\xi}^\varphi$. Let $W''' = W_\varphi - W''$. Observe that:

$$W_1 = W_s + W_3 \leq W_s + W_3 + W''' = W_2 + W_3,$$

as desired. $\square$

Lemma 8.25. $W_{\mathcal{A}_{FM}}(n, p, f_r + f_m) \leq n \cdot p$.

Proof. By the construction of algorithm AX, when processors are not able to exchange information about task execution due to regroupings, in the worst case, each processor has to perform all n tasks by itself. Since we can have at most p processors doing that the result follows. $\square$

Lemma 8.26. $W_{\mathcal{A}_{FM}}(n, p, f_r + f_m) \leq n \cdot f_r + n$.

Proof. To simplify notation, we let $\mathcal{W}(f_r, f_m)$ stand for $W_{\mathcal{A}_{FM}}(n, p, f_r + f_m)$. The proof is by induction on the number of views, denoted by ℓ, occurring in an execution. For a specific execution ξ_ℓ with ℓ views, let $f_r(\xi_\ell) = f_r^{(\ell)}$ be the fragmentation-number and $f_m(\xi_\ell) = f_m^{(\ell)}$ the merge-number.

Base Case: $\ell = 0$. Since $f_r^{(\ell)}$ and $f_m^{(\ell)}$ must also be 0, the base case follows from Lemma 8.22.

Inductive Hypothesis: Assume that for all $\ell \leq k$, $\mathcal{W}(f_r^{(\ell)}, f_m^{(\ell)}) \leq n \cdot f_r^{(\ell)} + n$.

Inductive Step: Need to show that for $\ell = k + 1$,

$$\mathcal{W}(f_r^{(k+1)}, f_m^{(k+1)}) \leq n \cdot f_r^{(k+1)} + n .$$

Consider a specific execution ξ_{k+1} with $\ell = k+1$. Let $\Gamma_{\xi_{k+1}}$ be the view-graph induced by this execution. The view-graph has at least one vertex such that all of its descendants are sinks (Fact 8.15). Let ν be such a vertex. We consider two cases:

Case 1: Vertex ν has a descendant μ that corresponds to a merge in the execution. Therefore all ancestors of μ in $\Gamma_{\xi_{k+1}}$ have outdegree 1. Since μ is a sink vertex, the group that corresponds to μ performs all the remaining (if any) tasks and does not perform any additional work. Let $\xi_k = \bar{\xi}_{k+1}^\mu$ (per Definition 8.20) be an execution in which this merge does not occur. In execution ξ_k, the number of views is k. Also, $f_r^{(k+1)} = f_r^{(k)}$ and $f_m^{(k+1)} = f_m^{(k)} + 1$. By inductive hypothesis, $\mathcal{W}(f_r^{(k)}, f_m^{(k)}) \leq n \cdot f_r^{(k)} + n$. By Lemma 8.23, the work performed in execution ξ_{k+1}, is no worse than the work performed in execution ξ_k. Hence, the total work complexity is:

$$\mathcal{W}(f_r^{(k+1)}, f_m^{(k+1)}) \leq \mathcal{W}(f_r^{(k)}, f_m^{(k)}) \leq n \cdot f_r^{(k)} + n = n \cdot f_r^{(k+1)} + n.$$

Case 2: Vertex ν has no descendants that correspond to a merge in the execution. Therefore, the group that corresponds to ν must fragment, say into q groups. These groups correspond to sink vertices in $\Gamma_{\xi_{k+1}}$, thus they perform all the remaining (if any) tasks and do not perform any additional work. Let $\xi_{k+1-q} = \bar{\xi}_{k+1}^\nu$ (per Definition 8.21) be an execution in which the fragmentation does not occur. In execution ξ_{k+1-q}, the number of views is $k+1-q \leq k$. Also, $f_r^{(k+1-q)} = f_r^{(k+1)} - q$ and $f_m^{(k+1-q)} = f_m^{(k+1)}$. By inductive hypothesis, $\mathcal{W}(f_r^{(k+1-q)}, f_m^{(k+1-q)}) \leq n \cdot f_r^{(k+1-q)} + n$. From Lemma 8.22, the work performed in each new group caused by the fragmentation is no more than n. Let W_σ be the total work performed in all q groups. Thus, $W_\sigma \leq qn$. By Lemma 8.24, the work performed in execution ξ_{k+1}, is no worse than the work performed in execution ξ_{k+1-q} and the work performed in all q groups. Hence, the total work complexity is:

$$\begin{aligned}
\mathcal{W}(f_r^{(k+1)}, f_m^{(k+1)}) &\leq \mathcal{W}(f_r^{(k+1-q)}, f_m^{(k+1-q)}) + W_\sigma \\
&\leq n \cdot f_r^{(k+1-q)} + n + W_\sigma \\
&= n \cdot \left(f_r^{(k+1)} - q \right) + n + W_\sigma \\
&\leq n \cdot \left(f_r^{(k+1)} - q \right) + n + qn \\
&= n f_r^{(k+1)} - qn + n + qn \qquad = n \cdot f_r^{(k+1)} + n.
\end{aligned}$$

This completes the inductive proof.   □

We now show the main result for task-oriented work of algorithm AX.

Theorem 8.27. *Algorithm AX solves the* Omni-Do$_{\mathcal{A}_{FM}}(n, p, f)$ *problem with task-oriented work*

$$W_{\mathcal{A}_{FM}}(n, p, f_r + f_m) \leq \min\{n \cdot f_r + n, \ n \cdot p\}.$$

Proof. It follows directly from Lemmas 8.25 and 8.26.   □

Note that in light of Theorem 8.1 algorithm AX is *work-optimal* under adversary $\mathcal{A}_{FM}$.

Also observe that task-oriented work complexity $W_{\mathcal{A}_{FM}}(n, p, f_r + f_m)$ does not depend on f_m. This of course does not imply that for any given execution, the work does not depend on merges. However, this observation substantiates the intuition that merges lead to a more efficient computation.

8.5.2 Message Complexity

We start by showing several lemmas that lead to the message complexity of the algorithm.

Lemma 8.28. *For algorithm AX, in any view v, including the initial view, if the group is not subject to any regroupings, and for each processor $i \in v.set$, D_i is the value of the state variable D at the start of its local round 1 in view v, then the number of messages M that are sent until all tasks are completed is $2(n - d) \leq M < 2(q + n - d)$ where $q = |v.set|$, and $d = |\bigcup_{i \in v.set} D_i|$.*

Proof. By the load balancing rule, the algorithm needs $\lceil \frac{n-d}{q} \rceil$ rounds to complete all tasks. In each round each processor sends one message to the coordinator and the coordinator responds with a single message to each processor. Thus, $M = 2q \cdot (\lceil \frac{n-d}{q} \rceil)$. Using the properties of the *ceiling*, we get: $2(n - d) \leq M < 2(q + n - d)$.   □

In the following lemma, groups $\mu, g_1, \ldots, g_k$ are defined as in Definition 8.20.

Lemma 8.29. *Let ξ^μ be an execution of Algorithm AX as in Definition 8.20. Let M_1 be the message cost of the algorithm in the execution ξ^μ. Let M_2 be the message cost of Algorithm AX in the execution $\bar{\xi}^\mu$. Then $M_1 < M_2 + 2p$.*

Proof. For the execution ξ^μ, let M' be the number of messages sent by the processors in $\mathcal{P} - \bigcup_{1 \leq i \leq k}(g_i.set) - \mu.set$. Observe that the number of messages sent by the processors in $\mathcal{P} - \bigcup_{1 \leq i \leq k}(g_i.set)$ in the execution $\bar{\xi}^\mu$ is equal to M'.

The number of messages sent by any processor j in $g_i.set$ prior to the NEWVIEW$(\mu)_j$ event in ξ^μ, is the same in both executions. Call this message cost $M_{i,j}$. Define $M'' = \sum_{i=1}^{k} \sum_{j \in g_i.set} M_{i,j}$. Define $M_s = M' + M''$. Thus, M_s is the same in both executions, ξ^μ and $\bar{\xi}^\mu$. Define M_μ to be the number of messages sent by all processors in $\mu.set$ in execution ξ^μ. For each processor j in $g_i.set$, let D_j be the value of the state variable D just prior to the NEWVIEW$(\mu)_j$ event in ξ^μ. For each g_i, define $d_i = |\bigcup_{j \in g_i.set} D_j|$. Thus there are at least $n - d_i$ tasks that remain to be done in each g_i.

In execution $\bar{\xi}^\mu$, the processors in each group g_i proceed and complete these remaining tasks. Let M_{g_i} be the number of messages sent by all processors in $g_i.set$ in order to complete the remaining tasks. By Lemma 8.28, $M_{g_i} \geq 2(n - d_i)$. In execution ξ^μ, groups $g_1, \ldots, g_k$ merge into group μ. The number of tasks that need to be performed by the members of μ is at most $n - d_j$, where $d_j = \max_i\{d_i\}$ for some j. By Lemma 8.28, $M_\mu < 2(q + n - d_j)$, where $q = |\mu.set|$. Observe that

$$\begin{aligned}
M_1 = M_s + M_\mu & \qquad < M_s + 2(q + n - d_j) \\
\leq M_s + 2q + 2\sum_{i=1}^{k}(n - d_i) & \leq M_s + 2q + \sum_{i=1}^{k} M_{g_i} \\
= M_2 + 2q & \qquad \leq M_2 + 2p,
\end{aligned}$$

as desired.   □

In the following lemma, groups $\varphi, g_1, \ldots, g_k$ are defined as in Definition 8.21.

Lemma 8.30. *Let ξ^φ be an execution of Algorithm AX as in Definition 8.21. Let M_1 be the message cost of the algorithm in the execution ξ^φ. Let M_2 be the message cost of Algorithm AX in the execution $\bar{\xi}^\varphi$. Then $M_1 \leq M_2 + M_3$, where M_3 is the number of messages sent by all processors in $\bigcup_{1 \leq i \leq k}(g_i.set)$ in the execution ξ^φ.*

Proof. For the execution ξ^φ, let M' be the number of messages sent by the processors in $\mathcal{P} - \bigcup_{1 \leq i \leq k}(g_i.set) - \varphi.set$. Observe that the number of messages sent by the processors in $\mathcal{P} - \varphi.set$ in the execution $\bar{\xi}^\varphi$ is equal to M'. The number of messages sent by processor j in $\varphi.set$ prior to the NEWVIEW$(g_i)_j$ event in ξ^φ, is the same in both executions. Call this message cost $M_{\varphi,j}$. Define $M'' = \sum_{j \in \varphi.set} M_{\varphi,j}$. Define $M_s = M' + M''$. Thus, M_s is the same in both executions, ξ^φ and $\bar{\xi}^\varphi$. Define M_φ to be the number of messages sent by all processors in $\varphi.set$ in execution $\bar{\xi}^\varphi$. Let $M''' = M_\varphi - M''$. Observe that

$$M_1 = M_s + M_3 \leq M_s + M_3 + M''' = M_2 + M_3,$$

as desired.   □

We now give the message complexity of algorithm AX.

Theorem 8.31. *Algorithm AX solves the Omni-Do$_{A_{FM}}(n, p, f)$ problem with message complexity*

$$M_{A_{FM}}(n, p, f_r + f_m) < 4 (n \cdot f_r + n + p \cdot f_m).$$

Proof. To simplify notation, we let $\mathcal{M}(f_r, f_m)$ stand for $M_{A_{FM}}(n, p, f_r + f_m)$. The proof is by induction on the number of views, denoted by ℓ, occurring in any execution. For a specific execution ξ_ℓ with ℓ views, let $f_r(\xi_\ell) = f_r^{(\ell)}$ be the fragmentation-number and $f_m(\xi_\ell) = f_m^{(\ell)}$ be the merge-number.

Base Case: $\ell = 0$. Since $f_r^{(\ell)}$ and $f_m^{(\ell)}$ must also be 0, the base case follows from Lemma 8.28.

Inductive Hypothesis: Assume that for all $\ell \leq k$,

$$\mathcal{M}(f_r^{(\ell)}, f_m^{(\ell)}) < 4(n \cdot f_r^{(\ell)} + n + p \cdot f_m^{(\ell)}).$$

Inductive Step: Need to show that for $\ell = k + 1$,

$$\mathcal{M}(f_r^{(k+1)}, f_m^{(k+1)}) < 4(n \cdot f_r^{(k+1)} + n + p \cdot f_m^{(k+1)}).$$

Consider a specific execution ξ_{k+1} with $\ell = k+1$. Let $\Gamma_{\xi_{k+1}}$ be the view-graph induced by this execution. The view-graph has at least one vertex such that all of its descendants are sinks (Fact 8.15). Let ν be such a vertex. We consider two cases:

Case 1: Vertex ν has a descendant μ that corresponds to a merge in the execution. Therefore all ancestors of μ in $\Gamma_{\xi_{k+1}}$ have outdegree 1. Since μ is a sink vertex, the group that corresponds to μ performs all the remaining (if any) tasks and no further messages are sent. Let $\xi_k = \bar{\xi}_{k+1}^\mu$ (per Definition 8.20) be an execution in which this merge does not occur. In execution ξ_k, the number of new views is k. Also, $f_r^{(k+1)} = f_r^{(k)}$ and $f_m^{(k+1)} = f_m^{(k)} + 1$. By inductive hypothesis, $\mathcal{M}(f_r^{(k)}, f_m^{(k)}) < 4(n \cdot f_r^{(k)} + n + p \cdot f_m^{(k)})$. Hence, the message complexity, using Lemma 8.29 is:

$$
\begin{aligned}
\mathcal{M}(f_r^{(k+1)}, f_m^{(k+1)}) &< \mathcal{M}(f_r^{(k)}, f_m^{(k)}) + 2p \\
&< 4(n \cdot f_r^{(k)} + n + p \cdot f_m^{(k)}) + 2p \\
&= 4(n \cdot f_r^{(k+1)} + n + p \cdot f_m^{(k+1)} - p) + 2p \\
&= 4n f_r^{(k+1)} + 4n + 4p f_m^{(k+1)} - 4p + 2p \\
&\leq 4(n \cdot f_r^{(k+1)} + n + p \cdot f_m^{(k+1)}).
\end{aligned}
$$

Case 2: Vertex ν has no descendants that correspond to a merge in the execution. Therefore, the group that corresponds to ν must fragment, say into q groups. These groups correspond to sink vertices in $\Gamma_{\xi_{k+1}}$, thus they perform all the remaining (if any) tasks and do not send any additional messages.

Let $\xi_{k+1-q} = \bar{\xi}^\nu_{k+1}$ (per Definition 8.21) be an execution in which the fragmentation does not occur. In the execution ξ_{k+1-q}, the number of new views is $k + 1 - q \leq k$. Also, $f_r^{(k+1-q)} = f_r^{(k+1)} - q$ and $f_m^{(k+1-q)} = f_m^{(k+1)}$. By inductive hypothesis, $\mathcal{M}_{f_r^{(k+1-q)}, f_m^{(k+1-q)}} < 4(n \cdot f_r^{(k+1-q)} + n + p \cdot f_m^{(k+1-q)})$. From Lemma 8.28, the message cost in each new group caused by a fragmentation is no more than $4n$. Let M_σ be the total number of messages sent in all q groups. Thus, $M_\sigma \leq 4qn$. By Lemma 8.30, the number of messages sent in execution ξ_{k+1}, is less than the number of messages sent in execution ξ_{k+1-q} and the number of messages sent in all q groups. Hence, the message complexity is

$$
\begin{aligned}
\mathcal{M}(f_r^{(k+1)}, f_m^{(k+1)}) &\leq \mathcal{M}(f_r^{(k+1-q)}, f_m^{(k+1-q)}) + M_\sigma \\
&< 4(n \cdot f_r^{(k+1-q)} + n + p \cdot f_m^{(k+1-q)}) + M_\sigma \\
&= 4(n \cdot f_r^{(k+1)} - qn + n + p \cdot f_m^{(k+1)}) + M_\sigma \\
&\leq 4n f_r^{(k+1)} - 4qn + 4n + 4p f_m^{(k+1)} + 4qn \\
&= 4(n \cdot f_r^{(k+1)} + n + p \cdot f_m^{(k+1)}),
\end{aligned}
$$

and this completes the proof. $\qquad\qquad\qquad\qquad\qquad\qquad\qquad\qquad\square$

8.5.3 Analysis Under Adversary $\mathcal{A}_F$

Algorithm AX solves the *Omni-Do* problem also under patterns of only fragmentations. Observe that $f = f_r$ and $f_m = 0$ for adversary $\mathcal{A}_F$. The following corollary is obtained on the basis of Theorems 8.27 and 8.31.

Corollary 8.32. *Algorithm AX solves the Omni-Do$_{\mathcal{A}_F}(n, p, f)$ problem with task-oriented work complexity $W_{\mathcal{A}_F}(n, p, f) \leq \min\{n \cdot f + n, \ n \cdot p\}$ and message complexity $M_{\mathcal{A}_F}(n, p, f) < 4(n \cdot f + n)$.*

Observe that Algorithm AX is asymptotically work-optimal under adversary $\mathcal{A}_F$ with respect to the lower bound of Theorem 8.1.

8.6 Open Problems

Algorithm AX uses a group communication service (GCS) with certain properties as a building block. The message analysis of the algorithm does not consider the cost of implementing the GCS. It would be interesting to investigate whether an algorithm with an embedded GCS could be developed that could achieve better message complexity.

Additionally, it is worthwhile to assess the total-work complexity of algorithm AX, but as with message complexity, for this to be meaningful, the work of a specific GCS implementation must be taken into account.

Finally, in some settings time complexity is another measure that is significant in practical applications. It is interesting to develop algorithms for *Omni-Do* that trade work efficiency for time efficiency.

8.7 Chapter Notes

The *Omni-Do* problem as presented here was introduced and studied by Dolev, Segala, and Shvartsman in [29]. They present a load balancing algorithm, called AF that solves the *Omni-Do* problem with group fragmentations (no merges), and under the assumption that all processors belong initially to a single group, with work $O(n + f \cdot n)$, where $f < n$ is the total number of groups that existed during the computation (this is different from our definition of fragmentation-number, see the comparison in [48]). The algorithm also uses a group communication service to handle group memberships and communication within groups, however the authors did not measure the message complexity of their algorithm. Georgiou and Shvartsman [48] extended the approach of [29] by considering the adversary that causes fragmentations and merges, and by evaluating message complexity as well as work complexity. The presentation in this chapter is based on that work.

Algorithm AX uses a group communication service (GCS) modeled after the VS service of Fekete, Lynch, and Shvartsman [33]. The safety and liveness properties of the GCS (Section 8.2). are given in the work of Chockler, Keidar, and Vitenberg [21] (the safety properties from Section 3 and the liveness properties from Section 10). Group communication services [97] provide membership and communication services to the group of processors. GCSs enable the application components at different processors to operate collectively as a group, using the service to multicast messages. There is a substantial amount of research dealing with specification and implementation of GCSs. Some GCS implementations are Isis [13], Transis [27], Totem [93], Newtop [32], Relacs [9], Horus [108], Consul [90] and Ensemble [55]. Some GCS specifications are presented in [98, 10, 33, 28, 23, 57, 92]. An extended study of GCS specifications can be found in [21].

Our exposition in this chapter focuses on work complexity of algorithms. In particular, we are not concerned about the overall time that it may take to complete a computation. There is evidence that algorithms that do not attempt to optimize work may have better time-to-completion. In this regard, a study performed by Jacobsen, Zhang, and Marzullo [62] suggests that algorithm AX may not be practical when using certain GCSs in wide-area networks. In particular, they showed via trace analysis, that algorithm AX performs poorly with respect to the total completion time. The authors argue that the reason for this is the use of GCSs that do not scale well in large networks, where communication is less likely to be transitive and symmetric (as assumed by group communications). However, as the authors point out, group communications can be used effectively in networks such as LANs, and hence algorithm AX is expected to perform well in such networks, especially with respect to its work complexity.

Omni-Do has an analogous counterpart in the shared-memory model of computation, called the *collect* problem, introduced by Shavit [103] and studied by Saks, Shavit, and Woll in [100]. There are p processors each with a shared register. The goal is to have all the processors learn (collect) all the register values. Computation is asynchronous, with the adversary controlling timing of the processors. Although the algorithmic techniques when dealing with the collect problem are different, the goal of having all processors to learn a set of values is similar to the goal of having all processor to learn the results of a set of tasks in *Omni-Do*.

Information on the Input/Output Automata mode, notation, and framework can be found in the work of Lynch and Tuttle, e.g., [80, 79]. A prototype computer-aided framework supporting specification in Input/Output Automata was developed at MIT [41]. A commercial framework, called Tempo, supporting specification, modeling, simulation, and verification of distributed systems using (timed and untimed) Input/Output Automata is available from VeroModo Inc. [61].

9

Competitive Analysis of Omni-Do in Partitionable Networks

THE efficiency of an algorithm solving the *Omni-Do* problem can only be partially understood through its worst case work analysis, such as we did for algorithm AX in the previous chapter. This is because the worst case upper and lower bounds might depend on unusual or extreme patterns of regroupings. In such cases, worst case work may not be the best way to compare the efficiency of algorithms. Hence, in this chapter, in order to understand better the practical implications of performing work in partitionable settings, we treat the *Omni-Do* problem as an on-line problem and we pursue *competitive analysis*, that is we compare the efficiency of a given algorithm to the efficiency of an "off-line" algorithm that has full knowledge of future changes in the communication medium. We consider asynchronous processors under arbitrary patterns of regroupings (including, but not limited to, fragmentation and merges). A processor crash is modeled as the creation of a singleton group (containing the crashed processor) that remains disconnected for the entire computation; the processors in such groups are charged for completing all remaining tasks, in other words, the analysis assumes the worst case situation where a crashed processor becomes disconnected, but manages to complete all tasks before the crash.

In this chapter we view algorithms as a rule that, given a group of processors and a set of tasks known by this group to be completed, determines a task for the group to complete next. We assume that task executions are atomic with respect to regroupings (a task considered for execution by a group is either executed or not prior a subsequent regrouping). Processors in the same group can share their knowledge of completed tasks and, while they remain connected, avoid doing redundant work. The challenge is to avoid redundant work "globally", in the sense that processors should be performing tasks with anticipation of future changes in the network topology. An optimal algorithm, with full knowledge of the future regroupings, can schedule the execution of the tasks in each group in such a way that the overall task-oriented work is the smallest possible, given the particular sequence of regroupings.

As an example, consider the scenario with 3 processors that, starting from isolation, are permitted to proceed synchronously until each has completed $n/2$ tasks; at this point an adversary chooses a pair of processors to merge into a group. It is easy to show that if N_1, N_2, and N_3 are subsets of $[n]$ of size $n/2$, then there is a pair (N_i, N_j) (where $i \neq j$) so that $|N_i \cap N_j| \geq n/6$: in particular, for *any* scheduling algorithm, there is a pair of processors which, if merged at this point, will have $n/6$ duplicated tasks; this pair alone must then expend $n + n/6$ task-oriented work to complete all n tasks. The optimal off-line algorithm that schedules tasks with full knowledge of future merges, of course, accrues only n task-oriented work for the merged pair, as it can arrange for zero overlap. Furthermore, if the adversary partitions the two merged processors immediately after the merge (after allowing the processors to exchanged information about task executions), then the task-oriented work performed by the merged and then partitioned pair is $n + n/3$; the task-oriented work performed by the optimal algorithm remains unchanged, since it terminates at the merge.

To focus on scheduling issues, we assume that processors in a single group work as a single virtual unit; indeed, we treat them as a single asynchronous processor. To this respect, we assume that communication within groups is instantaneous and reliable. We note that the above assumptions can be approximated by group communication services (such as the one considered in Section 8.2) if the reconfiguration time during which no tasks are performed is disregarded. However, in large scale wide-area networks the time performance (which we do not consider here) of *Omni-Do* algorithms can be negatively affected, as GCSs can be inefficient in such networks.

Chapter structure.

In Section 9.1 we present the model of adversity considered in this chapter, we define the notion of competitiveness and we present terminology borrowed from set theory and graph theory that we use in the rest of the chapter. In Section 9.2 we formulate a simple randomized algorithm, called algorithm RS, and we analyze its competitiveness. A result for deterministic algorithms is also given. In Section 9.3 we present lower bounds on the competitiveness of (deterministic and randomized) algorithms for *Omni-Do*, and we claim the optimality of algorithm RS. We discuss open problems in Section 9.4.

9.1 Model of Adversity, Competitiveness and Definitions

In this section we present Adversary $\mathcal{A}_{GR}$, the adversary assumed in this chapter, we formalize the notion of competitiveness, and we recall graph and set theoretic terminology used in the remainder sections.

9.1.1 Adversary $\mathcal{A}_{GR}$

We denote by $\mathcal{A}_{GR}$ an oblivious (off-line) adversary that can cause arbitrary regroupings. Consider an algorithm A that solves the *Omni-Do* problem under adversary $\mathcal{A}_{GR}$. The adversary determines, prior to the start of an execution of A, both the *sequence of regroupings* and the *number of tasks completed* by each group before it is involved in another regrouping. Taken together, this information determines, what we call, a *computation template*: this is a directed acyclic graph (DAG), each vertex of which corresponds to a group of processors that existed during the the computation; a directed edge is placed from group g_1 to group g_2 if g_2 is created by a regrouping involving g_1. We label each vertex of the DAG with the group of processors associated with that vertex and the total number of tasks that the adversary allows the group of processors to perform before the next reconfiguration occurs.

Specifically, if n is the number of *Omni-Do* tasks and p the number of participating processors, then such a computation template is a labeled and weighted DAG, which we call a (p, n)-DAG. More formally,

Definition 9.1. *A (p, n)-DAG is a DAG $C = (V, E)$ augmented with a weight function $h : V \to [n] \cup \{0\}$ and a labeling $\gamma : V \to 2^{[p]} \setminus \{\emptyset\}$ so that:*

1. *For any maximal path $(v_1, \ldots, v_k)$ in C, $\sum h(v_i) \geq n$. (This guarantees that any algorithm terminates during the computation described by the DAG.)*
2. *γ possesses the following "initial conditions":*

$$[p] = \dot{\bigcup_{v:\ in(v)=0}} \gamma(v).$$

3. *γ respects the following "conservation law":*
   there is a function $\phi : E \to 2^{[p]} \setminus \{\emptyset\}$ so that for each $v \in V$ with $indegree(v) > 0$,

$$\gamma(v) = \dot{\bigcup_{(u,v)\in E}} \phi((u,v)),$$

   and for each $v \in V$ with $out(v) > 0$,

$$\gamma(v) = \dot{\bigcup_{(v,u)\in E}} \phi((v,u)).$$

In the above definition, $\dot{\cup}$ denotes disjoint union, and $in(v)$ and $out(v)$ denote the in-degree and out-degree of v, respectively. Finally, for two vertices $u, v \in V$, we write $u \leq v$ if there is a directed path from u to v; we then write $u < v$ if $u \leq v$ and u and v are distinct.

Adversary $\mathcal{A}_{GR}$ is constrained to establish only the computation templates as defined above.

Example 9.2. Consider the $(12, n)$-DAG shown in Figure 9.1, where we let the following groups be represented: $g_1 = \{p_1\}$, $g_2 = \{p_2, p_3, p_4\}$, $g_3 = \{p_5, p_6\}$, $g_4 = \{p_7\}$, $g_5 = \{p_8, p_9, p_{10}, p_{11}, p_{12}\}$, $g_6 = \{p_1, p_2, p_3, p_4, p_6\}$, $g_7 = \{p_8, p_{10}\}$, $g_8 = \{p_9, p_{11}, p_{12}\}$, $g_9 = \{p_1, p_2, p_3, p_4, p_6, p_8, p_{10}\}$, $g_{10} = \{p_5, p_{11}\}$, and $g_{11} = \{p_9, p_{12}\}$.

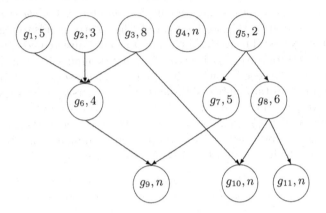

Fig. 9.1. An example of a $(12, n)$-DAG.

This computation template models all (asynchronous) computations with the following behavior.

(i) The processors in groups g_1 and g_2 and processor p_6 of group g_3 are regrouped during some reconfiguration to form group g_6. Processor p_5 of group g_3 becomes a member of group g_{10} during the same reconfiguration (see below). Prior to this reconfiguration, processor p_1 (the singleton group g_1) has performed exactly 5 tasks, the processors in g_2 have cooperatively performed exactly 3 tasks and the processors in g_3 have cooperatively performed exactly 8 tasks (assuming that $t > 8$).

(ii) Group g_5 is partitioned during some reconfiguration into two new groups, g_7 and g_8. Prior to this reconfiguration, the processors in g_5 have performed exactly 2 tasks.

(iii) Groups g_6 and g_7 merge during some reconfiguration and form group g_9. Prior to this merge, the processors in g_6 have performed exactly 4 tasks (counting only the ones performed after the formation of g_6 and assuming that there are at least 4 tasks remaining to be done) and the processors in g_7 have performed exactly 5 tasks.

(iv) The processors in group g_8 and processor p_5 of group g_3 are regrouped during some reconfiguration into groups g_{10} and g_{11}. Prior to this reconfiguration, the processors in group g_8 have performed exactly 6 tasks (assuming that there are at least 6 tasks remaining, otherwise they would have performed the remaining tasks).

(v) The processors in g_9, g_{10}, and g_{11} run until completion with no further reconfigurations.

(vi) Processor p_7 (the singleton group g_4) runs in isolation for the entire computation.

Given a (p, n)-DAG representing a computation template C, we say that two vertices (representing groups) are *independent* if there is no direct path connecting one to the other. Then, for the computation template C we define the *computation width of C*, $\mathbf{cw}(C)$, to be the maximum number of independent vertices reachable from any vertex in (p, n)-DAG. We give a formal definition at the conclusion of this section.

Let ξ is the execution of an algorithm solving *Omni-Do* under the computation template C represented by a (p, n)-DAG. We let the adversarial pattern $\xi|_{\mathcal{A}_{GR}}$ be represented by the (p, n)-DAG, or its appropriate subgraph[1]. Following the notation established in Section 2.2.3, we define the weight of $\xi|_{\mathcal{A}_{GR}}$ as the computation width of this graph, that is, $\|\xi|_{\mathcal{A}_{GR}}\| \leq \mathbf{cw}(C)$. (From the definition of the computation width it is easy to observe that given a subgraph H of a DAG G, $\mathbf{cw}(H) \leq \mathbf{cw}(G)$.)

9.1.2 Measuring Competitiveness

Before we formally define the notion of competitiveness, we introduce some terminology.

Let D be a deterministic algorithm for *Omni-Do* and C a computation template. We let $W_D(C)$ denote the task-oriented work expended by algorithm D, where regroupings are determined according to the computation template C. That is, if $\xi \in \mathcal{E}(D, \mathcal{A}_{GR})$ is an execution of algorithm D under computation template C, then $W_D(C)$ is the task-oriented work of execution ξ. We let OPT denote the optimal (off-line) algorithm, meaning that for each C we have $W_{\mathrm{OPT}}(C) = \min_D W_D(C)$. We now move to define competitiveness.

Definition 9.3. *Let α be a real valued function defined on the set of all (p, n)-DAGs (for all p and n). A deterministic algorithm D is α-**competitive** if for all computation templates C,*

$$W_D(C) \leq \alpha(C) W_{OPT}(C).$$

In this chapter we treat randomized algorithms as distributions over deterministic algorithms; for a set Z and a family of deterministic algorithms $\{D_\zeta \mid \zeta \in Z\}$ we let $R = \mathcal{R}(\{D_\zeta \mid \zeta \in Z\})$ denote the randomized algorithm where ζ is selected uniformly at random from Z and scheduling is done according to D_ζ. For a real-valued random variable X, we let $\mathbb{E}[X]$ denote its expected value. Then,

---

[1] The execution might terminate with all tasks performed before all regroupings specified by the computation template take place; this is possible in the case of randomized algorithm where the oblivious adversary does not know *a priori* how the algorithm would behave under the specific sequence of regroupings.

Definition 9.4. *Let α be a real valued function defined on the set of all (p, n)-DAGs (for all p and n). A randomized algorithm R is α-**competitive** if for all computation templates C,*

$$\mathbb{E}[W_{\mathrm{D}_\zeta}(C)] \leq \alpha(C) W_{OPT}(C),$$

this expectation being taken over uniform choice of $\zeta \in Z$.

Note that usually α is fixed for all inputs; we shall see in later sections that this would be meaningless in this setting. Presently, we use a function α that depends on a certain parameter of the graph structure of C, namely the computation width $\mathbf{cw}(C)$.

9.1.3 Formalizing Computation Width

We conclude this subsection with definitions and terminology that we use in the remainder of this chapter.

Definition 9.5. *A partially ordered set or poset is a pair $(P, \leq)$ where P is a set and $\leq$ is a binary relation on P for which (i) for all $x \in P$, $x \leq x$, (ii) if $x \leq y$ and $y \leq x$, then $x = y$, and (iii) if $x \leq y$ and $y \leq z$, then $x \leq z$. For a poset $(P, \leq)$ we overload the symbol P, letting it denote both the set and the poset.*

Definition 9.6. *Let P be a poset. We say that two elements x and y of P are comparable if $x \leq y$ or $y \leq x$; otherwise x and y are incomparable. A chain is a subset of P such that any two elements of this subset are comparable. An antichain is a subset of P such that any two distinct elements of this subset are incomparable. The width of P, denoted $\mathbf{w}(P)$, is the size of the largest antichain of P.*

Associated with any DAG $C = (V, E)$ is the natural *vertex poset* $(V, \leq)$ where $u \leq v$ if and only if there is a directed path from u to v. Then the *width of C*, denoted $\mathbf{w}(C)$, is the width of the poset $(V, \leq)$.

Definition 9.7. *Given a DAG $C = (V, E)$ and a vertex $v \in V$, we define the predecessor graph at v, denoted $P_C(v)$, to be the subgraph of C that is formed by the union of all paths in C terminating at v. Likewise, the successor graph at v, denoted $S_C(v)$, is the subgraph of C that is formed by the union of all the paths in C originating at v.*

Using the above definitions and terminology we give a formal definition of the computation width of a given computation template.

Definition 9.8. *The computation width of a DAG $C = (V, E)$, denoted $\mathbf{cw}(C)$, is defined as*

$$\mathbf{cw}(C) = \max_{v \in V} \mathbf{w}(S_C(v)).$$

Note that the processors that comprise a group formed during a computation template C may be involved in many different groups at later stages of the computation, but no more than $\mathbf{cw}(C)$ of these groups can be computing in ignorance of each other's progress.

Example 9.9. In the $(12, n)$-DAG of Figure 9.1, the maximum width among all successor graphs is 3: $\mathbf{w}(S((g_5, 2))) = 3$. Therefore, the computation width of this DAG is 3. Note that the width of the DAG is 6 (nodes $(g_1, 5), (g_2, 3), (g_3, 8), (g_4, n), (g_7, 5)$ and $(g_8, 6)$ form an antichain of maximum size).

9.2 Algorithm RS and its Analysis

In this section we formulate algorithm RS (Random Select), analyze its competitiveness, and present a result on the competitiveness of deterministic algorithms.

9.2.1 Description of Algorithm RS

We consider the natural randomized algorithm RS where a processor (or group) with knowledge that the tasks in a set $K \subset [n]$ have been completed selects to next complete a task at random from the set $[n] \setminus K$. (Recall that we treat randomized algorithms as distributions over deterministic algorithms.) More formally, let $\Pi = (\pi_1, \ldots, \pi_p)$ be a p-tuple of permutations, where each π_i is a permutation of $[n]$. We describe a deterministic algorithm D_Π so that

$$\mathrm{RS} = \mathcal{R}(\{\mathrm{D}_\Pi \mid \Pi \in (\mathcal{S}_n)^p\});$$

here $\mathcal{S}_n$ is the collection of permutations on $[n]$. Let G be a group of processors and $q \in G$ the processor in G with the lowest processor identifier. Then the deterministic algorithm D_Π specifies that the group G, should it know that the tasks in $K \subset [n]$ have been completed, next completes the first task in the sequence $\pi_q(1), \ldots, \pi_q(n)$ which is not in K.

9.2.2 Analysis of Algorithm RS

We now analyze the competitiveness (in terms of task-oriented work) of algorithm RS. For a computation template C we write $W_{\mathrm{RS}}(C) = \mathbb{E}[W_{\mathrm{RS}}(C)]$, this expectation taken over the random choices of the algorithm. Where C can be inferred from context, we simply write W_{RS} and W_{OPT}.

We first recall Dilworth's Lemma, a duality theorem for posets:

Lemma 9.10. (Dilworth's Lemma) *The width of a poset P is equal to the minimum number of chains needed to cover P. (A family of nonempty subsets of a set Q is said to cover Q if their union is Q.)*

We will also use a generalized degree-counting argument:

Lemma 9.11. *Let $G = (U, V, E)$ be an undirected bipartite graph with no isolated vertices and $h : V \to \mathbb{R}$ a non-negative weight function on G. For a vertex v, let $\Gamma(v)$ denote the vertices adjacent to v. Suppose that for some $B_1 > 0$ and for each vertex $u \in U$ we have $\sum_{v \in \Gamma(u)} h(v) \leq B_1$ and that for some $B_2 > 0$ and for each vertex $v \in V$ we have $\sum_{u \in \Gamma(v)} h(u) \geq B_2$, then $\dfrac{\sum_{u \in U} h(u)}{\sum_{v \in V} h(v)} \geq \dfrac{B_2}{B_1}.$*

Proof. We compute the quantity $\sum_{(u,v) \in E} h(u)h(v)$ by expanding according to each side of the bipartition:

$$B_1 \sum_{u \in U} h(u) \geq \sum_{u \in U} \left(h(u) \cdot \sum_{v \in \Gamma(u)} h(v) \right) = \sum_{(u,v) \in E} h(u)h(v)$$

$$= \sum_{v \in V} \left(h(v) \cdot \sum_{u \in \Gamma(v)} h(u) \right) \geq B_2 \sum_{v \in V} h(v).$$

As $B_1 > 0$ and $\sum_v h(v) \geq B_2 > 0$, we conclude that $\dfrac{\sum_{u \in U} h(u)}{\sum_{v \in V} h(v)} \geq \dfrac{B_2}{B_1}$, as desired. $\square$

We now establish an upper bound on the competitiveness of the algorithm RS.

Theorem 9.12. *Algorithm RS is $(1 + \mathbf{cw}(C)/e)$-competitive for any (p, n)-DAG $C = (V, E)$.*

Proof. Let C be a (p, n)-DAG; recall that associated with C are the two functions $h : V \to \mathbb{N}$ and $\gamma : V \to 2^{[p]} \setminus \{\emptyset\}$. For a subgraph $C' = (V', E')$ of C, we let $H(C') = \sum_{v \in V'} h(v)$. Recall that $P_C(v)$ and $S_C(v)$ denote the predecessor and successor graphs of C at v. Then, we say that a vertex $v \in V$ is *saturated* if $H(P_C(v)) \leq n$; otherwise, v is *unsaturated*. Note that if v is saturated, then the group $\gamma(v)$ must complete $h(v)$ tasks *regardless of the scheduling algorithm used*. Along these same lines, if v is an unsaturated vertex for which $n > \sum_{u < v} h(u)$, the group $\gamma(v)$ must complete at least $\max(h(v), n - \sum_{u < v} h(u))$ tasks under any scheduling algorithm. As these portions of C which correspond to computation which must be performed by any algorithm will play a special role in the analysis, it will be convenient for us to rearrange the DAG so that all such work appears on saturated vertices. To achieve this, note that if v is an unsaturated vertex for which $\sum_{u < v} h(u) < n$, we may replace v with a pair of vertices, v_s and v_u, where all edges directed into v are redirected to v_s, all edges directed out of v are changed to originate at v_u, the edge (v_s, v_u) is added to E, and h is redefined so that

$$h(v_s) = n - \sum_{u < v} h(u) \qquad \text{and} \qquad h(v_u) = h(v) - h(v_s).$$

Note that the graph C' obtained by altering C in this way corresponds to the same computation, in the sense that $W_{\mathrm{D}}(C) = W_{\mathrm{D}}(C')$ for any algorithm D. For the remainder of the proof we will assume that this alteration has been made at every relevant vertex, so that the graph C satisfies the condition

$$v \text{ unsaturated } \Rightarrow \sum_{u < v} h(u) \geq n. \tag{9.1}$$

Finally, for a vertex v, we let T_v be the random variable equal to the number of tasks that RS completes at vertex v. Note that if v is saturated, then $T_v = h(v)$. Let $\mathcal{S}$ and $\mathcal{U}$ denote the sets of saturated and unsaturated vertices, respectively. Given the above definitions, we immediately have

$$W_{\mathrm{OPT}} \geq \sum_{s \in \mathcal{S}} h(s)$$

and, by linearity of expectation,

$$W_{\mathrm{RS}} = \mathbb{E}\Big[\sum_v T_v\Big] = \sum_{s \in \mathcal{S}} h(s) + \sum_{u \in \mathcal{U}} \mathbb{E}[T_u] \leq W_{\mathrm{OPT}} + \sum_{u \in \mathcal{U}} \mathbb{E}[T_u]. \tag{9.2}$$

Our goal is to conclude that for some appropriate β,

$$\mathbb{E}\Big[\sum_{u \in \mathcal{U}} T_u\Big] \leq \beta \cdot \sum_{s \in \mathcal{S}} h(s) \leq \beta \cdot W_{\mathrm{OPT}}$$

and hence that RS is $1 + \beta$ competitive. We will obtain such a bound by applying Lemma 9.11 to an appropriate bipartite graph, constructed next.

Given $C = (V, E)$ construct the (undirected) bipartite graph $G = (\mathcal{S}, \mathcal{U}, E_G)$ where $E_G = \{(s, u) \mid s < u\}$. As in Lemma 9.11, for a vertex v, we let $\Gamma(v)$ denote the set of vertices adjacent to v. Now assign weights to the vertices of G according to the rule $h^*(v) = \mathbb{E}[T_v]$. Note that for $s \in \mathcal{S}, h^*(s) = h(s)$ and hence by condition (9.1) above, we immediately have the bound

$$\forall u \in \mathcal{U}, \quad \sum_{s \in \Gamma(u)} h^*(s) \geq n. \tag{9.3}$$

We now show that $\forall s \in \mathcal{S}$,

$$\sum_{u \in \Gamma(s)} h^*(u) \leq \mathbf{cw}(C) \cdot \frac{n}{e}. \tag{9.4}$$

Before proceeding to establish this bound, note that equations (9.3) and (9.4), together with Lemma 9.11 imply that

$$W_{\mathrm{RS}}(C) \leq \sum_{s \in \mathcal{S}} h(s) + \sum_{u \in \mathcal{U}} h^*(u) \leq \Big(1 + \frac{\mathbf{cw}(C)}{e}\Big) \sum_{s \in \mathcal{S}} h(s)$$

$$\leq \Big(1 + \frac{\mathbf{cw}(C)}{e}\Big) W_{\mathrm{OPT}}(C),$$

as desired.

Returning now to equation (9.4), let $s \in \mathcal{S}$ be a saturated vertex and consider the successor graph (of C) at s, $S_C(s)$. By Lemma 9.10 (Dilworth's Lemma), there exist $w \triangleq \mathbf{w}(S_C(s)) \leq \mathbf{cw}(C)$ paths in $S_C(s)$, $P_1, P_2, \ldots P_w$ so that their union covers $S_C(s)$. Let X_i be the random variable whose value is the number of tasks performed by RS on the portion of the path P_i consisting of unsaturated vertices. Note that if $u \in V$ is unsaturated and $u \leq v$, then v is unsaturated and hence, for each path P_i, there is a first unsaturated vertex u_i^0 after which every vertex of P_i is unsaturated. Note now that for a fixed individual task τ, conditioned upon the event that τ is not yet complete, the probability that τ is *not* chosen by RS for completion at a given selection point in $P_C(u_i^0)$ is no more than $(1 - 1/n)$. Let L_i be the random variable whose value is the set of tasks left incomplete by RS at the formation of the group $\gamma(u_i^0)$. As u_i^0 is unsaturated, $\sum_{v < u_i^0} h(v) \geq n$ by condition (9.1) and hence, for each i,

$$\Pr[\tau \in L_i] \leq (1 - 1/n)^n \leq 1/e.$$

As there are a total of n tasks,

$$\mathbb{E}[|L_i|] \leq n/e.$$

Of course, since RS completes a new task at each step, $X_i \leq |L_i|$ so that $\mathbb{E}[X_i] \leq n/e$ and by the linearity of expectation

$$\mathbb{E}\left[\sum_i X_i\right] \leq w \cdot n/e.$$

Now every unsaturated vertex in $S_C(s)$ appears in some P_i and hence

$$\sum_{u \in \Gamma(s)} h^*(u) \leq \mathbb{E}\left[\sum_i X_i\right] \leq wn/e \leq \mathbf{cw}(C) \cdot n/e,$$

as desired.   □

9.2.3 Deterministic Algorithms

The analysis of algorithm RS can be altered to yield an upper bound result on the competitiveness of deterministic algorithms. Recall that a deterministic algorithm D for the *Omni-Do* problem in this setting is a rule which, given a processor (or group of processors) and a collection of tasks known to be completed, determines the next task for this processor (or group) to complete. Specifically, an algorithm is a function $D : 2^{[p]} \times 2^{[n]} \to [n]$; Furthermore, we assume that $D(P, T) \notin T$ for all $P \subset [p]$ and for all $T \subsetneq [n]$, which is to say that the algorithm never chooses to complete a task it already knows to be completed (thus we restrict our attention to nontrivial algorithms). Then,

Theorem 9.13. *Any (nontrivial) deterministic algorithm* D *for Do-* $All_{A_{GR}}(n, p, f)$ *is* $(1 + \mathbf{cw}(C))$*-competitive for any* (p, n)*-DAG* $C = (V, E)$.

Proof. In the proof of Theorem 9.12, $h^*(v)$ was defined as the expected number of tasks performed by algorithm RS at node v. For algorithm D, if we define $h^*(v)$ to be the actual number of tasks performed by the algorithm at node v, then it is not difficult to see that equation (9.4) becomes $\sum_{u \in \Gamma(s)} h^*(u) \leq \mathbf{cw}(C) \cdot t$ (provided that no processor in D performs a task that already knows its result). This leads to the thesis of the theorem. $\qquad\square$

9.3 Lower Bounds

We now show that the competitive ratio achieved by algorithm RS is tight. We begin with a lower bound for deterministic algorithms. This is then applied to give a lower bound for randomized algorithms in Corollary 9.15.

Theorem 9.14. *Let* $a : \mathbb{N} \to \mathbb{R}$ *and* D *be a deterministic algorithm for Omni-Do so that* D *is* $a(\mathbf{cw}(\cdot))$*-competitive (that is* D *is* α*-competitive, for a function* $\alpha = a \circ \mathbf{cw}$*)). Then* $a(c) \geq 1 + c/e$.

Proof. Fix $k \in \mathbb{N}$. Consider the case when $n = p = g \gg k$ and $n \bmod k = 0$, g being the number of initial groups. We consider a computation template $C_{\mathbf{G}}$ determined by a tuple $\mathbf{G} = (G_1, \ldots, G_{n/k})$ where each $G_i \subset [n]$ is a set of size k and $\bigcup_i G_i = [n]$. Initially, the computation template $C_{\mathbf{G}}$ has the processors synchronously proceed until each has completed n/k tasks; at this point, the processors in G_i are merged and allowed to exchange information about task executions. Each G_i is then immediately partitioned into c groups. Note that the off-line optimal algorithm accrues exactly n^2/k work for this computation template (it terminates prior to the partitions of the G_i).

We will show that for any D, there is a selection of the G_i so that

$$W_D(C_{\mathbf{G}}) \geq n^2/k \left[1 + c\left(1 - \frac{1}{k}\right)^k - o(1) \right],$$

and hence that $a(c) \geq 1 + c/e$. Consider the behavior of D when the $\mathbf{G}$ is selected at random, uniformly among all such tuples. Let $P_i \subset [n]$ be the subset of n/k tasks completed by processor i before the merges take place; these sets are determined by the algorithm D. We begin by bounding

$$\mathbb{E}_{\mathbf{G}} \left[\left| \bigcup_{i \in G_1} P_i \right| \right].$$

To this end, consider an experiment where we select k sets $Q_1, \ldots, Q_k$, each Q_i selected independently and uniformly from the set $\{P_i\}$. Now, for a specific task τ, let $p_\tau = \Pr_{Q_1}[\tau \notin Q_1]$, so that $\Pr_{Q_i}[\tau \notin \bigcup_i Q_i] = p_\tau^k$. As the Q_i are selected independently,

$$\mathbb{E}_{Q_i}\left[\left|[n] - \bigcup_i Q_i\right|\right] = \sum_\tau p_\tau^k.$$

Observe now that

$$\sum_\tau (1 - p_\tau) = \sum_\tau \Pr_{Q_1}[\tau \in Q_1] = \mathbb{E}_{Q_1}[|Q_1|] = n/k$$

and hence $\sum_\tau p_\tau = n(1 - 1/k)$. As the function $x \mapsto x^k$ is convex on $[0, \infty)$, $\sum_\tau p_\tau^k$ is minimized when the p_τ are equal and we must have

$$\mathbb{E}_{Q_i}\left[\left|[n] - \bigcup_i Q_i\right|\right] \geq n \cdot \left(1 - \frac{1}{k}\right)^k.$$

Now observe that, conditioned on the Q_i being distinct, the distribution of $(Q_1, \ldots, Q_k)$ is identical to that of $(P_{g_1^1}, \ldots, P_{g_k^1})$ where the random variable $G_1 = \{g_1^1, \ldots, g_k^1\}$. Considering that $\Pr[\exists i \neq j, Q_i = Q_j] \leq k^2/n$, we have

$$\mathbb{E}_{Q_i}\left[\left|[n] - \bigcup_i Q_i\right|\right] \leq \left(1 - \frac{k^2}{n}\right) \mathbb{E}_{\mathbf{G}}\left[n - \left|\bigcup_{i \in G_1} P_i\right|\right] + 1 \cdot \frac{k^2}{n}$$

and hence as $n \to \infty$ we see that the expected number of tasks remaining for those processors in group G_1 is

$$\mathbb{E}_{\mathbf{G}}\left[n - \left|\bigcup_{i \in G_1} P_i\right|\right] \geq n(1 - 1/k)^k - o(1).$$

Of course, the distribution of each G_i is the same, so that

$$\mathbb{E}_{\mathbf{G}}\left[\sum_{i=1}^{n/k}\left(n - \left|\bigcup_{j \in G_i} P_j\right|\right)\right] = [1 - o(1)]\left(\frac{n}{k}\right) \cdot n \left(1 - \frac{1}{k}\right)^k.$$

In particular, there must exist a specific selection of $\mathbf{G} = (G_1, \ldots, G_{n/k})$ which achieves this bound. Recall that every G_i is partitioned into c groups. Therefore, for such $\mathbf{G}$, the total work is at least

$$\frac{n^2}{k} \cdot \left(1 + [1 - o(1)] \cdot c \cdot \left(1 - \frac{1}{k}\right)^k\right).$$

As $\lim_{k \to \infty}(1 - \frac{1}{k})^k = \frac{1}{e}$, this completes the proof.   □

The above lower bound result together with the upper bound result given in Theorem 9.13 show that there is a gap of a factor of $1/e$ on the competitiveness of deterministic algorithms. Closing this gap remains an open problem.

As the above stochastic computation template $C_{\mathbf{G}}$ is independent of the deterministic algorithm D, this immediately gives rise to a lower bound for randomized algorithms:

Corollary 9.15. Let $\mathcal{R}(\{D_\zeta \mid \zeta \in Z\})$ be a randomized algorithm for Omni-Do that is $(a \circ \mathbf{cw})$-competitive, where $a : \mathbb{N} \to \mathbb{R}$. Then $a(c) \geq 1 + c/e$.

Proof. Assume for contradiction that for some c, $a(c) < 1 + c/e$ and let k be large enough so that $(1 - \frac{1}{k})^k > a(c) - 1$. For this k we proceed as in the proof above, considering a random $\mathbf{G}$ and the computation template $C_\mathbf{G}$ with $n = g = p$ congruent to $0 \bmod k$, g being the number of initial groups. Then, as above,

$$\mathbb{E}_\mathbf{G}\left[\mathbb{E}_\zeta\left[W_{D_\zeta}(C_\mathbf{G})\right]\right] = \mathbb{E}_\zeta\left[\mathbb{E}_\mathbf{G}\left[W_{D_\zeta}(C_\mathbf{G})\right]\right] \geq \min_\zeta\left[\mathbb{E}_\mathbf{G}\left[W_{D_\zeta}(C_\mathbf{G})\right]\right]$$

$$\geq \frac{n^2}{k} \cdot \left(1 + [1 - o(1)] \cdot c \cdot \left(1 - \frac{1}{k}\right)^k\right).$$

Hence there exists a $\mathbf{G}$ so that $\mathbb{E}_\zeta\left[W_{D_\zeta}(C_\mathbf{G})\right] \geq \frac{n^2}{k} \cdot (1 + [1 - o(1)]\frac{c}{e})$, which completes the proof. $\square$

The above result yields the optimality of algorithm RS. Specifically, RS achieves the optimal competitive ratio over the set of all computation templates with a given computation width.

9.4 Open Problems

One outstanding open question is how to derandomize the schedules used by task-performing algorithms in this chapter. Specifically, we would like to construct deterministic scheduling algorithms that are $(1 + \mathbf{cw}(C)/e)$-competitive for any computation template C, thus closing the gap of factor $1/e$ identified in the previous section.

An interesting direction is to study the competitiveness of *Omni-Do* algorithms with respect to their message complexity. Another promising direction is to study the task-performing paradigm in the models of computation that combine network regroupings with processor failures. The goal is to establish complexity results that show how performance of task-performing algorithms depends both on the extent of regroupings and on the number of processor failures.

9.5 Chapter Notes

Dolev, Segala, and Shvartsman [29] performed the first study of the *Omni-Do* problem in the partitionable setting. Assuming $p = n$, they model regrouping patterns for which the termination time of any on-line task-performing algorithm is greater than the termination time of an off-line task-performing algorithm by a factor linear in p.

Malewicz, Russell, and Shvartsman [83, 86] introduced the notion of k-*waste* that measures the worst-case redundant work performed by k groups (or processors) when started in isolation and merged into a single group at some later time. They developed several efficient constructions that allow processors to compute locally, without coordination, while controlling waste. These results are deterministic, and they adequately describe such computation to the point of the first regrouping, where the regrouping is assumed to merge groups. (This is the topic of the next Chapter.)

Georgiou and Shvartsman [48] give upper bounds on work for an algorithm that performs work in the presence of network fragmentations and merges using a group communication service where processors initially start in a single group (this is the topic of Chapter 8). They establish an upper bound of $O(\min(n \cdot p, \ n + n \cdot g(C)))$ onw work, where $g(C)$ is the total number of new groups formed during the computation pattern C. Note that $\mathbf{cw}(C) \leq g(C)$, and there can be an arbitrary gap between $\mathbf{cw}(C)$ and $g(C)$.

The presentation in this chapter is based on the work of Georgiou, Russell, and Shvartsman [46]. For a proof of the Dilworth's lemma see [26].

The notion of competitiveness was introduced by Sleator and Tarjan [105]. See also Bartal, Fiat, and Rabani [11], Awerbuch, Kutten, and Peleg [8], and Ajtai, Aspnes, Dwork, and Waarts [3].

Cooperation in the Absence of Communication

I N the setting where the *Omni-Do* (and *Do-All*) problem needs to be solved by distributed message-passing processors there exists a trade-off between computation and communication: both resources must be managed to decrease redundant computation and to ensure efficient computational progress. In this chapter we specifically examine the extreme situation of collaboration *without communication*. That is, we consider the extent to which efficient collaboration is possible if all resources are directed to computation at the expense of communication. Of course there are also cases where such an extreme situation is not a matter of choice: the network may fail, the mobile nodes may have intermittent connectivity, and when communication is unavailable it may take a long time to (re)establish connectivity. The results summarized in this section precisely characterize the ability of distributed agents to collaborate on a known collection of independent tasks by means of local scheduling decisions that require no communication and that achieve low redundant work in task executions. Such scheduling solutions exhibit an interesting connection between the distributed collaboration problem and the mathematical design theory. The lower bounds presented here along with the randomized and deterministic schedule constructions show the limitations on such low-redundancy cooperation and show that schedules with near-optimal redundancy can be efficiently constructed by processors working in isolation.

Let us consider an asynchronous setting, where processors communicate by means of a *rendezvous*, i.e., two processors that are able to communicate can perform state exchange. The processors that are not able to communicate via rendezvous have no choice but to perform all n tasks. Consider the computation with a single rendezvous. There are $p - 2$ processors that are unable to communicate, and they collectively must perform exactly $n \cdot (p - 2)$ work units to learn all results. Now what about the remaining pair of processors that are able to rendezvous? In the worst case they rendezvous after performing all tasks individually. In this case no savings in work are realized. Suppose they rendezvous having performed $n/2$ tasks each. In the best case, the two processors performed mutually-exclusive subsets of tasks and they learn the complete set of results as a consequence of the rendezvous. In particular if these two processors know that they will be able to rendezvous in the future, they could schedule their work as follows: one processor performs the tasks in the order $1, 2, \ldots, n$, the other in the order $n, n - 1, \ldots, 1$. No matter when they happen to rendezvous, the number of tasks they both perform is minimized. Of course the processors do not know *a priori* what pair will be able to rendezvous. Thus it is interesting to produce task execution schedules for all processors, such that upon the first rendezvous of any two processors the number of tasks performed redundantly is minimized.

This setting we have just described is interesting for several reasons. If the communication links are subject to failures, then each processor must be ready to execute all of the n tasks, whether or not it is able to communicate. In realistic settings the processors may not initially be aware of the network configuration, which would require expenditure of computation resources to establish communication, for example in radio networks. In distributed environments involving autonomous agents, processors may *choose* not to communicate either because they need to conserve power or because they must maintain radio silence. Finally, during the initial configuration of a dynamic network or a middleware service (such as a group communication service) the individual processors may start working in isolation pending the completion of system configuration. Regardless of the reasons, it is important to direct any available computation resources to performing the required tasks as soon as possible. In all such scenarios, the n tasks have to be scheduled for execution by all processors. The goal of such scheduling must be to control redundant task executions in the absence of communication and during the period of time when the communication channels are being (re)established.

Chapter structure.

In Section 10.1 we describe the adverse setting, formalize the notions of schedules, waste associated with redundant task execution in schedules, and present basic design theory. In Section 10.2 we present a lower bound on redundancy without communication. Section 10.3 explores the behavior of random schedules. Derandomization of schedules is the topic of Section 10.4. Discussion of open problems is in Section 10.5.

10.1 Adversity, Schedules, Waste, and Designs

The adversarial setting. In our abstract setting there are p asynchronous processors that need to perform n tasks. The processors have unique identifiers from the set $[p] = \{1, \ldots, p\}$, and the tasks have unique identifiers from the set $[n] = \{1, \ldots, n\}$. Initially each processor knows the tasks that need to be performed and their identifiers (otherwise no fault-tolerant distributed solution is possible). For this setting, the adversary initially isolates the processors, which forces them to perform tasks without being able to coordinate their activity with other processors. The adversary then allows the processors to rendezvous, but with the goal of maximizing the redundant work performed by the processors prior to the rendezvous.

For the purposes of this chapter, we define a simplified adversary, called $\mathcal{A}_R$, that starts processors in isolation, and then causes a rendezvous. We also define a parameterized adversary $\mathcal{A}_R^{(r)}$ to be the adversary that causes at most a r-way rendezvous. Following our established notation, for an algorithm A, let $\mathcal{E} = \mathcal{E}(A, \mathcal{A}_R^{(r)})$ be the set of all executions of the algorithm in our model of computation subject to adversary $\mathcal{A}_R^{(r)}$. For a particular execution $\xi \in \mathcal{E}$, the adversarial pattern $\xi|_{\mathcal{A}_R^{(r)}}$ establishes that the processors $q_1, \ldots, q_k$, where $k \leq r$, rendezvous for the first time when each processor q_i performs a_1 tasks prior to the rendezvous. Note that each a_i can be very different due to asynchrony. We define the *weight* $\|\xi|_{\mathcal{A}_R^{(r)}}\|$ of the adversarial pattern corresponding to this execution to be the vector $\boldsymbol{a} = (a_1, \ldots, a_k)$.

We are interested in studying how the magnitude of the redundant work depends on the weight of the adversarial pattern.

Schedules and waste. A (p, n)-*schedule* is a tuple $(\sigma_1, \ldots, \sigma_p)$ of p permutations of the set $[n]$. When $p = 1$ it is elided and we simply write n-*schedule*. A (p, n)-schedule immediately gives rise to a strategy for p isolated processors who must complete n tasks until communication between some pair (or group) is established: the processor i simply proceeds to complete the tasks in the order prescribed by σ_i. Suppose now that an adversarial pattern causes some k of these processors, say $q_1, \ldots, q_k$, to rendezvous at a time when the ith processor in this group, q_i, has completed a_i tasks (i.e., the weight of the corresponding adversarial pattern is $\boldsymbol{a} = (a_1, \ldots, a_k)$). Ideally, the processors would have completed disjoint sets of tasks, so that the total number of tasks completed is $\sum_i a_i$. As this is too much to hope for in general, it is natural to attempt to bound the gap between $\sum_i a_i$ and the actual number of distinct tasks completed. This gap we call *waste* (here and throughout, if $\phi : X \to Y$ is a function and $L \subset X$, we let $\phi(L) = \{\phi(x) \mid x \in L\}$):

Definition 10.1. *If L is a (p, n)-schedule and $(a_1, \ldots, a_k) \in \mathbb{N}^k$, the **waste** function for L is*

$$\mathfrak{W}_L(a_1, \ldots, a_k) = \max_{(q_1, \ldots, q_k)} \left(\sum_i^k a_i - \left| \bigcup_i^k \sigma_{q_i}([a_i]) \right| \right),$$

this maximum taken over all k tuples $(q_1, \ldots, q_k)$ of distinct elements of $[p]$.

For a specific vector $\boldsymbol{a} = (a_1, \ldots, a_k)$ representing the weight of an adversarial pattern, $\mathfrak{W}_L(\boldsymbol{a})$ captures the worst-case number of redundant tasks performed by any collection of k processors when the ith process has completed the first a_i tasks of its schedule.

One immediate observation is that bounds on *pairwise* waste can be naturally extended to bounds on *k-wise* waste: specifically, note that if L is a (p, n)-schedule then

$$\mathfrak{W}_L(a_1, \ldots, a_k) \leq \sum_{i<j} \mathfrak{W}_L(a_i, a_j)$$

just by considering the first two terms of the standard inclusion-exclusion rule. Moreover, it appears that this relationship is fairly tight as it is nearly attained by randomized schedules (see Section 10.3). With this justification we shall content ourselves to focus mainly on pairwise waste—the function $\mathfrak{W}_L(a, b)$.

Designs as schedules. Set systems with prescribed intersection properties have been the object of intense study by both the design theory community and the extremal set theory community. Despite this, the study of *waste* in distributed cooperative settings is new. We shall, however, make substantial use of some design-theoretic constructions, which we describe below.

Definition 10.2. *A ℓ-(v, k, λ) design is a family of subsets $\mathcal{L} = (L_1, \ldots, L_t)$ of the set $[v]$ with the property that each $|L_i| = k$ and any set of ℓ elements of $[v]$ is a subset of precisely λ of the L_i. (N.B. The subsets L_i are typically referred to as blocks.)*

Observe that if $\mathcal{L}$ is a ℓ-(v, k, λ) design, then it is also a $(\ell - 1)$-$(v, k, \hat{\lambda})$ design where

$$\hat{\lambda} = \lambda \frac{(v - \ell + 1)}{(k - \ell + 1)}.$$

To see this, note that if T is a subset of elements of size $\ell - 1$, then there are exactly $v - (\ell - 1)$ sets of size ℓ which contain T; let $U_i, i \in [v - (\ell - 1)]$, denote these sets. By assumption, each U_i appears in exactly λ of the L_j. Of course, if U_i is a subset of some L_j, then in fact exactly $k - (\ell - 1)$ if the U_i are subsets of L_j. Hence T appears in exactly $\lambda(v - \ell + 1)/(k - \ell + 1)$ of the L_j, as desired.

To see the connection between such designs and our problem, let $\mathcal{D}$ be a 2-(p, k, λ) design consisting of n sets $L_1, \ldots, L_n$. For each $i \in [p]$, let $T_i = \{j \mid i \in L_j\}$. Note now that for any $i \neq j$,

$$T_i \cap T_j = \{k \mid \{i, j\} \subset L_k\}$$

and hence that $|T_i \cap T_j| = \lambda$. Based on the observation above, we see also that $\forall i, j, |T_i| = |T_j|$ and let a denote this common cardinality. Now, let $\Sigma = (\sigma_1, \ldots, \sigma_t)$ be any sequence of permutations of $[n]$ for which $\sigma_i([a]) = T_i$. It is clear that these form an (p, n)-schedule for which

$$\mathfrak{W}_\Sigma(a, a) = \lambda.$$

Unfortunately, the above construction offers satisfactory control of 2-waste only for the specific pair (a, a). Furthermore, considering that the construction only determines the *sets* $\sigma_i([a])$ and $\sigma_i([p] \setminus [a])$, the ordering of these can be conspiratorially arranged to yield poor bounds on waste for other values. Our goal is construct schedules with satisfactory control on waste for all pairs (a, b).

While designs do not appear to immediately induce a solution to this problem, we will apply the following design-theoretic construction several times in the sequel. Let $\mathrm{GF}(q)$ denote the finite field with q elements, where q is a prime power. Treating $\mathrm{GF}(q)^3$ as a vector space over $\mathrm{GF}(q)$, the design will be given by the lattice of linear subspaces of $\mathrm{GF}(q)^3$. It is easy to check that there are $t = q^2 + q + 1$ distinct one dimensional subspaces of $\mathrm{GF}(q)^3$, which we denote $\ell_1, \ldots, \ell_t$. We say that two subspaces ℓ_i and ℓ_j are *orthogonal* if $\forall u \in \ell_1, \forall v \in \ell_2, \langle u, v \rangle = \sum u_j v_j \bmod q = 0$; in this case we write $\ell_i \perp \ell_j$. It is a fact that for any one dimensional subspace there are exactly $q + 1$ one dimensional subspaces to which it is orthogonal. The design consists of the $n = q^2 + q + 1$ sets $S_u = \{\ell_i \mid \ell_i \perp \ell_u\}$. It is easy to show that any pair of such sets intersect at a single ℓ_i, and that this forms a $2\text{-}(q^2 + q + 1, q + 1, 1)$ design.

For concreteness, we fix a specific (arbitrary) ordering of each of these sets L_u: let K_u denote a canonical sequence $\langle k_u^1, \ldots, k_u^r \rangle$ where $L_u = \{\ell_{k_u^i} \mid 1 \leq i \leq q + 1\}$; i.e., the one dimensional subspaces $\ell_{k_u^i}$, $i = 1, \ldots, q + 1$, are precisely those orthogonal to ℓ_u. For convenience, for two sequences A and B, we let $A \cap B$ and $A \cup B$ denote the corresponding union or intersection of the sets of objects in the sequences. We record the above discussion in the following proposition.

Proposition 10.3. *Let $t = q^2 + q + 1$, where q is a prime power. Then the sequences $\mathcal{K}_t = \langle K_1, \ldots, K_t \rangle$ possess the following properties: each K_u has length $q + 1$, for each $u \neq v$, $|K_u \cap K_v| = 1$, and any element appears in exactly $q + 1$ distinct sequences. We note also that if q is prime, the first element of each sequence can be calculated in $O(\log t)$ time; each subsequent element can be calculated in $O(1)$ time.*

In the sequel we will use these designs with $t = p$, the number of processors. We assume throughout that addition or multiplication of two $\log(\max\{p, n\})$-bit numbers can be performed in $O(1)$ time.

10.2 Redundancy without Communication: a Lower Bound

Controlling global computation redundancy in the absence of communication is a futile task. This is because no amount of algorithmic sophistication can compensate for the possibility of individual processors, or groups of processors, becoming disconnected during the computation. In general, an adversary that is able to partition the processors into g groups that cannot communicate with each other will cause any task-performing algorithm to have work $\Omega(n \cdot g)$, even if each group of processors performs no more than the optimal number of $\Theta(n)$ tasks. In the extreme case where all processors are isolated from the beginning, the work of any algorithm is $\Omega(n \cdot p)$, which is at least the work of an oblivious algorithm, where each processor performs all tasks.

Of course it is not surprising that substantial redundancy cannot be avoided in the absence of communication, furthermore, the lower bound on work of $\Omega(n \cdot p)$ is not very interesting. However, as we pointed out earlier, it is possible to schedule the work of a pair of processors so that each can perform up to $n/2$ tasks without a single task performed redundantly. Thus it is very interesting to consider the intersection properties of pairs of processor schedules, i.e., 2-waste.

If we insist that among the p total processors, any two processors, having executed the same number of tasks n', where $n' < n$, perform *no* redundant work, then it must be the case that $n' \leq \lfloor n/p \rfloor$. In particular, if $p = n$, then the pairwise waste jumps to one if any processor executes more than one task. The next natural question is: how many tasks can processors complete before the lower bound on pairwise redundant work is 2? In general, if any two processors perform n_1 and n_2 tasks respectively, what is the lower bound on pairwise redundant work? In this section we answer these questions. The answers contain both good and bad news: given a fixed t, the lower bound on pairwise redundant work starts growing slowly for small n_1 and n_2, then grows quadratically in the schedule length as n_1 and n_2 approach t.

Now we proceed to the lower bound for the case when two processors execute *different* number of tasks prior to their rendezvous (this lower bound generalizes the second Johnson Bound).

Theorem 10.4. *Let $\Pi = \langle \pi_1, \ldots, \pi_p \rangle$ be a (p, n)-schedule and let $0 \leq a \leq b \leq n$. Then*

$$\mathfrak{W}_\Pi(a, b) \geq \frac{p\, a^2}{(p-1)(n-b+a)} - \frac{a}{p-1}.$$

For example, when processors perform the same number of tasks $a = b$ and $p = n$, then the worst case number of redundant tasks for any pair is at least $\frac{a^2 - a}{n - 1}$. This means that (for $p = n$) if a exceeds $\sqrt{n} + 1$, then the number of redundant task is at least 2.

Corollary 10.5. *For $n = p$, if $a > \sqrt{n - 3/4} + \frac{1}{2}$ then any p-processor schedule of length a for n tasks has worst case pairwise waste at least 2.*

10.3 Random Schedules

As one would expect, schedules chosen at random perform quite well. In this section we explore the behavior of the (p, n)-schedules obtained when each permutation is selected uniformly (and independently) at random among all permutations of $[n]$.

Randomized schedules

When the processors are endowed with a reasonable source of randomness, a natural candidate scheduling algorithm is one where processors select tasks by choosing them uniformly among all tasks they have not yet completed. This amounts to the selection, by each processor i, of a random permutation $\pi_i \in \mathcal{S}_{[n]}$ which determines the order in which this processor will complete the tasks. ($\mathcal{S}_{[n]}$ denotes the collection of all permutations of the set $[n]$.) We let $\mathcal{R}$ be the resulting system of schedules.

Our objective now is to show that random schedules $\mathcal{R}$ have controlled waste with high probability. This amounts to bounding, for each pair i, j and each pair of numbers a, b, the overlap $|\pi_i([a]) \cap \pi_j([b])|$. Observe that when these π_i are selected at random, the expected size of this intersection is ab/n. By showing that the actual waste is very likely to be close to this expected value, one can conclude the waste if bounded for *all* long enough prefixes.

Theorem 10.6. *Let $\mathcal{R}$ be a system of p random schedules for n tasks constructed as above. Then with probability at least $1 - \frac{1}{pn}$, $\forall a, b$ such that*

$$7\sqrt{n} \ln (2pn) \leq a, b \leq n, \ \mathfrak{W}_{\mathcal{R}}(a, b) \leq \frac{ab}{n} + \Delta(a, b) \ , \ \text{where } \Delta(a, b) =$$

$$11\sqrt{\frac{ab}{n} \ln(2pn)} \ .$$

Observe that Theorem 10.4 shows that (p, n)-schedules must have waste $\mathfrak{W}(a, a) = \Omega(a^2/n)$ (as $p \to \infty$); hence such randomized schedules offer nearly optimal waste for this case.

k-Waste for random schedules

For random schedules, one can apply martingale techniques to directly control k-wise waste. We mention one such result.

Theorem 10.7. *Consider the random schedule $\mathcal{R}$ as given above. Then with probability at least $1 - 1/p$,*

$$\mathfrak{W}_{\mathcal{R}}(a, \ldots, a) \leq \sum_{s=2}^{k} (-1)^s \binom{k}{s} \frac{a^s}{n^{s-1}} + \Delta_{a,k},$$

where $\Delta_{a,k} = (2k + 1)\sqrt{a \ln p}$.

Note that again this bounds the distance of the k-waste from its expected value, which can be computed by inclusion-exclusion to be $\sum_{s=2}^{k}(-1)^s \binom{k}{s} \frac{a^s}{n^{s-1}}$. The proof, which we omit, proceeds by considering the martingale which exposes the ith element of all schedules at step i. The theorem then follows by noting that the expected value can change by at most k during a single exposure and applying Azuma's inequality.

10.4 Derandomization via Finite Geometries

We now consider a method for derandomizing these schedules using the design discussed in Section 10.1.

Schedules for $p = n$

We construct a system of schedules of length p by arranging tasks from the sequences of $\mathcal{K}_p$ in a recursive fashion. (Recall that while the sequences of $\mathcal{K}_p$ have strong intersection properties, they are only roughly $\sqrt{p}$ in length.) In preparation for the recursive construction, we record the following lemma about the pairwise intersections of the elements in the sequence of $\mathcal{K}_p$ *indexed* by a specific subspace K_u.

Lemma 10.8. *Let* $\mathcal{K}_p = \langle K_1, \ldots, K_p \rangle$ *be the collection of sequences constructed in Proposition 10.3, and let* $K_u = \langle k_u^1, \ldots, k_u^{q+1} \rangle$, $1 \leq u \leq p$. *Then for any* $i \neq j$, *we have* $K_{k_u^i} \cap K_{k_u^j} = \{u\}$.

As a result of this lemma, there is *only a single repeated element* in the sequences $K_{k_u^1}, K_{k_u^2}, \ldots, K_{k_u^{q+1}}$; this element is u. This fact suggests the following construction of a system of schedules $\mathcal{Q}_p$. Let Q_u, $1 \leq u \leq p$, be the sequence whose first element is u, and whose remaining elements are given by concatenating the $q+1$ sequences $K_{k_u^1}, \ldots, K_{k_u^{q+1}}$ after removing u from each. Specifically,

$$Q_u = \langle u \rangle \circ (\bigcirc_{i \in K_u}(K_i - u)),$$

where $\circ$ denotes concatenation and $K_i - u$ denotes the sequence K_i with u deleted. Note now that since the total length of Q_u is evidently $(q+1)q+1 = p$, each element of $[p]$ must appear exactly once in each Q_u; these Q_u thus give rise to a family of permutations π_u, where $\pi_u(i)$ is the ith element of Q_u. Let $\mathcal{Q}_p = (\pi_1, \ldots, \pi_p)$.

We conceptually divide the sequences Q_u (associated with the permutations π_u) into $q+1$ *segments* of elements. The first segment contains the first $q+1$ elements (including the initial element u); the remaining q segments contain q consecutive elements each.

This recursive construction yields a straightforward bound on pairwise waste, recorded below.

Theorem 10.9. *Let* q *be a prime power,* $p = q^2 + q + 1$. *Let* $a = 1 + iq$, $b = 1 + jq$, $0 \leq i, j \leq q+1$. *Then*

$$\mathfrak{W}_{\mathcal{Q}_p}(a, b) \leq \begin{cases} 0, & i + j = 0, \\ 1, & i = 0, j \geq 1 \text{ or } i \geq 1, j = 0, \\ q + ij, & i \cdot j \geq 1. \end{cases}$$

We mention that the construction can be done on-line. For each schedule the first element can be calculated in $O(1)$ time. For the remaining $q(q+1)$ elements, at the beginning of every sequence of q elements we need to invert at most two elements in $\mathrm{GF}(q)$. When q is prime this can be done in $O(\log p)$ using the extended Euclidean algorithm. Other elements of the schedule can be found in $O(1)$ time.

Note that when $n = \kappa p$ for some $\kappa \in \mathbb{N}$, the above construction can be trivially applied by placing the n tasks into p chunks of size κ. In this case, of course, when a single overlap occurred in the original construction, this penalty is amplified by κ.

Controlling waste for short prefixes

One disadvantage of $\mathcal{Q}_p$ is that the first segment may repeat, so that $(q+1)$ waste may be incurred when a prefix of length $\hat{a} = (q+1)$ is executed. To postpone this increase one would like to rearrange the segments in each Q_u so that the first segment is distinct across the resulting schedules. This can be accomplished by finding a bijection $\rho : [p] \rightarrow [p]$ such that the sequence K_u contains task $\rho(u)$. (In other words ℓ_u must be orthogonal to $\ell_{\rho(u)}$.) This bijection can then be used to select distinct segments as the first segments of schedules in $\mathcal{Q}_p$.

Consider the bipartite graph $G_p = (U_p, V_p, E_p)$ where $U_p = V_p = [p]$ and $p = q^2 + q + 1$; here q is a prime power. Both U_p and V_p can be placed in one-to-one correspondence with the one dimensional subspaces of $\mathrm{GF}(q)^3$. An edge is placed between $\ell_u \in U_p$ and $\ell_v \in V_p$ when they are orthogonal. Based on the structure of $\mathrm{GF}(q)^3$, it is not hard to show that G_p is $(q+1)$-regular. By Hall's theorem, there is always a perfect matching in a d-regular bipartite graph and note that such a matching yields a permutation ρ with the desired properties. In particular if the edge (u, v) appears in the perfect matching, then we put $\rho(u) = v$. This matching can be found using the Hopcroft-Karp algorithm that runs in time $O(\sqrt{|U| + |V|} \cdot |E|) = O(p^2)$.

We use ρ to construct the system of schedules $\mathcal{G}_p$ such that the first segments are distinct. Specifically, given $\mathcal{K}_p$, the system of schedules $\mathcal{G}_p = \langle \gamma_1, \ldots, \gamma_p \rangle$ is defined as follows. For any $1 \leq u \leq p$, the sequence G_u is given by

$$G_u = \langle u \rangle \circ (K_{\rho(u)} - \{u\}) \circ (\bigcirc_{i \in K_u - \rho(u)} (K_i - u)).$$

Then γ_u is the permutation associated with G_u.

Theorem 10.10. *Let q be a prime power, $p = q^2 + q + 1$. Let $a = 1 + iq$, $b = 1 + jq$, $0 \leq i, j \leq q + 1$. Then:*

$$\mathfrak{W}_{\mathcal{G}_p}(a, b) \leq \begin{cases} 0, & i + j = 0, \\ 1, & i = 0, j \geq 1 \text{ or } i \geq 1, j = 0, \\ 1, & i \cdot j = 1, \\ q + ij, & i \cdot j > 1. \end{cases}$$

Observe that this construction is time-optimal as it produces p^2 elements and runs in $O(p^2)$ time. However, the algorithm requires $O(p^2)$ time to construct even a single permutation.

10.5 Open Problems

We surveyed results that characterize the ability of p isolated processors to collaborate on a common known set of n tasks. The good news is that the isolated processors can deterministically construct schedules locally, equipped only with the knowledge of n, p, and their unique processor identifiers in $[p]$. Moreover, the cost of constructing such schedules can be largely amortized over the performance of tasks. It is nevertheless interesting to seek more efficient constructions and deterministic constructions that help control k-waste. Although the lower bounds on wasted work mandate that waste must grow quadratically with the number of executed tasks (from 1 to n), such schedules control wasted work for surprisingly long prefixes of tasks. Another worthwhile problem is to design deterministic strategies that control waste for arbitrary patterns of rendezvous, for example, as in the setting of Chapter 9. Finally, for the settings where communication is deemed expensive or undesirable, it is interesting to develop algorithmic and scheduling strategies that intentionally force processors to work in isolation, and to analyze these strategies in terms of waste, work, and message complexity.

10.6 Chapter Notes

The material in this chapter is based on the work of Malewicz, Russell, and Shvartsman [83, 84, 85, 86] and follows the presentation in [99]. The proofs of the theorems and lemmas stated in this Chapter can be found in [86]. Additional results in this area can be found in Malewicz's thesis [81].

The problem of assessing redundant work for distributed cooperation in the absence of communication was studied by Dolev, Segala, and Shvartsman in [29]. The authors showed that for the case of dynamic changes in connectivity, the termination time of any on-line task assignment algorithm can be greater than the termination time of an off-line task assignment algorithm by a factor linear in n. This means that an on-line algorithm may not be able to do better than the trivial solution that incurs linear overhead by having each processor perform all the tasks. With this observation [29] develops an effective strategy for managing the task execution redundancy and proves that the strategy provides each of the $p \leq n$ processors with a schedule of $\Theta(n^{1/3})$ tasks such that at most one task is performed redundantly by any two processors.

Other approaches to dealing with limited communication have also been explored. Papadimitriou and Yannakakis [95] study how limited patterns of communication affect load-balancing. They consider a problem where there are 3 agents, each of which has a job of a size drawn uniformly at random from $[0, 1]$, and this distribution of job sizes is known to every agent. Any agent A can learn the sizes of jobs of some other agents as given by a directed graph of three nodes. Based on this information each agent has to decide to which of the two servers its job will be sent for processing. Each server has capacity 1, and it may happen that when two or more agents decide to send their jobs to the same server the server will be overloaded. The goal is to devise cooperative strategies for agents that will minimize the chances of overloading any server. The authors present several strategies for agents for this purpose. They show that adding an edge to a graph can improve load balancing. These strategies depend on the communication topology. This problem is similar to our scheduling problem. Sending a job to server number $x \in \{0, 1\}$ resembles doing task number x in our problem. The goal to avoid overloading servers resembles avoiding overlaps between tasks. The problem of Papadimitriou and Yannakakis is different because in our problem we are interested in structuring job execution where the number of tasks can be arbitrary $n \geq 1$.

Georgiades, Mavronicolas, and Spirakis [42] study a similar load-balancing problem. On the one hand their treatment is more general in the sense that they consider arbitrary number of agents n, and arbitrary computable decision algorithms. However it is more restrictive in the sense that they consider only one type of communication topology where there is no communication between processors whatsoever. The two servers that process jobs have some given capacity that is not necessarily 1. They study two families of decision algorithms: algorithms that cannot see the size of jobs before making a decision which server to send a job to for processing, and algorithms that can make decisions based on the size of the job. They completely settle these cases by showing that their decision protocols minimize the chances of overloading any server.

For additional information on the design theory and the extremal set theory see the survey of Hughes and Piper [60]. See [64] for information about the second Johnson Bound. For a discussion of discrete exposure martingales and Azuma's inequality see Alon and Spencer [4]. For Hall's theorem see, e.g., Harary [54]. For Hopcroft-Karp algorithm see [58].

11

Related Cooperation Problems and Models

IN this last chapter we survey selected additional problems involving distributed cooperation in a variety of settings, including shared-memory models and message-passing model using broadcast channels, and we discuss the connection between the *Do-All* problem and the *Consensus* problem for distributed systems.

Chapter structure.

We survey the results for *Do-All* in shared-memory models in Section 11.1. There we include the main algorithmic results, lower bounds, and selected open problems. In Section 11.2 we present several results for the *Do-All* problem obtained for the distributed setting where the message passing is implemented using broadcasts. Finally, in Section 11.3, we overview the *Consensus* Problem for distributed systems and we discuss how, for certain models, *Do-All* algorithms can be used to solve consensus.

11.1 *Do-All* in Shared-Memory

In shared-memory models, the *Do-All* problem is known as the *Write-All* problem, introduced and studied by Kanellakis and Shvartsman [66].

> **Write-All:** *Given a zero-valued array of n elements and p processors, write value 1 into each array location in the presence of adversity.*

The *Write-All* problem captures and abstracts the computational progress that can be achieved in unit time by n correct synchronous processors. Despite its simplicity, solutions for *Write-All* can be used in constructing more complex robust algorithms and for simulations of synchronous parallel algorithms on asynchronous or undependable parallel processors, e.g., [24, 70, 89, 104]. Following the initial work [66], the *Write-All* problem was studied in a variety of shared-memory settings e.g., [5, 7, 14, 51, 65, 68, 69, 82, 87, 88, 89].

A monograph by Kanellakis and Shvartsman [67] presents many of the early results for the *Write-All* problem.

In the design of practical parallel programs one needs to ensure good performance and dependability on multiprocessors with unpredictable load patterns. Here a common challenge is to efficiently perform n independent tasks on p processors, e.g., [56]. Such tasks could be copying a large array, searching a collection of data, or applying a function to all elements of a matrix [40, 51]. In such cases a *Write-All* algorithm can be used with the only change being that the assignment to a particular array element is preceded by a performance of distinct task, where the recording of 1 in the *Write-All* array signifies the completion of the task. The main difference between the *Do-All* problem in message-passing models and the *Write-All* problem in shared-memory models is that in *Do-All* the tasks may be supplied to the processors from some external source, while in *Write-All* the tasks are stored in shared-memory accessible to all processors.

Algorithmics and Lower Bounds. The first algorithm for *Write-All*, and still the most efficient deterministic algorithm as of this writing for synchronous crash-prone processors is due to Kanellakis and Shvartsman [66]. This deterministic algorithm, called algorithm W, solves *Write-All* under processor crashes with total-work $S = O(n + p \log n \log p / \log \log p)$. The algorithm uses binary trees for estimating the number of operational processors, the number of completed tasks (elements of the input array that have value 1) and for balancing the loads of the operational processors. In particular, the elements of the input array are associated with the leaves of a binary tree of depth $O(\log \min\{n, p\})$, called the *progress tree*. The processors are initially distributed to the leaves of the progress tree where each of them performs a task and writes 1 to the corresponding tree location. Then the processors traverse the tree bottom-up recording the progress that it made. This gives an (under)estimate of the number of done tasks. The processors also traverse, bottom-up, a tree of depth $O(\log p)$, called the *processor enumeration tree* to estimate the number of operational processors. Using the two estimated values, the processors traverse the progress tree top-down until they reach to a leaf of the tree. This evenly distributes the operational processors onto undone tasks. The processors perform the task associated with the leaf they reached, and then traverse the progress tree up to the root to record the new progress. This is repeated until all tasks are performed.

Observe that the bound on work for algorithm W as given above does not include f, the number of processor crashes. Georgiou, Russell and Shvartsman [45] presented a failure-sensitive analysis of algorithm W using the techniques we presented in Chapter 3. They showed that algorithm W has total-work $S = O(n + \log n \log p / \log(p/f))$ when $f \leq p \log p$, and work $S = O(n + \log n \log p / \log \log p)$ when $f > p \log p$.

Kedem, Palem, and Spirakis [70] performed an average case analysis of algorithm W [66] considering *random* processor crashes (each processor may crash with a fixed probability). They showed that algorithm W can solve the *Write-All* problem with expected time $O(\log p \log n)$ and expected total-work $O((p+n)\log n)$. This shows that algorithm W performs well under random failures. In the same paper, Kedem *et al.* developed a simple algorithm, called algorithm PS, which is a trivial modification of the straightforward pointer-doubling algorithm (PS is short for pointer shortcutting). The algorithm improves on the expected time of algorithm W, while obtaining the same expected work complexity. Specifically, algorithm PS solves the *Write-All* problem under random failures with expected time $O(\log n)$ and expected work $O(n \log n)$.

Kanellakis, Michailidis and Shvartsman [65] developed a deterministic synchronous algorithm, called algorithm $W_{CR/W}^{opt}$, that solves *Write-All* under processor crashes while controlling the read and write memory access concurrency. The algorithm uses the same data structures as algorithm W to record the progress of the computation and to perform load balancing, and it uses two additional data structures to control the memory access concurrency: (a) *processor priority trees* are used to determine which processors are allowed to read or write each shared location that has to be accessed concurrently by more than one processor, and (b) *broadcast arrays* are used to disseminate values among readers and writers. The write concurrency, denoted ω, measures the redundant write memory accesses as follows: Consider a step of a synchronous parallel computation, where a particular location is written by $x \le p$ processors. Then $x - 1$ of these writes are "redundant", because a single write should suffice. Hence, the write concurrency for this step is $x - 1$. The read concurrency, denoted ρ, is measured in a similar manner. Algorithm $W_{CR/W}^{opt}$ was shown to have total-work $S = O(n + p \log^2 n \log^2 p / \log \log n)$, write concurrency $\omega \le f$ and read concurrency $\rho \le f \log n$, f being the number of crashes.

Observe from above that although the bounds on the read and write concurrencies are given as a function of f, the bound on work is not given as a function of f. Georgiou, Russell, and Shvartsman [47] presented a failure-sensitive analysis on the work of algorithm $W_{CR/W}^{opt}$. They showed that the algorithm achieves total-work $S = O(n + p \log^2 n \log^2 p / \log(p/f))$ when $f \le p / \log p$, and work $S = O(n + p \log^2 n \log^2 p / \log \log p)$ when $f > p / \log p$. This is due to the model of failures, where a crashed processor loses its local memory.

Algorithm V [14] is a variation of algorithm W that solves *Write-All* with synchronous restartable crash-prone processors. As in algorithm W, the processors use binary trees of depth $O(\log n)$ to perform load balancing. Restarted processors join the computation at a pre-defined phase. Algorithm V requires work $S = O(n + p \log^2 n + f \log n)$, where f is the number of processor crashes and restarts. Observe that since f can be arbitrarily large, the work of algorithm V might not be bounded by a function of n and p.

Anderson and Woll [5] developed the best deterministic asynchronous algorithm for *Write-All*. We call this algorithm AW^T. Algorithm AW^T has work $S = O(np^\varepsilon)$, for arbitrary $0 < \varepsilon < 1$. The algorithm uses a q-ary tree, called *progress* tree to load balance processors to tasks (array elements) and a list of $q \leq p$ permutations of $[q]$, used in conjunction with processor identifiers to let the processors know in what order to traverse each of the q subtrees of each interior node in the progress tree. The work complexity does not account for the time required for these permutations to be computed; it is assumed that they are known before the execution of the algorithm. The authors of [5] provide a construction (exponential in q processing time) of permutations needed by their algorithm.

Groote, Hesselink, Mauw, and Vermeulen [51] introduced a different approach that does not use permutation lists and hence no pre-processing is needed. They present an algorithm that has work $S = O(np^{\log(\frac{x+1}{x})})$ where $x = n^{\frac{1}{\log p}}$. The authors argue that their algorithm performs better than AW^T under practical circumstances where $p \ll n$, e.g., when $n = p^2$.

Another practical algorithm, that does not require a precomputed set of permutations is algorithm X of Buss, Kanellakis, Ragde, and Shvartsman [14]. Algorithm X is a special case of algorithm AW^T, where $q = 2$ and it has work $S = O(np^{0.59})$.

Kedem, Palem, Raghunathan, and Spirakis [69] showed that any execution of an algorithm designed to solve *Write-All* deterministically for $n = p$ with crash-prone processors requires time $\Omega(\log n)$ and work $\Omega(n \log n)$. Martel and Subramonian [88] extended these lower bounds for randomized algorithms. Specifically they showed that the lower bound on expected time and expected work on randomized algorithms for *Write-All* is $\Omega(\log n)$ and $\Omega(n \log n)$, for $n = p$, respectively (these lower bounds apply to both synchronous crash-prone and asynchronous processors). Martel, Park, and Subramonian [87] developed a randomized asynchronous algorithm for *Write-All* that matches the above lower bound on the expected work for randomized algorithms. Their algorithm proceeds as follows: the locations of the input array are viewed as n leaves of a binary tree that is $\Theta(\log n)$ deep (this is similar to the progress tree of algorithm X [14]). Initially all tree nodes are unmarked. Each processor selects a tree node at random. If the node v is a leaf node or if its children are marked, then node v is also marked. This is repeated until the root is marked.

Complexity of *Write-All* and Open Problems. Algorithm W [66] has optimal work of $O(n)$ when $p \leq n \log \log n / \log^2 n$. However, the $\Omega(n \log n)$ lower bound of Kedem et al. [69] shows that no optimal algorithm for *Write-All* exists for the full range of processors ($p = n$). Although a small gap of $\log n / \log \log n$ remains between the upper and lower bounds, the problem can be considered substantially solved for synchronous processors.

Solutions for the *Write-All* problem are significantly more challenging when asynchrony is introduced. As we pointed out, the most efficient deterministic asynchronous *Write-All* algorithm is the elegant algorithm of Anderson and Woll [5] that has work $O(n \cdot p^\varepsilon)$ for $p \leq n$ and any $\xi > 0$. The strongest corresponding lower bound, due to Buss, Kanellakis, Ragde, and Shvartsman [14], is $\Omega(n + p \log p)$, and it holds even if no processor crashes. Note that in complexity-theoretic terms, the relative gap between these bounds on work is very large (i.e., polynomial in p, being p^ε for $p = n$), since the lower bound is only a logarithm away from linear work. Given that this gap is now over 15 years old, and that this problem continues to be of interest, it appears that narrowing this gap is extremely challenging.

Thus we formulate a two-pronged, open problem as follows: (*a*) *can a stronger than $\Omega(n \log n)$ lower bound on work be shown for asynchronous Write-All problem, and/or (b) is there an algorithm for asynchronous processors that solves the problem with work asymptotically lower than $O(n^{1+\varepsilon})$ for $p = n$?*

Next observe that an optimal algorithm for *Write-All* must have work $\Theta(n)$, however the lower bounds on work of $\Omega(n + p \log p)$ make optimality out of reach when $p = \Omega(n)$. Also note that the asynchronous algorithm [5] has work complexity $\omega(n)$ for all but a trivial number p of processors. The quest then is to obtain work-optimal solutions for this problem using the largest possible, and non-trivial compared to n, number of processors p in order to maximize the parallelism of the solution.

Malewicz [82] presented the first qualitative advancement in the search for optimal work complexity by exhibiting a deterministic asynchronous algorithm for the *Write-All* problem that has work $S = O(n + p^4 \log n)$. This is the first asynchronous *Write-All* algorithm that obtains optimal work for a non-trivial number g of processors, where $g = \sqrt[4]{n/\log n}$. This compares very favorably to all previously known deterministic algorithms that require as much as $\omega(n)$ work when $p = n^{1/c}$, for any fixed $c > 1$. The algorithm operates on *collision* detection: each processor has a collection of intervals of the input array and iteratively selects an interval to work on. The processor proceeds from one edge of the interval toward the other edge, executing the tasks associated with the cells in the interval. When processors "collide", meaning that they are allocated to the same input element, they exchange appropriate information and schedule their future work accordingly. The algorithm uses Test-And-Set instructions to detect collisions, as opposed to the previous algorithms that used only atomic Read/Write instructions.

Using different techniques, Kowalski and Shvartsman [76] exhibited an algorithm that has work complexity of $O(n + p^{2+\varepsilon})$, achieving optimality for a substantially larger range of processors, specifically for $p = O(n^{1/(2+\varepsilon)})$, essentially squaring the number of processors g [82] for which optimality was previously shown to be possible.

Consequently, we formulate another important open problem as follows: *Is it possible to solve the asynchronous Write-All problem with optimal work $O(n)$ using the number of processors $p = n^\delta$ for $\delta > 1/2$?*

Simulations. *Write-All* algorithms can be used *iteratively* to simulate parallel algorithms formulated for synchronous failure-free processors (see the works of Kedem, Palem, and Spirakis [70], Kedem, Palem, Raghunathan, and Spirakis [69], Martel, Park, and Subramonian [87], Martel, Subramonian, and Park [89], and Shvartsman [104]). It was shown that the execution of a single n-processor step on p failure-prone processors does not exceed the complexity of solving a n-size instance of *Write-All* using p failure-prone processors. This commonly requires that (i) the individual processor steps are made idempotent (since they may have to be performed multiple times due to failures or asynchrony), and that (ii) a linear in the number of processors auxiliary memory is made available (to be used as a "scratchpad" and to store intermediate results). While the former can be solved with the help of an automated tool, e.g., a compiler, the latter requires sophisticated solutions because of the difficulty of (re)using the auxiliary memory due to "late writers" (i.e., processors that are slow and that unknowingly write stale values to memory). Examples of randomized solutions addressing these problems include the works of Aumann and Rabin [7], and Kedem, Palem, Rabin, and Raghunathan [68]. Another important aspect of algorithm simulations is the use of an optimistic approach, where the computation may proceed for several steps assuming that all tasks assigned to active processors are successfully completed. Such approach was used by Kedem, Palem, Raghunathan, and Spirakis [69]. In some deterministic models optimal simulations are possible, e.g., as presented by Shvartsman [104]), however randomized solutions are able to achieve (expected) optimality for broader ranges of models and algorithms. An example of a practical implementation is discussed by Dasgupta, Kedem and Rabin [24].

11.2 *Do-All* with Broadcast Channels

Chlebus, Kowalski, and Lingas [20] studied the *Do-All* problem in the setting of broadcast networks where crash-prone processors (or stations as they call them) communicate over a multiple access channel [39], synchronized by a global clock. In such networks, if exactly one processor broadcasts at a time, then the message is delivered to all processors. If more than one processor broadcasts then *collision* occurs and no message is delivered.

The authors provide randomized and deterministic solutions with and without collision detection, and for various size-bounded adversaries causing crashes. An adversary is f-bounded if it may crash at most $f < p$ processors. If f is a constant fraction of p, then the adversary is called linearly bounded. An f-bounded adversary is weakly adaptive if it pre-selects (prior to a start of the computation) a subset of processors that might crash later in the computation (at any time). An f-bounded adversary is strongly adaptive if the upper bound f on the number of crashes is the only restriction on failure occurrences in a computation.

First, the authors prove that $\Omega(n + p\sqrt{n})$ total-work is required for any (deterministic or randomized) *Do-All* algorithm even when no crashes occur.

For the channel where collision detection is available, they develop an optimal deterministic *Do-All* algorithm, called GROUPS-TOGETHER, that achieves total-work $O(n + p\sqrt{n})$ against the f-bounded adversary. The authors also show that randomization does not help to improve efficiency of deterministic algorithms under any adversary.

For the channel where collision detection is not available, Chlebus et al. develop a deterministic *Do-All* algorithm, called TWO-LISTS, that achieves total-work $O(n + p\sqrt{n} + p\min\{f, n\})$ against the f-bounded adversary. The algorithm is shown to be optimal by providing a matching lower bound result for the strongly-adaptive f-bounded adversary. Futhermore, the authors show that randomization does not help to improve efficiency of deterministic algorithms under the strongly-adaptive f-bounded adversary. However, they develop a randomized algorithm, called MIX-RAND, and show that it achieves expected total-work $O(n+p\sqrt{n})$ against certain weakly-adaptive size-bounded adversaries. This demonstrates that randomization can help if collision detection is not available and the adversary is sufficiently weak.

Finally, Chlebus et al. show that if $f = p(1 - o(1/\sqrt{n}))$ and $n = o(p^2)$, then a weakly-adaptive f-bounded adversary can force any *Do-All* algorithm for the channel where collision detection is to available to perform asymptotically more than $\Omega(n + p\sqrt{n})$ total-work.

Following the work of Chlebus et al., Clementi, Monti, and Silvestri [22] considered the *Do-All* problem in broadcast networks without collision detection under an omniscient f-bounded crash-causing adversary, while assuming that f, the maximum number of crashes, is *a priori known* to the processors. More specifically, they introduced the notion of f-*reliability*: a *Do-All* algorithm is f-reliable if it solves the problem against any f-bounded adversary, for a known f. Note that the work of Chlebus et al. [20] considered $(p - 1)$-reliable algorithms, as f was not known a priori and the algorithms were designed to work even in the case that up to $p - 1$ processors crashed (the f appearing in the complexity analyses of those algorithms is the actual number of processor crashes in a given execution).

Clementi et al., produced tight bounds on the completion time (total time for the *Do-All* problem to be solved) and total-work of f-reliable algorithms. In particular, they showed that the completion time of f-reliable algorithms in broadcast networks without collision detection is $\Theta(\frac{n}{p-f} + \min\{\frac{nf}{p}, f + \sqrt{n}\})$ and the total-work is $\Theta(n + f \cdot \min\{n, f\})$. The algorithm yielding the upper bound result for total work is based on a version of algorithm TWO-LISTS of Chlebus et al. [20] modified to exploit the knowledge of f. It is noted that the two lower bounds on completion time and total-work hold even when crashes take place at the very beginning of the algorithm execution.

11.3 Consensus and its Connection to *Do-All*

Consensus is the abstract problem of having p processors to agree on a common value. This problem is one of the fundamental problems of distributed computing, and solutions to this problem are used as building blocks in various distributed applications [79].

The *Consensus* problem is defined as follows.

> **Consensus:** *For a collection of processors, where each starts with some initial input value, each processor must decide upon an output value, subject to the following constraints:*
> *(Agreement) All non-faulty processors must agree on the output.*
> *(Validity) If all non-faulty processors begin with the same input value, that value must be the output value of all non-faulty processors.*
> *(Termination) All non-faulty processors eventually decide.*

Processors are subject to failures, e.g., crashes, but communication is assumed to be reliable. Consensus is also referred to as the *Byzantine agreement problem*. When the processors are subject to Byzantine failures, consensus is also known as *Byzantine generals problem*. This problem was introduced by Lamport, Shostak, and Pease [78]. Here p processors, a subset of which may be faulty, must eventually agree (termination) on a value broadcast by a distinguished processor, called the *sender* or the *general*, in such a way that all non-faulty processors decide the same value (agreement), and when the general is non-faulty, they decide on the value the general sent (validity). The number of faulty processors is bounded in advance, by a fixed number f. It is also shown that it is impossible to reach agreement when $p = 3f$.

Dwork, Halpern, and Waarts [30] developed an algorithm that can use a *Do-All* algorithm as a building block to solve the Byzantine agreement problem for synchronous crash-prone processors. Their algorithm proceeds in two stages: first the general broadcasts its value to processors with PID $= 1, \ldots, f + 1$. Then these $f + 1$ processors use one of the *Do-All* algorithms (Protocols $\mathcal{B}$, $\mathcal{C}$ or $\mathcal{D}$) to perform the "work" of informing processors $1, \ldots p$ about the general's value. Hence, performing a *Do-All* task here means sending a message containing the general's value. Initially all processors have the initial value 0 as the general's value (the general of course has it own value as initial value). When a processor receives a message about a value for the general different from its current value, it adopts the new value. Finally, at a predetermined time by which the underlying *Do-All* algorithm is guaranteed to have terminated, each processor decides on its current value for the general. Using protocol $\mathcal{C}$ as the *Do-All* algorithm the authors solve the Byzantine agreement problem for synchronous crash-prone processors in $O(2^p)$ time and with $O(p + f \log f)$ message complexity. When they use protocol $\mathcal{B}$ they obtain a Byzantine agreement solution of $O(p)$ time and $O(p + f\sqrt{f})$ message complexity. When p and f are comparable, the second solution has the same asymptotic time complexity as the algorithms presented in [79] (best known for this problem) and substantially better message complexity. This demonstrates that *Do-All* solutions can yield efficient solutions to the Byzantine agreement problem (and to the consensus problem in general).

Galil, Mayer and Yung [38] developed an algorithm that solves Byzantine agreement for synchronous crash-prone processors that uses a linear number of messages ($O(p)$) and super-linear time ($O(p^{1+\varepsilon})$). They also improved the message complexity of the *Do-All* algorithm of De Prisco *et al.* [25]. This algorithm relies on two agreement-like protocols: (a) the check-point protocol that processors use to agree on the set of operational processors, and (b) the synchronization protocol that processors use to agree on the time that the next check-point protocol will begin. Given the full details of the protocols, it is not difficult to observe that these protocols solve multiple instances of the Byzantine agreement problem. Also, as we have seen in Section 6.3.1, algorithm Majority makes use of check-pointing, agreement-like protocols to solve the *Do-All* problem under synchronous processors prone to Byzantine failures. Therefore, efficient solutions to consensus can lead to efficient solutions to *Do-All*.

We conclude with a noteworthy observation. The impossibility result shown by Fischer, Lynch and Paterson [36] states that consensus cannot be solved in asynchronous models, even if there is only one processor crash. More precisely, no asynchronous deterministic algorithm with only one possible crash can guarantee agreement, that is, if such an algorithm terminates, it may violate agreement. This reveals a fundamental (although not surprising) difference between the *Consensus* and *Do-All* problems: although it is possible for consensus not to have a solution in certain models, the *Do-All* problem is always solvable, as long as one processor remains correct for the entire course of the computation. For example, *Do-All* is trivially solved by having each processor perform all tasks.

References

1. M. Abdelguerfi and S. Lavington. *Emerging Trends in Database and Knowledge-Base Machines: The Application of Parallel Architectures to Smart Information Systems.* IEEE Press, 1995.
2. C. Aguirre, J. Martinez-Munoz, F. Corbacho, and R. Huerta. Small-world topology for multi-agent collaboration. In *Proceedings of the 11th International Workshop on Database and Expert Systems Applications*, pages 231–235, 2000.
3. M. Ajtai, J. Aspnes, C. Dwork, and O. Waarts. A theory of competitive analysis for distributed algorithms. In *Proceedings of the 35th Symposium on Foundations of Computer Science (FOCS 1994)*, pages 401–411, 1994.
4. N. Alon and J.H. Spencer. *The Probabilistic Method.* J. Wiley and Sons, Inc., second edition, 2000.
5. R.J. Anderson and H. Woll. Algorithms for the certified Write-All problem. *SIAM Journal of Computing*, 26(5):1277–1283, 1997.
6. H. Attiya and J. Welch. *Distributed Computing: Fundamentals, Simulations and Advanced Topics.* Wiley-Interscience, second edition, 2004.
7. Y. Aumann and M.O. Rabin. Clock construction in fully asynchronous parallel systems and PRAM simulation. In *Proceedings of the 33rd IEEE Symposium on Foundations of Computer Science (FOCS 1992)*, pages 147–156, 1992.
8. B. Awerbuch, S. Kutten, and D. Peleg. Competitive distributed job scheduling. In *Proceedings of the 24th ACM Symposium on Theory of Computing (STOC 1992)*, pages 571–580, 1992.
9. O. Babaoglu, R. Davoli, L. Giachini, and M. Baker. Relacs: A communication infrastructure for constructing reliable applications in large-scale distributed systems. In *Proceedings of the 28th Hawaii International Conference on System Science (HICSS 1995)*, pages 612–621, 1995.
10. O. Babaoglu, R. Davoli, and A. Montresor. Group communication in partitionable systems: Specification and algorithms. *Software Engineering*, 27(4):308–336, 2001.
11. Y. Bartal, A. Fiat, and Y. Rabani. Competitive algorithms for distributed data management. In *Proceedings of the 24th ACM Symposium on Theory of Computing (STOC 1992)*, pages 39–50, 1992.
12. S. Ben-David, A. Borodin, R. Karp, G. Tardos, and A. Wigderson. On the power of randomization in on-line algorithms. *Algorithmica*, 11(1):2–14, 1994.

13. K.P. Birman and R. van Renesse. *Reliable Distributed Computing with the Isis Toolkit.* IEEE Computer Society Press, 1994.

14. J. Buss, P.C. Kanellakis, P. Ragde, and A.A. Shvartsman. Parallel algorithms with processor failures and delays. *Journal of Algorithms*, 20(1):45–86, 1996.

15. B. Chlebus, R. De-Prisco, and A.A. Shvartsman. Performing tasks on restartable message-passing processors. *Distributed Computing*, 14(1):49–64, 2001. A preliminary version has appeared in WDAG 1997.

16. B.S. Chlebus, L. Gasieniec, D.R. Kowalski, and A.A. Shvartsman. Bounding work and communication in robust cooperative computation. In *Proceedings of the 16th International Symposium on Distributed Computing (DISC 2002)*, pages 295–310, 2002.

17. B.S. Chlebus and D.R. Kowalski. Randomization helps to perform independent tasks reliably. *Random Structures and Algorithms*, 24(1):11–41, 2004. A preliminary version appeared as "Randomization helps to perform tasks on processors prone to failures" in DISC 1999.

18. B.S. Chlebus and D.R. Kowalski. Robust gossiping with an application to consensus. *Journal of Computer and System Sciences*, 72(8):1262–1281, 2006. A preliminary version appeared as "Gossiping to reach consensus" in SPAA 2002.

19. B.S. Chlebus and D.R. Kowalski. Time and communication efficient consensus for crash failures. In *Proceedings of the 20th International Symposium on Distributed Computing (DISC 2006)*, pages 314–328, 2006.

20. B.S. Chlebus, D.R. Kowalski, and A. Lingas. The Do-All problem in broadcast networks. *Distributed Computing*, 18(6):435–451, 2006. A preliminary version appeared in PODC 2001.

21. G.V. Chockler, I. Keidar, and R. Vitenberg. Group communication specifications: A comprehensive study. *ACM Computing Surveys*, 33(4):1–43, 2001.

22. A.E.F. Clementi, A. Monti, and R. Silvestri. Optimal F-reliable protocols for the Do-All problem on single-hop wireless networks. In *Proceedings of the 13th International Symposium on Algorithms and Computation (ISAAC 2002)*, pages 320–331, 2002.

23. F. Cristian. Group, majority and strict agreement in timed asynchronous distributed systems. In *Proceedings of the 26th Conference on Fault-Tolerant Computer Systems (FTCS 1996)*, pages 178–187, 1996.

24. P. Dasgupta, Z. Kedem, and M. Rabin. Parallel processing on networks of workstation: A fault-tolerant, high performance approach. In *Proceedings of the 15th IEEE International Conference on Distributed Computer Systems (ICDCS 1995)*, pages 467–474, 1995.

25. R. De-Prisco, A. Mayer, and M. Yung. Time-optimal message-efficient work performance in the presence of faults. In *Proceedings of the 13th ACM Symposium on Principles of Distributed Computing (PODC 1994)*, pages 161–172, 1994.

26. R.P. Dilworth. A decomposition theorem for partially ordered sets. *Annals of Mathematics*, 51:161–166, 1950.

27. D. Dolev and D. Malki. The transis approach to high availability cluster communications. *Communications of the ACM*, 39(4):64–70, 1996.

28. D. Dolev, D. Malki, and R. Strong. A framework for partitionable membership service. Technical Report TR 95-4, Institute of Computer Science, The Hebrew University of Jerusalem, 1995.

29. S. Dolev, R. Segala, and A.A. Shvartsman. Dynamic load balancing with group communication. *Theoretical Computer Science*, 369(1–3):348–360, 2006. A preliminary version appeared in SIROCCO 1999.

30. C. Dwork, J. Halpern, and O. Waarts. Performing work efficiently in the presence of faults. *SIAM Journal on Computing*, 27(5):1457–1491, 1998. A preliminary version appears in the *Proceedings of the 11th ACM Symposium on Principles of Distributed Computing (PODC 1992)*, pages 91–102, 1992.

31. R. Elmasri and S.B. Navathe. *Fundamentals of Database Systems*. Addison-Wesley publishing company, second edition, 1994.

32. P. Ezhilchelvan, R. Macedo, and S. Shrivastava. Newtop: A fault-tolerant group communication protocol. In *Proceedings of the 15th IEEE International Conference on Distributed Computing Systems (ICDCS 1995)*, pages 296–306, 1995.

33. A. Fekete, N. Lynch, and A.A. Shvartsman. Specifying and using a partition-able group communication service. *ACM Transactions on Computer Systems*, 19(2):171–216, 2001. A preliminary version appeared in PODC 1997.

34. A. Fernández, Ch. Georgiou, L. Lopez, and A. Santos. Reliably executing tasks in the presence of untrusted entities. In *Proceedings of the 25th IEEE Symposium on Reliable Distributed Systems (SRDS 2006)*, pages 39–50, 2006.

35. A. Fernández, Ch. Georgiou, A. Russell, and A.A. Shvartsman. The Do-All problem with byzantine processor failures. *Theoretical Computer Science*, 333(3):433–454, 2005. A preliminary version appeared in SIROCCO 2003.

36. M.J. Fischer, N.A. Lynch, and M.S. Paterson. Impossibility of distributed consensus with one faulty process. *Journal of the ACM*, 32(2):374–382, 1985.

37. J.D. Foley, A. van Dam, S.K. Feiner, and J.F. Hughes. *Computer Graphics: Principle and Practice*. Addison-Wesley publishing company, second edition, 1996.

38. Z. Galil, A. Mayer, and M. Yung. Resolving message complexity of byzan-tine agreement and beyond. In *Proceedings of the 36th IEEE Symposium on Foundations of Computer Science (FOCS 1995)*, pages 724–733, 1995.

39. G.R. Gallager. A perspective on multi-access channels. *IEEE Transactions on Information Theory*, 31(2):124–142, 1985.

40. Hui Gao, Jan Friso Groote, and Wim H. Hesselink. Lock-free dynamic hash tables with open addressing. *Distributed Computing*, 18(1):21–42, 2005.

41. S. Garland and N. Lynch. The IOA language and toolset: Support for designing, analyzing, and building distributed systems. Technical Report MIT/LCS/TR-762, Laboratory for Computer Science, Massachusetts Institute of Technology, Cambridge, MA, 1998.

42. S. Georgiades, M. Mavronicolas, and P. Spirakis. Optimal, distributed decision-making: The case of no communication. In *Proceedings of the 12th International Symposium on Foundamentals of Computation Theory (FCT 1999)*, pages 293–303, 1999.

43. Ch. Georgiou. *Robust Distributed Cooperation in the Presence of Quantified Adversity*. PhD thesis, The University of Connecticut, Storrs, CT, 2003.

44. Ch. Georgiou, D.R. Kowalski, and A.A. Shvartsman. Efficient gossip and robust distributed computation. *Theoretical Computer Science*, 347(1):130–166, 2005. A preliminary version appeared in DISC 2003.

45. Ch. Georgiou, A. Russell, and A.A. Shvartsman. The complexity of syn-chronous iterative Do-All with crashes. *Distributed Computing*, 17:47–63, 2004. A preliminary version appeared in DISC 2001.

46. Ch. Georgiou, A. Russell, and A.A. Shvartsman. Work-competitive scheduling for cooperative computing with dynamic groups. *SIAM Journal on Computing*, 34(4):848–862, 2005. A preliminary version appeared in STOC 2003.

47. Ch. Georgiou, A. Russell, and A.A. Shvartsman. Failure-sensitive analysis of parallel algorithms with controlled memory access concurrency. *Parallel Processing Letters*, 17(2):153–168, 2007. A preliminary version appeared in OPODIS 2002.

48. Ch. Georgiou and A.A. Shvartsman. Cooperative computing with fragmentable and mergeable groups. *Journal of Discrete Algorithms*, 1(2):211–235, 2003. A preliminary version appeared in SIROCCO 2000.

49. A. Gharakhani and A.F. Ghoniem. Massively parallel implementation of a 3D vortex-boundary element method. In *Proceedings of the European Series in Applied and Industrial Mathematics*, volume 1, pages 213–223, 1996.

50. S.A. Green. *Parallel Processing for Computer Graphics*. MIT Press/Pitman Publishing, 1991.

51. J.F. Groote, W.H. Hesselink, S. Mauw, and R. Vermeulen. An algorithm for the asynchronous Write-All problem based on process collision. *Distributed Computing*, 14(2):75–81, 2001.

52. R. Guerraoui and Luis Rodrigues. *Introduction to Reliable Distributed Programming*. Springer, 2006.

53. V. Hadzilacos and S. Toueg. Fault-tolerant broadcasts and related problems. In *Distributed Systems*, chapter 5, pages 97–145. ACM Press/Addison-Wesley, 1993.

54. F. Harary. *Graph Theory*. Addison-Wesley, 1994.

55. M. Hayden. *The Ensemble System*. PhD thesis, Cornell University, 1998.

56. W.H. Hesselink and J.F. Groote. Waitfree distributed memory management by Create and Read until Deletion (CaRuD). *Distributed Computing*, 14(1):31–39, 2001.

57. M. Hiltunen and R. Schlichting. Properties of membership services. In *Proceedings of the 2nd International Symposium on Autonomous Decentralized Systems*, pages 200–207, 1995.

58. J.E. Hopcroft and R.M. Karp. An $n^{5/2}$ algorithm for maximum matching in bipartite graphs. *SIAM Journal on Computing*, 2(4):225–231, 1973.

59. J. Hromkovic, R. Klasing, A. Pelc, P. Ruzicka, and W. Unger. *Dissemination of Information in Communication Networks: Broadcasting, Gossiping, Leader Election, and Fault-Tolerance*. Springer, 2005.

60. D.R. Hughes and F.C. Piper. *Design Theory*. Cambridge University Press, 1985.

61. Veromodo Inc. Tempo toolkit. http://www.veromodo.com.

62. K. Jacobsen, X. Zhang, and K. Marzullo. Group membership and wide-area master-worker computations. In *Proceedings of the 23rd IEEE International Conference on Distributed Computing Systems (ICDCS 2003)*, pages 570–581, 2003.

63. C.B. Jenssen. *Parallel Computational Fluid Dynamics 2000: Trends and Applications*. Elsevier Science Ltd., first edition, 2001.

64. S.M. Johnson. A new upper bound for error-correcting codes. *IEEE Transactions on Information Theory*, 8(3):203–207, 1962.

65. P.C. Kanellakis, D. Michailidis, and A.A. Shvartsman. Controlling memory access concurrency in efficient fault-tolerant parallel algorithms. *Nordic Journal of Computing*, 2(2):146–180, 1995.

66. P.C. Kanellakis and A.A. Shvartsman. Efficient parallel algorithms can be made robust. *Distributed Computing*, 5(4):201–217, 1992. A preliminary version appears in the *Proceedings of the 8th ACM Symposium on Principles of Distributed Computing (PODC 1989)*, pages 211–222, 1989.

67. P.C. Kanellakis and A.A. Shvartsman. *Fault-Tolerant Parallel Computation*. Kluwer Academic Publishers, 1997.

68. Z.M. Kedem, K.V. Palem, M.O. Rabin, and A. Raghunathan. Efficient program transformations for resilient parallel computation via randomization. In *Proceedings of the 24th ACM Symposium on Theory of Computing (STOC 1992)*, pages 306–318, 1992.

69. Z.M. Kedem, K.V. Palem, A. Raghunathan, and P. Spirakis. Combining tentative and definite executions for dependable parallel computing. In *Proceedings of the 23rd ACM Symposium on Theory of Computing (STOC 1991)*, pages 381–390, 1991.

70. Z.M. Kedem, K.V. Palem, and P. Spirakis. Efficient robust parallel computations. In *Proceedings of the 22nd ACM Symposium on Theory of Computing (STOC 1990)*, pages 138–148, 1990.

71. D.E. Knuth. *The Art of Computer Programming*, volume 3. Addison-Wesley Publishers, third edition, 1998.

72. K. M. Konwar, S. Rajasekaran, and A.A. Shvartsman. Robust network supercomputing with malicious processes. In *Proceedings of the 20th International Symposium on Distributed Computing (DISC 2006)*, pages 474–488, 2006.

73. E. Korpela, D. Werthimer, D. Anderson, J. Cobb, and M. Lebofsky. SETI@home: Massively distributed computing for SETI. *Computing in Science and Engineering*, 3(1):78–83, 2001.

74. D.R. Kowalski, M. Momenzadeh, and A.A. Shvartsman. Emulating shared-memory Do-All algorithms in asynchronous message-passing systems. In *Proceedings of the 7th International Conference on Principles of Distributed Systems (OPODIS 2003)*, pages 210–222, 2003.

75. D.R. Kowalski, P. Musial, and A.A. Shvartsman. Explicit combinatorial structures for cooperative distributed algorithms. In *Proceedings of the 25th International Conference on Distributed Computing Systems (ICDCS 2005)*, pages 48–58, 2005.

76. D.R. Kowalski and A.A. Shvartsman. Writing-all deterministically and optimally using a non-trivial number of asynchronous processors. In *Proceedings of the 16th ACM Symposium on Parallel Algorithms and Architectures (SPAA 2004)*, pages 311–320, 2004.

77. D.R. Kowalski and A.A. Shvartsman. Performing work with asynchronous processors: message-delay-sensitive bounds. *Information and Computation*, 203(2):181–210, 2005. A preliminary version appeared in PODC 2003.

78. L. Lamport, R. Shostak, and M. Pease. The Byzantine generals problem. *ACM Transactions on Programming Languages and Systems*, 4(3):382–401, 1982.

79. N.A. Lynch. *Distributed Algorithms*. Morgan Kaufmann Publishers, 1996.

80. N.A. Lynch and M.R. Tuttle. An introduction to Input/Output automata. *CWI Quarterly*, 2(3):219–246, 1989.

81. G. Malewicz. *Distributed Scheduling for Disconnected Cooperation*. PhD thesis, The University of Connecticut, Storrs, CT, 2003.

82. G. Malewicz. A work-optimal deterministic algorithm for the certified Write-All problem with a nontrivial number of asynchronous processors. *SIAM Jour-*

nal on Computing, 34(4):993–1024, 2005. A preliminary version appeared in PODC 2003.

83. G. Malewicz, A. Russell, and A.A. Shvartsman. Distributed cooperation during the absence of communication. In *Proceedings of the 14th International Symposium on Distributed Computing (DISC 2000)*, pages 119–133, 2000.

84. G. Malewicz, A. Russell, and A.A. Shvartsman. Local scheduling for distributed cooperation. In *Proceedings of the IEEE International Symposium on Network Computing and Applications (NCA 2001)*, 2001.

85. G. Malewicz, A. Russell, and A.A. Shvartsman. Optimal scheduling for disconnected cooperation. In *Proceedings of the 8th International Colloquium on Structural Information and Communication Complexity (SIROCCO 2001)*, pages 259–274, 2001.

86. G. Malewicz, A. Russell, and A.A. Shvartsman. Distributed scheduling for disconnected cooperation. *Distributed Computing*, 18(6):409–420, 2006.

87. C. Martel, A. Park, and R. Subramonian. Work-optimal asynchronous algorithms for shared memory parallel computers. *SIAM Journal on Computing*, 21(6):1070–1099, 1992.

88. C. Martel and R. Subramonian. On the complexity of certified Write-All algorithms. *Journal of Algorithms*, 16(3):361–387, 1994.

89. C. Martel, R. Subramonian, and A. Park. Asynchronous PRAMs are (almost) as good as synchronous PRAMs. In *Proceedings of the 31st IEEE Symposium on Foundations of Computer Science (FOCS 1990)*, pages 590–599, 1990.

90. S. Mishra, L.L. Peterson, and R.D. Schlichting. Consul: A communication substrate for fault-tolerant distributed programs. *Distributed Systems Engineering Journal*, 1(2):87–103, 1993.

91. S. Molnar, J. Eyles, and J. Poulton. PixelFlow: High-speed rendering using image composition. *Computer Graphics*, 26(2):231–240, 1992.

92. L.E. Moser, Y. Amir, P.M. Melliar-Smith, and D.A. Agarwal. Extended virtual synchrony. In *Proceedings of the 14th IEEE International Conference on Distributed Computing Systems (ICDCS 1994)*, pages 56–65, 1994.

93. L.E. Moser, P.M. Melliar-Smith, D.A. Agarawal, R.K. Budhia, and C.A. Lingley-Papadopolous. Totem: A fault-tolerant multicast group communication system. *Communications of the ACM*, 39(4):54–63, 1996.

94. P.M. Musial. Computational requirements of the beam-space post-doppler space time adaptive processing algorithm. Master's thesis, University of Connecticut, 2001.

95. C.H. Papadimitriou and M. Yannakakis. On the value of information in distributed decision-making. In *Proceedings of the 10th ACM Symposium on Principles of Distributed Computing (PODC 1991)*, pages 61–64, 1991.

96. A. Pelc. Fault-tolerant broadcasting and gossiping in communication networks. *Networks*, 28(3):143–156, 1996.

97. D. Powell, editor. *Special Issue on Group Communication Services*, volume 39(4) of *Communications of the ACM*. ACM Press, 1996.

98. A. Ricciardi, A. Schiper, and K. Birman. Understanding partitions and the "no partition" assumption. In *Proceedings of the 4th Workshop on Future Trends of Distributed Computing Systems*, pages 354–360, 1993.

99. A. Russell and A.A. Shvartsman. Distributed computation meets design theory: Local scheduling for disconnected cooperation. *Bulletin of the European Association for Theoretical Computer Science*, 77:120–131, 2002.

100. M. Saks, N. Shavit, and H. Woll. Optimal time randomized consensus – making resilient algorithms fast in practice. In *Proceedings of the 2nd ACM-SIAM Symposium on Discrete Algorithms (SODA 1991)*, pages 351–362, 1991.

101. R. Samanta, J. Zheng, T. Funkhouser, K. Li, and J.P. Singh. Load balancing for multi-projector rendering systems. In *SIGGRAPH/Eurographics Workshop on Graphics Hardware*, pages 107–116, 1999.

102. R.D. Schlichting and F.B. Schneider. Fail-stop processors: An approach to designing fault-tolerant computing systems. *ACM Transactions on Computing Systems*, 1(3):222–238, 1983.

103. N. Shavit. *Concurrent Time Stamping*. PhD thesis, The Hebrew University of Jerusalem, Israel, 1989.

104. A.A. Shvartsman. Achieving optimal CRCW PRAM fault-tolerance. *Information Processing Letters*, 39(2):59–66, 1991.

105. D. Sleator and R. Tarjan. Amortized efficiency of list update and paging rules. *Communications of the ACM*, 28(2):202–208, 1985.

106. D.R. Stinson. *Cryptography: Theory and practice*. CRC PRess, 1995.

107. M. Tambe, J. Adibi, Y. Alonaizon, A. Erdem, G.A. Kaminka, S. Marsella, and I. Muslea. Building agent teams using an explicit teamwork model and learning. *Artificial Intelligence*, 110(2):215–239, 1999.

108. R. van Renesse, K.P. Birman, and S. Maffeis. Horus: A flexible group communication system. *Communications of the ACM*, 39(4):76–83, 1996.

109. S.G. Ziavras and P. Meer. Adaptive multiresolution structures for image processing on parallel computers. *Journal of Parallel and Distributed Computing*, 23(3):475–483, 1994.

Index

Chryssis Georgiou is on the faculty of the Department of Computer Science at the University of Cyprus, Cyprus, since 2004. He earned his B.Sc. degree in Mathematics at the University of Cyprus, and M.S. and Ph.D. degrees in Computer Science and Engineering at the University of Connecticut, U.S.A. His research interests span theory and practice of distributed computing, in particular, design, analysis, verification, and implementation of algorithms; fault-tolerance and dependability; communication protocols; cooperative distributed computing; and dynamic computing environments.

Alexander Allister Shvartsman is a Professor of Computer Science and Engineering at the University of Connecticut and a Co-Founder of VeroModo Inc. He earned his B.S. degree from Stevens Institute of Technology, M.S. degree from Cornell University, and Ph.D. from Brown University, all in Computer Science. The author is a winner of the NSF Career Award in principles and practices of dependable distributed computing, and he is an established authority in this area. He is an author of over 100 technical publications. The author served on program committees of numerous technical conferences, and he chaired several conference committees in distributed computing.